P9-DEY-740

BIG WAVE
STORIES OF RIDING THE
WORLD'S WILDEST WATER

EDITED BY CLINT WILLIS

Thunder's Mouth Press
New York

For Margaret Anne Murphey,
My only aunt

BIG WAVE: STORIES OF RIDING THE WORLD'S WILDEST WATER

Compilation copyright © 2003 by Clint Willis
Introductions copyright © 2003 by Clint Willis

Published by
Thunder's Mouth Press
An Imprint of Avalon Publishing Group Incorporated
245 West 17th Street, 11th floor
New York, NY 10011

AVALON
publishing group incorporated

Book design: Sue Canavan

All rights reserved. No part of this book may be reproduced in any
form without prior written permission from the publishers and the
copyright owner, except by reviewers who wish to quote brief passages.

Library of Congress Cataloging-in-Publication Data is available.

ISBN: 1-56025-501-3
ISBN 13: 978-1-56025-501-7

9 8 7 6 5 4 3

Printed in the United States of America
Distributed by Publishers Group West

contents

Introduction

I know a couple of guys who like to go surfing in the winter off the coast of Maine. Their version of surfing doesn't look much like what goes on at Hawaii's North Shore or California's Malibu Beach. They wear heavy wetsuits and paddle out to catch small waves—but they always come back stoked.

Surfing is one of those pointless activities that seems to draw power from its very pointlessness. A wave shows up and you ride it; the wave is gone. You can't point to it the way climbers can point to a mountain they've climbed; on the other hand, no one else will ever ride that wave. You have created a private moment in your history that cannot be duplicated or known to anyone else.

Of course, every moment is like that—but they rarely seem that way. We share our cities, our roads, our best-sellers and our television events; we share the very air we must breathe, however filthy it may be from the factories and cars that support our shared lifestyle. We share our buildings and streets with strangers; we share our homes with family members (who also may be strangers to us). It is hard to think of any thing or experience that we don't in some sense share with someone.

Surfers sometimes surf to escape all of this; to find solitude. Riding a wave is one way to make everything else go away. Surfing—like other solitary vocations that occur in the wilderness or at its fringes—is a version of meditation. It forces the surfer to be present in a world that as it turns out is absolutely gorgeous. Once you've seen that world from any angle you want to go back and see it again.

The stories in this collection are about (and mostly by) surfers. The surfers include 18th-century kings, California golden boys who hung out with Gidget, big-wave riders on Hawaii's North Shore and die-hard kids who commute from Brooklyn to Queens to get their rides at Rockaway Beach. They don't try to explain why they surf; the answer is out there in the water—you can't carry something like that around in your head. But they do offer answers to the question you might be asking yourself by the time you've read a few of their stories: Why not go surfing?

—Clint Willis
Series Editor, Adrenaline Books

from Caught Inside: A Surfer's Year on the California Coast

by Daniel Duane

Daniel Duane's (born 1967) 1996 account of a year spent surfing in Santa Cruz, California, makes you want to spend a year surfing in Santa Cruz, California—and makes you wonder whether you'd last the whole 12 months.

found out, over time, that the sea otter here at the Point, with his gray whiskers, black eyes, and powerful hands, preferred to dine on mussels and urchins, purple urchins like those in the tide pools among the rocks. Which was fine, given that urchins—spiky little spherical herbivores that they are—mow down kelp forests to leave kelp-free *urchin barrens*. And since kelp helps surf hold its shape by dampening out short-period wind chop and letting long-period groundswell roll through, the otter did more than scenic duty in making this place beautiful: he actually contributed to wave quality with every meal. The otter also occasionally ate crab, the purple rock crabs that lived in every little crevice like walking mouthfuls, but he didn't touch much else. Taking after the legendary Hawaiian surfer, waterman, and Olympic Gold Medal swimmer Duke Kahanamoku, I'd decided never again to eat shark—bad karma—but at a cedar-paneled sushi place I tried the otter's diet, with variations: urchin in nori over rice (textured much like pudding), crab in a California roll. I had a little wasabi and hot sake, of course, for that lovely, drippy-eyed sushi buzz, but ate the seafood as did the otter: sashimi. And when I considered his other options, things like turban snails, tube worms, and tunicates, I decided he had pretty good taste, though he missed out on clam and abalone and appeared not, as some local otters do, to hunt and kill large sea birds (cormorant, grebe, and gull had all been observed as prey).

On a drizzly dawn, I locked the truck near a deer that had been literally blown all over the highway in a terrifying, ghastly smear, as if made by an eighteen-wheeler at a hundred miles an hour. An enormous, blunt-headed owl loped across the carcass in its last hunt before light, then over the first brussels-sprout field torn up by the harvesters. Crossing the empty, silent road, I got that sweet, deserted-highway peace that makes you want to lie down and nap or do some stretching on the yellow line. But a young farm supervisor with no thumbs sat reading the newspaper nearby in his pickup, so I continued on my way, past two farmworkers hunched and bobbing down the rows, sprinkling something from buckets, silhouetted black against a flat gray sky. Full-grown sprouts still weighted the other fields, sage green and damp under the mist, and "Peligro/Poison" signs with skulls and crossbones stood along the dirt road warning of pesticide spraying the night before; permissible levels were apparently determined by average annual consumption, and as the basic human ate about one brussels sprout per year, they could saturate this place with chemical weapons. Since all the hemlock's tarlike, sticky death a few weeks ago, it had parched to a forest of broken stalks full of flitting sparrows; another autumnal death in the nadir of the year's growth cycle. High-tide surf washed quietly under the sound-dampening fog. Out at the Point, on an offshore rock, a family of harbor seals had taken up residence. As I changed in the half light, clouds pulled through the cypress and beaded on the grass and dirt. Someone's Coke can and soiled underwear lay in the open, and one of the seals let out a horribly displeased whine, the kind of predawn conversation that would give a sailor just cause for superstition. I felt somehow intrusive, as if eavesdropping on squabbling neighbors. I drank the last of my herbal tea and paddled out alone, watched long, warbled lines roll in out of the south. From a last South Pacific winter storm, these waves were yet another lingering vestige of summer, reflecting the very tilt of the earth in the angle of their approach. The first wave I caught was wound tight, bunched up, and glassy as I rose and fell with each bowl. The sky faded into a gray-blue as the fog began to break up, and eventually another man joined me. It was the older of those two friends, the one who always got so many waves. Off such a rocky and remote shore, this midmorning appearance implied far different motivation than idle fun in the sun. A week before, we'd had one laconic, surfer-jargon conversation that ended too soon when a few others paddled out. But I still wondered what he did for a living: somehow "surfer" just didn't suffice. Tradesman? Independently wealthy? He'd been distant at first, as we gave each other the requisite stern-faced nods. Sat side by side looking out to sea, not talking in spite of our solitude; one often does this while surfing, gives others a chance to be alone with their thoughts. Few people drive up here and make these walks out of a desire for company. He spoke a truncated English when I did try to chat.

"Fun ones, huh?" I said, offering a stock phrase as an opener.

"Tide's getting too low."

"When's the low?"

" 'Bout now," he said. Then be turned and paddled for a wave. The Point, I'd also discovered, had as daily regulars only this guy and a few others. He was by far the most dedicated, here every time I came and obviously at home. After a small but smooth wave, gentle turns and soft banks off the lip, we paddled back out together.

"All right," I said, fishing, "fess up. Trust fund? Unemployed?" So many people *were* being laid off, with the economy turning down and construction all but halting. A lot of middle-aged guys were getting more waves than usual.

"Vince Collins," he offered, although I hadn't asked. Then he looked carefully at me and said he was a lecturer in math up at the university. He smiled a tight little grin, knowing why I'd asked, then laughed out loud and looked down at his board. "Pathetic," he said, "I know." His demeanor softened immediately, and I found out later this was typical of him—as much as he'd savagely berate the follies of other surfers and rant about smashing windshields and keying the cars of outsiders, it all melted to kindness in the face of another human.

Straight-edged little waves came clean and gray through the still rain with nobody to ride them but us two. Everything water—me, sea, air . . . him. Then he paddled away, suddenly but not frantically, just putting one hand in front of the other, head down. Nothing antisocial about this, although he certainly didn't encourage me to follow; one simply stayed alert, responded to the water, and kept moving. Seemed to me he was blowing it, though; most waves were hitting right where I was. In water, rise and fall makes a paced view: nothing from the troughs, the horizon from the peaks. A rill lifted him and he paddled over it, dropped out of sight behind. A bull kelp bulb the size of a grapefruit surfaced in the little boil in front of me—a medusan sea hag waving its long seaweed hair—and the otter floated on its back, wrapped in a kelp strand as a mooring against the current, little pointed ears catching the plunge of a pelican, the approach of a wave. Against the flat anvil-stone again on his belly, he smacked something new, a mussel perhaps (taking a big flavor risk). He reached high with his paw and smashed it down with a loud crack, then gnawed at it the way you'd crack a nut. Never seen him use anything but a stone, though otters are known to use soft-drink bottles to dislodge shellfish, to break open beer cans for resident octopi. A gull floated a few feet from him, upright and white against the gray water, waiting for scraps. The placid inner waters of the cove struck a surprising symmetry against the chaotic lines of land, like an Alpine lake below broken crags; water always an element that, like fire, one can watch endlessly.

Then I, too, rose with the rill and saw Vince, far off to my left, dropping into the biggest wave of the day, as if he'd *felt* it coming, didn't want to tip me off. After all, who knew how many there'd be? On his feet early, he took a high line, nothing fancy. He just moved from peak to trough and back again, arcing into the curl when the wall slowed down, stepping forward and trimming high when it sped up—the board an easy expression of unobtrusive desire. Many shortboarders— that is, riders of pointed boards under seven feet, as opposed to long- boarders, riders of rounded boards over eight feet—ride as though glued in one stance. But Vince's style had been formed by a youth on the big longboards of the 1960s and the loose little twin-fins of the 1970s; he kept his feet in play, flicking the board about as much with his toes as with heavy weight shifts. I was cold and not surfing well, kept mistiming the suck and pitch, getting thrown headfirst. On my way down, I'd see Vince drop right in on the same wave, having politely watched and waited. In a long lull between sets of waves, through which surfers often sit silently, I mentioned how beautiful I thought the place was.

He looked at me a little askance, and for a moment I felt embar- rassed at the sentiment. But then he smiled with surprise and looked behind us at the cliffs and hills.

"It's the most beautiful place on earth," he said quite seriously. "And I've had a look around." It only took him five minutes to get out that he was the first person to surf this place, that he'd been surfing here for thirty years, and that back then the reef had been quite different, much better. And best of all, there'd been nobody else here, ever: no fish- ermen, no weekend sunbathers, no mountain-bike geeks, and, most important, no surfers. "We used to park a mile up the highway," Vince said, "and walk down here just to throw off the Valleys. Only about ten guys even knew this place existed, and whenever some geek parked too close—this was in my wilder days—we'd smash their headlights and leave a note on the windshield telling them where to park and how to walk down here. We held on to this place five years longer by doing that, five more years before it finally got overrun." (I felt unclear about where I fit in, since I was obviously a recent arrival from inland, but his tone somehow included me in the camp of the good guys.) Back then, Vince said, the farmer still hadn't yielded a public right-of-way across his fields, but for some reason he'd liked Vince and often gave him rides in the back of his truck.

"You weren't here yesterday," Vince said suddenly, changing the subject. He took some mischievous pleasure in the announcement.

It had looked messy to me, much too windy, but I'd walked out anyway just to have lunch and watch the void shuffle around under the sun.

"Perfect in the morning," he said with a grin.

"Perfect?"

"Slaphappy."

"What?"

"Perfect."

We talked more between waves, with occasional lapses as we chased separate peaks—different parts of the reef causing distinct breaks quite near each other. Mostly we just floated, happy to sense some shared points of view. When I asked how he'd started surfing, he described what most surfers will: that first childhood moment of standing up on a board and knowing right then, with absolute certainty, that he was a surfer for life. He'd grown up in the 1950s in Chico, in the northern Central Valley, stealing cars and joyriding through cherry orchards, tow-surfing the irrigation canals by ropes tied to the bumpers. Back then Santa Cruz had been a low-budget summer destination for Central Valley families seeking to escape the stultifying valley heat. While the San Francisco country club set headed farther south to Carmel and Pacific Grove—London's and Sterling's haunts—the plebeians rode roller coasters and strolled the boardwalk. Once he'd picked up the surfing habit on a family trip, Vince and a few friends had taken to siphoning gas, stealing bottles to redeem for food money, speeding out to the coast. Maybe break into an empty beach house and have a little party. He apparently stole two hundred and fifty cars by the time he was a high-school senior, although it was all for kicks, and he never sold a single one of them. But he told all this without brag-gadocio, the way a sober alcoholic talks of drinking. He was just explaining how surfing, far from a bad influence, had slowed down his delinquency and put him on the right track. Now, presumably, he had a teacher's flexible schedule, a good pickup truck. And then, another set; Vince once again found his way to the right spot on the best wave and took off with a single paddle. Other sports so often require you to generate all the energy—one stares up at the inert mountain, laces up the running shoes—but surfing, however exhausting, is a system one plugs into.

The otter never came ashore, by the way. Otters can live their whole lives without coming to land, with fur four times as insulating as fat keeping them warm, buoyant, and waterproof. And they're quiet: no barking or baying like sea lions and seals; the otter just drifts alone, diving for food, staying in his small home range, tending his garden, holding a good feeding ground to court females. Otters are said to sleep curled up on the sand, paws over their noses, but this one did all his dozing among the slimy green patches of surface kelp (unless he beached elsewhere, along some cliff without enough sand for sunbathers or waves for surfers). He had the air of a nervous, irritated busybody, with none of the languid curiosity of a seal; but to be fair, he *did* have to eat a third of his body weight daily just to stay warm.

Then the fog pulled back, and for a while the view to sea could've been a winter stormscape, while the view immediately behind, to land, sparkled with bright blues and greens, leaving the late morning warm over the clearest water I'd seen. Ten feet down, grass waved among red algae and urchins, and the water tasted kelpy clean. Vince drifted away altogether when another fellow paddled out—being shy perhaps, or not gregarious enough to squander his attentions. The new surfer had a very northern European look to him: "Holland," he said, when I asked a little abruptly where he was from, "but I grew up in Liberia." He was happy to chat, and said his father did foreign development, still lived in Africa—had once seen a surfing picture in an airline magazine and decided he and his three boys ought to try it; on a stop-over in Spain he'd bought a couple of used boards. Then the Dutch surfer turned suddenly and paddled away—a good, shoulder-high wave—made a late drop, smacked the lip, and fell. Came up with a smile and paddled back out. "Well," he said, lying on his board, "we'd never even seen videos, much less the real thing. We just knew you caught waves and somehow ended up standing like the guy in the picture. It was hilarious." He said they got some better boards and a copy of *Surfer* magazine through a Pan Am steward whose circuit took him through California; they'd met him in a café in Monrovia, put in orders, and waited. Three months later he showed. "And there was this old Liberian man," he said, "a fisherman, who lived by the water and could predict swells. Not big storm swells, but local ones. He'd be like, 'There'll be waves tomorrow,' and he'd be right." So brothers and father had reinvented the surfing wheel, alone, in West Africa; now, scattered around the globe, they got together once a year—this year at a fabled left-point break in Tanzania. This brother now lived with his American wife in San Francisco, wondered if I was married. I mentioned my quasi girlfriend, now a graphic artist in San Francisco, and he asked if she surfed.

I just laughed, as would she have.

"You know," he said with great sincerity, "if she ever wants to try, I've got a brand-new, never-used foam board and a wetsuit that'd fit her."

"Never used at all, huh?"

"Nope."

"Wife's?"

"How'd you guess?"

An hour later, the Dutch surfer gone and Vince onshore changing clothes, I started paddling in; the otter looked up suddenly when I came too close, raised his silver-flecked head high out of the water to focus, then tucked the stone under one arm and dove. I dressed on shore and knew my toes were never going to dry out in this drizzle; even my T-shirt was damp. As Vince bent over to put on his pants, I noticed a tattoo on his butt, leaned a little closer to make the thing out, then realized it was like one of those tailgating bumper stickers: IF YOU CAN READ THIS, YOU'RE TOO CLOSE.

"If someone asks," Vince said suddenly, standing up, "what I've done with my life, what'll I say? Surfed the Point and taught math?"

He shook his head with a laugh. "Raw mediocrity." It didn't, of course, strike me that way, and I wanted to tell him but couldn't think how. I also wanted to ask if I could meet him surfing some time, maybe share the drive; but I knew it was too soon. The fog now well offshore, and fingers of wind printing deep-blue splotches on the light-blue sea, we started back and I got to wondering about a culture that marked his life that way, a man who'd mastered a skill he deeply loved, learned to truly know an element. On campus, he explained as we walked, boards under our arms, he had to lie about irregularities of schedule, fabricate false travel itineraries for sabbaticals; the frivolous aura of surfing having invalidated the great achievement of his life. No social cachet at all—just a guy who couldn't grow up. And then the oddest thing happened: a cougar stood in the road, a hundred yards off, its long, supple tail swinging slowly from side to side. As we walked closer, it stepped into the dead hemlock on the side of the road, looked back out with its brown head, and then disappeared. As we approached the point where the cat had entered the brush, Vince suggested that the petting-zoo concept might not be appropriate, thought we ought to give the beast a little room. We stepped off the far side of the road, and as we came even with the bush, Vince said, "Is that it? There it is, right?"

Ten feet away, waiting under a willow: a cat the size of a very large dog, a wild thing on a scale quite different from the raptors and their rodents. We both froze. And suddenly it vanished like a ghost— unafraid, unhurried. One second it lay watching, the next it was gone. None of the coyote's slinking or the deer's bolting. A visitation in a backwater place, all part of the wet skin and salty eyelashes, draining sinuses and muscles loose in the way only water can make them. We were both stunned, and Vince said that in thirty years he'd never seen a cougar before. Big predators change your whole sense of an ecology: sharks in the water, lions on the land, a hawk overhead.

"By the way," Vince said, as we walked back up the path, "get a new surfboard." A few hippie farming interns stood smiling in the field, having fun—not, after all, getting paid.

"Because of the lion?"

"No, because you need one." Surfboard shape changes constantly in a blend of technical advancement and fashion; Vince made a point of eschewing whatever the current trend. At the moment, the young pros had made wafer-thin little blades the craze; Vince told me to steer clear of that baloney, get something with a little heft. "Nobody in their right mind rides one of those ridiculous potato chips," he said, "but as long as they do, guys like you and me will paddle circles around them, which is fine." As we got our last glimpse of ocean, Vince said an evening surf was out of the question.

Why? How could he tell? The winds seemed right, plenty of swell . . .

"Color—wind'll be onshore." The gradations in the ocean's blue had tipped him off; not genius, but an intimate knowledge of place, an eye adapted to particular minutiae. Still, nothing learned, gained, or earned in a public way, just his secret discipline, his private pleasure.

Vince's suggestion led to my discovering another surfing peculiarity: off-the-rack boards cost more, generally speaking, than custom boards. Many serious surfers simply don't buy boards out of shops; they develop a relationship with a particular shaper in their town and have every board made slightly differently in an ongoing search for the perfect combination of elements. The endless play with length, thickness, bottom contour, outline curve, fin placement, and other considerations gives the surfer, over time, a phenomenally complex relationship to his tool. Even more peculiar is that there is no substantial price difference between the very best and the very worst boards: they all use largely the same materials in largely the same amounts. Longboards cost more than shortboards, but good longboards don't cost much more than lousy ones, and likewise for shortboards. There's simply no such thing as a "starter" model and a "top of the line" model; no deluxe edition with loads of expensive extras, no latest high-tech pricey material or heat treatment. There are boards better suited for learning, others better for tube riding or big waves, but the *quality* distinction is quite subtle and subjective.

Tom Blake, in his 1935 *Hawaiian Surfriders,* explains the way it used to be in the islands: the commoner's nine-foot *alaia* board, for *kakala,* a curling, deadly wave; and the nobleman's eighteen-foot *olo* board, for *opuu,* a gentle roller. One chose a tree—hardwood breadfruit for the *alaia,* porous wiliwili for the *olo*—then placed an offering of red *kumu* fish at the trunk, cut down the tree, dug a hole in the root, and left the fish there with a prayer. Then one chipped the trunk with a stone adze until a board emerged; corrugated coral helped smooth out the adze marks, and a paint made from *mole-ki* root and burned kukui nuts gave it a glossy finish. Burying the board in mud sealed the wood pores, and a last rubbing with oil gave it a final polish. Stateside, into the 1920s, the surfboard was still a six- to nine-foot flat-bottomed piece of solid redwood: one bought a plank at the lumberyard, chopped it into shape with an ax, and whittled it down with a knife. Three and a half inches thick and over a hundred pounds, with no fin or keel. Tom Blake's own 1926 hollow boards came next. Blake had grown up in Wisconsin, spent his first few years after high school hoboing on freight trains, and eventually landed in Los Angeles. There, with no formal training, he set the world record in the open ten-mile swim and eventually designed his revolutionary boards: long, closed canoes, beautiful pieces of maritime architecture designed largely for open-water paddling races. Then, in 1934, two southern Californians got sick of "sliding ass" while trying to carve turns on faster waves. C. R. Stecyk writes in *The Surfer's Journal* that the two went home after a frustrating session, hacked the rear of the plank into a V, and sanded it smooth—soon they were working their wooden slabs into gorgeously organic, curved hulls with keels carved into the bottom shape.

The next big leaps in surfboard design came, Stecyk writes, during the Second World War, from a young man named Bob Simmons who was unfit for military service because of a left arm damaged in a bicycling accident. Simmons remains one of the sport's oddest heroes: brother of a very successful inventor and a high-school dropout with total recall, he tested into Caltech and performed extraordinarily, going on to work as a machinist and eventually as a mathematician for Douglas Aircraft. During the lean war years—few people on the beaches, gasoline and tires tightly rationed—Simmons also took to hopping freight cars at the Pasadena rail yard, riding the coast looking for waves. Quitting his mathematician's job when the surf came up, getting re-hired when it dropped, he eventually gutted a 1937 Ford flatbed to put in a mattress and camping supplies, mixed in a little kerosene to stretch his mileage. Surfers were already shaping boards out of balsa, but it took this mathematician and trained engineer to understand the technological advances offered by military war research. Simmons used a U.S. naval report on planing hulls to apply research on aspect ratio—the ideal balance of length to width, developed in aircraft wing design—to his surfboards. He also took the report's recommendation on the strengthening of planing hulls with fiberglass. Styrofoam had been used in the war as well, for fuselage radar domes, and by 1947 Simmons was pouring his own foam in a backyard mold and laminating it with fiberglass. Stecyk writes that Simmons integrated the new materials and hull designs with military research on the dynamics of waves, originally meant to aid in amphibious landings. The results were what Simmons called his "hydrodynamic planing hulls," boards faster and much easier to control than their predecessors. He was killed in 1954 in big surf at Windansea, but his boards are still coveted artifacts.

Until the late 1960s, boards were ten to eleven feet long and four inches thick; by the early seventies they were in the seven-foot range. The old longboard style has a wonderful grace to it: on a stable, heavy board, your feet are in constant play up and down its length, stepping back to stall, forward to speed, planting a foot in the rear to weight a turn, then scampering up to hang your toes off the front. The great old longboard moves revolved partly around classic postures—a static elegance—and partly around the loose, walking, casual cool of nose riding. The new shortboard style is geared more to fast, slashing turns, a kind of aggressive gymnastic. Design variations also become, over time, increasingly precise and arcane. The obvious considerations are length and width, both of which affect volume and therefore flotation. The better a board floats, the faster it will paddle, and the faster it paddles, the better it will catch waves; but at higher speeds, extra bulk will make the board plane on top of the water rather than carve through it, compromising control. Other differences lie in side rail shape (where and to what degree the curve of the board's edge becomes a hard angle), the location of the board's widest point, and the extent of its lengthwise flat spot. Tail shape is also crucial: a stiletto-pointed pin tail will keep the center point of the board close to the wave, holding a high, fast line on a steep wave; a wide, flat-bottomed tail will give the board a loose, broad pivot for skateboardlike sudden turns. Still finer distinctions lie in the contours of the board's underside—distinctions that can be difficult to make out visually. A shaper can build very subtle convex or concave areas running the board's length, channeling the water's flow for particular effects.

In 1994, the Beach Lifestyle Industry Group reported that 310,000 surfboards were sold in the United States, and yet not a single large producer dominates the market. While a few Australian and southern California shapers sell their boards worldwide, it is primarily a cottage industry, and every little surf town has its local shaper or two, guys with a shop in their garage and a loyal following. So, heeding Vince's advice, I made an appointment with his shaper across town at Ocean Groove Surfboards—an old garage on a shady, cottage-lined street of redwoods and wispy, scented eucalyptus. Jack Bence, a journeyman carpenter who'd finally committed to shaping full-time, was an underground big-wave hero with sound local credentials; he'd been surfing the Lane for twenty years but could also talk Pipeline, Grajagan, Jeffrey's Bay. Vince had recommended him highly. Jack bought his house back before the market blew and had put in yellow roses and a Japanese rock garden. Loose-limbed in jeans and an old chinchilla jacket, hair full of foam dust, he stood in his garage with the door up, a beer open, a game on the radio. When I parked and stepped into the windless fog, he pulled off his face mask and shook my hand; then he took a sheet of paper from a box. He asked questions like a therapist with a new client: "How do you surf?"

"I don't know," I said. "I mean, I've only been surfing a few years, but I want to shred, you know? Not just cruise."

"Where do you surf?" He looked right at me as he asked, and I noticed deep crow's feet, smile wrinkles by his mouth—time spent in sun and salt. His hands were surprisingly delicate.

"Up north," I said, trying to sound bored, "town when it's huge."

He wrote a note, appeared to make a tough decision. Along the wall hung photographs of pretty women and deep, sucking tubes.

"So you don't get out in the big stuff?" he asked.

"Huh?" What a question! "Ahhh . . . no, I mean, pretty big. Double overhead, I guess. Maybe bigger, sometimes."

He nodded and wrote down a few numbers.

"Where do you want to take your surfing?"

"Floaters, aerials . . . I mean, I'm twenty-seven, and I know that's old, but I grew up skateboarding so I want to rip."

He nodded as if to say, Yes, my son, this is healthy. "So . . . lot of tail rocker?"

Three more unfiberglassed boards hung from a rack, each with an airbrushed pattern drying: flames, a sunburst, a naked woman of exaggerated proportions.

"Rocker? Well, my seven-two projects me too parallel to the lip. I need something I can smack it square with. So . . ."

"You want to watch me start?"

Through his shop, past foam blanks—raw surfboard forms piled along the walls—to a partitioned room at the back of the garage. In the black-walled cubicle, a seven-foot blank rested flat on a stand. Along the walls were waist-high fluorescent strips to throw subtle curves into shadowed relief. With a power planer connected to a vacuum hose, Jack skinned the blank quickly into a thing distinct and sharp in its form. Wearing expensive basketball shoes, he walked up and down the length of the board like an old ballroom dancer. Then he picked up a long piece of plywood, a curve template that would determine the arc of the board's outline. He traced one onto the rear of the board, another toward the nose, then cut them out with a handsaw, again walking the length of the board in a steady sweep. The subtleties of bottom shape and rail curve went in with still more walking, passing strips of sanding gauze across each part of the board, never making a change that he didn't carry all the way through the board's shape. And although he made many measurements, followed lines and marks and patterns, he also paused several times to turn the board upright and run his hands down its length. Then he'd flip it back onto the stand to smooth something, fix an irregularity. Back and forth from the measured to the felt in a fast, physical rendering of a complex of theories and desires, running through a kata of moves that rendered a unique, functional sculpture with a life of its own. On the wall, a graffito: "Yes, Grasshopper, now that you have learned to laminate, you may begin to sand."

He stopped eventually for a break, said he had the basic outline in place and would fine-tune later. So we stepped back into the garage, and I asked him again about the overall shape.

"Oh, pretty basic," he said. "Enough tail rocker to let you come real vertical off the bottom. Pretty clipped-up nose'll be nice on late drops, and I gave you a rounded squash tail so it'll feel pretty loose, but it should hold a big turn just fine. Little extra thickness under your chest'll give you some paddling, but I domed it down to pretty nimble rails, so it's not a cork at all. Also, I generally do a single to double concave in the bottom, but it's real subtle."

Sounded good.

As a paying, full-price customer—and thus in no way an insider—I could be assured that delivery of my board would be at the bottom of Jack's schedule. But an idle surfer has plenty to think about, like sharks: naturally, one takes an interest in them, studies photographs of their gaping, bloody mouths—prostrate on the decks of fishing boats or on municipal piers, great whites always seem a ghastly and naked smear of triangular teeth and pale, fleshy gums. And when stared at all afternoon, the stuffed great white at the San Francisco Aquarium— thirteen feet long and somewhat deflated in its freezer case—serves reasonably well as an embodiment of one's relationship to fate: you know they're out there, you even know they're more likely to be at one place than another, and, yet, the odds are on your side. You either quit surfing (unthinkable), or accept a sentiment commonly shared in the water: "Yeah, I figure, if a shark's going to eat me, he's going to eat me." Sensible enough, although one feels compelled to ask how many aspects of late-twentieth-century American life involve the possibility of being devoured by a two-thousand-pound predator with razor teeth. A kid I knew in high school had once seen coroner's pho- tographs of a Monterey surfer bitten almost in half—he repeatedly told me how most of the man's rib cage was gone and how his organs spilled across the table. The board had beached first, with a classic cookie-cutter bite missing; the body drifted in the cold currents for nearly two weeks before it was found. Years later, another local man was having a great time at a remote reef when he felt as if someone had dropped a VW on his back—suddenly he was underwater facing a huge eye. And in Oregon, a shark bit the board out from under a surfer who was sitting in wait for a wave; that awful mouth surged up and chomped onto the fiberglass between his legs. The shark bolted with the board in its teeth, dragging the surfer along by the ankle leash; when the shark turned to charge, the surfer grabbed its tail—two other surfers witnessed this—and they wheeled around in circles together before it let go.

There were whole weeks that fall when the Point was no good; I'd even walked out the dirt road several times in the rain, as if visiting a lover never quite in the mood. Somehow Vince and his friend, whose name was Willie Gonzales, were never even checking it on those days, having apparently predicted its conditions through remote observa- tions. But that's one of the sport's mysteries: one must be available, flexible, always in shape. A storm could break for one day and produce the greatest four hours your reef has seen in a decade, only to pick up the next and blow the waves apart. One comes to welcome serendipity into the patterns of daily life, accept the fleeting nature of happiness, and avoid all unnecessary time constraints. But even when I could find waves, the cold occasionally felt like a kind of oppressive duty; sometimes I wanted to just hide indoors, drink some hot tea. On one such stormy afternoon, I took coffee and a big Toll House cookie (my unqualified favorite food) over to the Santa Cruz Surf Museum at the lighthouse for a look at the obligatory chewed-up board. A small room with the air of a temple, the museum had a historical range of boards hung all over the walls, from redwood planks to the latest big-wave elephant guns. Old black-and-white photographs showed smiling boys in simpler times; an older gentleman wearing a satin Santa Cruz Longboarders Association jacket mentioned that the winter of '41 was a beaut. And then I found it: huge teeth had crunched the fiberglass like a potato chip, tangible evidence of a phantom reaper, like the footprints of a yeti or film footage of a ghost. A glass case held photographs of Erik Larsen, the victim, in bed, with heavily bandaged arms; handwritten doctor's reports described deep lacerations and massive blood loss. Pieces of wetsuit, also behind glass, looked as if they'd been shredded by a tree mulcher. A photo caption compared territorial bites to feeding bites, said Larsen was slated for dinner. Expecting fatty seal meat instead of fiberglass and neoprene, lean muscle and bone, sharks usually spit surfers out; but the one that got Larsen had come back for a second bite.

Still, tide dropping, big storm on the way and time wasting, I said my mantras—"more likely to be killed by a drunk driver, more likely to be struck by lightning"—and drove north. All the way up the coast, I felt the dread of true wilderness, of getting an upward view in the food chain—something humans have worked hard at avoiding, like exposure to the elements and procreative sex. I changed into my wetsuit with a little reggae on the tape deck: "Kill de white man, kill de white man . . ." On the path, panicked cottontails scampered into the dead hemlock as I passed. I paddled out in water slate-gray and disappointingly flat, caught a little nothing of an ankle-high wave, then drifted about and took comfort in the water's murkiness—concentrated on surfaces, ignored the way my legs faded down into the milky green. Smelled the brine, watched granite-colored light wave along the still outer waters. There's a rare quality of sun and shade here on cloudy days, with the dramatic contrasts of black-and-white film. Sunbeams bit a patch of outer sea with glaring intensity, the water so bright against the black distance as to appear shivering and splashing in response to the light. Vince was nowhere to be seen, hadn't been for a few days. I rose and fell a little, lying down, eyes at water level. Ishmael again: "These are the times of dreamy quietude . . . when beholding the tranquil beauty and brilliancy of the ocean's skin, one forgets the tiger heart that pants beneath it; and would not willingly remember, that this velvet paw but conceals a remorseless fang." Willie Gonzales drifted far outside, arms folded, watching the shifts in shadows and holding a kelp strand as an anchor against the current. A seal's shiny head surfaced quietly behind him, undetected. It watched Willie's back for a minute, then leapt out of the water and came down with a terrific slap: thrashing and kicking, Willie spun around on his board, utterly hysterical, face white, screaming, "What was that!? What the *hell* was that!?"

And I didn't blame him: you can think you're thinking only about the super chicken burrito you intend to have for lunch, brush your leg against a thick boa kelp stalk and absolutely flip with terror, find that death by devouring lurks just a thought below your mind's surface. *Sharkiness:* state of mind spoken as a state of place—"Getting kinda sharky out here, dontcha think?"—a combination of a break's history, water depth, and exposure to open ocean, maybe crowd level, fog density, and even just sheer distance from the highway. I paddled over to a patch of kelp to hide from the deep, and, thinking of the guy who'd been dragged around, sat up to avoid decapitation. A neighbor of mine had been sitting on his board near here just recently, thinking what a drag it would be if a shark appeared. There were so few waves, he'd have had to paddle in. And just then, he'd seen a four-foot dorsal fin ten feet away from him, a huge, swirling wake displacing as it moved slowly past. He told me his eyes couldn't quite process it at first, kept trying to see a seal or a sea lion; but then another surfer had *leaned* around the fin and nodded frantically with an expression that said, *Uh huh, that's exactly what you think it is!* As they paddled for the beach, my neighbor turned around once to see the fin slowly following; decided right then not to look back again. When they'd screamed the other surfers ashore, one diehard remained in the water, unbelieving. I had actually mistaken a sealion flipper for a fin once and discovered a peculiar human dynamic: guys want to scorn your misplaced fear, are ever ready to laugh at he who cries wolf, but never quite do. The danger is simply too legitimate for teasing. Nearly everyone, no matter how gruff and grim, is scared witless at the thought of being torn apart while conscious, of watching a spreading slick of one's own blood. Nevertheless, Skinny once felt convinced he'd seen a great white inside a wave: he'd paddled for shore and left without telling any of the other ten surfers in the water, didn't want to be ridiculed. But great whites were, after all, nowhere more common than right here on this coast. The patch of ocean from Monterey, just south of where I floated, out to the Farallon Islands off San Francisco and north to Bodega Bay just north of the Golden Gate had become known—in wonderfully oblique terms—as the Red Triangle. And, indeed, I'd been out alone at the Point one morning at just the hour when several surfers sighted a great white less than a mile north.

So many disturbing traits, once you look into them—with a some-what morbid curiosity, I'd begun prowling around the University Science Library, an airy new building with gestures toward native construction materials, a self-conscious sensitivity to the surrounding redwoods, and the rational and antiseptic calm of too many quantitative minds padding silently down well-carpeted corridors. A few tid-bits: sharks are the world's only known *intrauterine cannibals*; as eggs hatch within a uterus, the unborn young fight and devour each other until one well-adapted predator emerges. (If the womb is a battle-ground, what then the sea?) Also, without the gas-filled bladders that float other fish, sharks, if they stop swimming, sink. This explains their tendency to lurk along the bottom like twenty-one-foot, 4,600-pound benthic land mines with hundred-year life spans. Hard skin bristling with tiny teeth sheaths their flexible cartilage skeletons—no bone at all. Conical snouts, black eyes without visible pupils, black-tipped pectoral fins. Tearing out and constantly being replaced, their serrated fangs have as many as twenty-eight stacked spares (a bite meter embedded in a slab of meat once measured a dusky shark's bite at eighteen tons per square inch). And all of the following have been found in shark bellies: a goat, a tomcat, three birds, a raincoat, overcoats, a car license plate, grass, tin cans, a cow's head, shoes, leggings, buttons, belts, hens, roosters, a nearly whole reindeer, even a headless human in a full suit of armor. Swimming with their mouths open, great whites are indiscriminate recyclers of the organic—my sensitive disposition, loving family and affection for life, my decent pickup, room full of books, preoccupation with chocolate in the afternoons, and tendency to take things too personally: all immaterial to my status as protein.

Leftovers from premammalian times, survivors of the dinosaur extinction, sharks evolved completely and always in the sea, never in fresh water. First appearing 350 million years ago, they've descended from sixty-foot, fifty-ton prehistoric monsters, truly over-determined predators—in one photo a group of scientists stands comfortably inside a pair of fossilized jaws. Great whites are capable of between forty and seventy knots—calculated from photographic blur—and one writer describes a diver in the Mediterranean being hit so hard he exploded. Another mentions a white shark leaping clear out of the water to pull a seal off a rock, and writes that "in most attacks, witnesses see neither seal nor shark, only a sudden explosion blasting spray fifteen feet high, then a slick of blood on the surface." One never sees the white before it strikes, no speeding fin: it surges up in ambush, jaw distended, and tears out fifty-pound chunks of flesh. Death coming truly like a stroke of lightning; in that vast, three-dimensional world of the sea, the surfer's world is quite two-dimensional, all surface and shore, with neither depth nor open sea. Aiding the shark's stealth are jelly-filled subcutaneous canals on its head and sides that are lined with neuromasts called ampullae of Lorenzini, a kind of prey radar detecting faint electrical fields. (As a surfer waits for a wave, his very life force pulses like a homing beacon.) And their powerful eyes—with optic nerves thick as ropes—see detail quite poorly, are adapted only to separating prey from background. Among the world's most efficient predators, great whites have a kill rate better than ninety percent, while the hawks just inland strike all day without luck.

I popped a kelp bulb just as a seal rose and looked at me, processing my presence. Perhaps wondering why I'd be stupid enough to dress like him in this part of town.

"Don't like seeing seals," said a surfer nearby.

Now I was nervous, having always seen seals as good news.

"Just paranoid," he answered, when I asked why, "because . . . I'm Erik Larsen." He sounded almost apologetic.

I looked closely, saw the resemblance to the bandaged figure in the photographs. He rolled up his wetsuit sleeve to show deep scars the length of his forearm; I let a little wave pass—had to ask.

"Kind of foggy out there," he said, telling a much-told tale, "and my brother had just gone in. I got this weird feeling a big animal was under me. Really hoping it was a sea lion. Then I saw teeth, like coming up at me."

Willie drifted over to listen.

"And then my whole leg was in the thing's mouth," Larsen said, slouching like a beaten veteran. "It cut my thigh muscle in half and severed my femoral artery." He looked outside at a three-wave set; clouds still a gray continuum. Willie said he'd heard you bled to death if your femoral artery got cut.

"If you slit it, you do," Larsen said, "but it's like a rubber band, so if you cut it all the way like mine, it'll snap back and close a little."

Not a distinction I enjoyed picturing. Willie looked toward the beach.

Larsen explained how the shark let go, circled, and attacked again, this time at his head. "I put up my arms," he said, crossing them before his face, "and it cut all the adductor tendons and my right brachial artery—the really big one under your bicep. My arms were all flopping around in its mouth. Yeah, I totally remember thinking how much room there was in there, like plenty for me. But I got one arm out and hit it in the eye."

He took a breath. I was stunned, couldn't be patient—and then?

"It let go," he said. "And I actually got on my board. No shit. And the miracle is, I could even paddle because I still had the tendons that pulled down, even though it cut the ones that lift up. I actually caught a wave." He laughed a little. "Yeah, a little one. Belly-rode it in, and a lady came out with her kid and I told them how to tie tourniquets. When the chopper got there I'd lost a third of my blood."

The end of the story left an awkward silence: what to say? Larsen stroked into a waist-high right and surfed it casually, did what the wave wanted. I floated awhile alone, then caught one in—waves kind of small, not real interesting.

from # In Search of Captain Zero
by Allan C. Weisbecker

Surfer and journalist Allan C. Weisbecker in 1996 sold his home in Montauk, Long Island, and set out to find his surfer friend Christopher, who had disappeared into Central America.

'm smoking crack these days," were the next few words Christopher spoke to me upon our reunion, after saying that God had sent me to him, and that everything would be all right now.

I stood there looking at him and the silence wore on.

"We're going to make millions," he said then, as if the gobs of coming money were a corollary to, a result of, the fact that he was smoking crack.

"We'll have to put a stop to that," I said, in reference to the crack smoking.

But we were on different wavelengths now. "It's all about my Hogfish Philosophy."

Hogfish Philosophy?

"You were the last of everybody I figured'd show up here," Christopher said as we rumbled down the dirt track toward the beach, with six dogs, Shiner plus Christopher's pack, trotting behind.

"Really. Why?"

"You? Mister Hollywood? What would you be doing here?"

Mister Hollywood? Notwithstanding my relatively modest successes in the screen trade, "Mister Hollywood" was definitely not how I'd ever thought of myself. In fact, if anything, quite the opposite. I'd always considered myself an outlander on that coast. "Well, buddy," I said, "Hollywood done ran me out of town. So here I am."

"You still got your connections there, I bet," Christopher said as we pulled up to the polished hardwood facade of the Puerto Viejo Hotel.

"Who cares?" Even with the money I still had coming in from screenplay options and TV residuals, that part of my life was the last thing I wanted to think about.

As it turned out, Christopher cared. Sitting in the hotel's rustic little eatery sipping some much-needed *café con leche*, I listened with feigned interest as he rambled on about what he called his Hogfish Philosophy, which he said would form the basis of a full-length animated feature film that would not only make us millions, but very likely change the world as we know it.

"Show me Hogfish Ranch," I interrupted, mainly to change the subject.

I'd gone right by the place in my initial search for Christopher. It was the most run-down of the shacks on the track that formed the inland border of the town. Suspended over a rickety, cockeyed little gate was a rough-cut, oblong chunk of hardwood, upon which was emblazoned a grotesquely surreal but not unamusing pig's head, the body trailing behind that of a fish. *"Hogfish Ranch"* proclaimed a flourished, fading legend. Tendrils of jungle vine and a maze of creepers had wound around the gate supports and were reaching upward toward the weather-beaten artwork as if straining to snatch it. My initial impression of Hogfish Ranch was that it was on the verge of assimilation by the jungle itself. But perhaps, once I crossed the threshold, the grounds out back would open up to reveal the surf camp Bob Rotherham had mentioned: a sprawl of *cabinas* or platformed tents, surfboards scattered about, shaggy dudes swaying in shaded hammocks, poised for the arrival of a groundswell that would set the offshore reef to cracking with that object of great desire, the heralded but currently elusive serious wave of the Talamanca coast.

"All right," I muttered at my first look at the interior of Christopher's abode. "Wow." I mean what *do* you say when after nearly six years an old friend proudly displays his digs, apparently unaware that it's a filthy hovel reeking of cat piss and foul bedding, with a pair of ratty, askew chairs as the only appointments, the hanging and wall decor a zoomorphically motile disarrangement of darting minisaurians along with fist-sized arachnids and their flossy nets.

I stepped to the back door and surveyed the grounds of Hogfish Ranch. A lawn of some long-gone era was a waist-high tangle of underbrush and rotting vegetation. Dead leaves, thin and brown as old parchment, hung limp and forlorn from a cluster of untended banana trees.

The air inside was heavy and fetid; not a breath was stirring. "You have a fan we can fire up?"

"No electricity at the moment. The bank fucked me up over the bill."

I scanned the shack for surfsticks but there were none to speak of, just a lime-green old monstrosity in the eaves overhead; a virtually unridable relic, jaggedly dinged and filigreed with cobwebs.

"Where're your surfboards?" I asked. "The Brewer."

"Don't have one right now."

"What do you mean?"

"I mean I don't have one."

"Where's the Brewer?"

"Sold it a few months ago."

"Wait . . . You haven't had a surfboard for a *few months*?"

I still hadn't gotten the picture.

I spent my first night in Puerto Viejo parked in front of Hogfish Ranch, retiring early after dinner with Christopher, who, in a state of edgy impatience bolted from the restaurant (I still had food on my plate) with the words "I'm a man on a mission," after hitting me up for five thousand *colones* (about $15) and assuming I'd pick up the check, which I did. The mission he was on, I suspected—no, I *knew*—was to score crack.

Odd thing was, although we had both occasionally done cocaine recreationally back in our pot smuggling days, it had been Christopher who was the more temperate in consumption. In fact, he'd often abstain altogether and retire for the night, while I, and the party, roared on.

Over dinner, I had tried to sound him out on the evolution of this apparent change in attitude and habits, but he'd waved me off, saying he'd rather not discuss it, adding with an odd finality that *he'd learned a lot about himself through crack cocaine.* When he then asked to borrow money, it occurred to me that the reason he had, upon our reunion, almost instantly brought up the fact that he was smoking the stuff was that he was hoping I'd suggest an immediate buy; he was broke and looking for a toke. When I failed to take the hint, the subject was no longer of any interest. The depressing point was that his first thought, the very first thing that occurred to him, when I'd finally tracked him down after well over half a year of searching, was, *here's someone who can finance my next high.*

The one thing I knew for sure about the situation was that I had to somehow help. It was with this thought that I finally drifted off into fitful sleep, somewhere around midnight.

Chaos commenced about 4 a.m., when two girls, one whom I'd met through Christopher that afternoon—a slinky *gringa* named Wanda— began pounding on his door and yelling for Christopher to come out. The pair banged and blabbered incessantly for a good half hour, unable to grasp the obvious fact that no one was home.

Christopher finally pulled up, riding shotgun in a vintage Dodge rag-top. The driver was a scraggly fellow with shoulder-length hair and one leg; he was shirtless and his slug-pale skin was bedecked with a swirling mass of tattoos. The tattered cuff of his vacant pant leg dragged the ground as he hopped sprightly toward the gate, using his crutch to keep himself upright and on course. Through my back window, I watched as all four entered Christopher's shack.

The edgy cackling of a crack party began as first light spread its soft, clement blush over the high reaches of the rain forest above the road, although the coastal plain upon which sprawled the town remained in deep, lugubrious gloom until dawn itself.

"You a friend of Christopher?"

It was about 9 a.m. and I was sitting on my back-door stoop sipping coffee and yawning when the kid appeared. Diminutive, fragile, with a wide, open face and astonishingly long eyelashes, he looked to be seven or eight years old. A local kid, a black kid.

"Yes," I said. "I've known Christopher a long time."

"You shouldn't be stayin' heah at night." He looked over at Hog-fish Ranch; it had been quiet in there for an hour or so. The crack had run out, I assumed, and the party had deteriorated to a squirmy group jones.

"Why not?"

"De stone men come at night," he said. "Dey steal, mebbe killin' your dog."

Pieces of crack are called stones. Stone men. Crack addicts. "How do you know this?"

He pointed up the street. "I livin' dere. I see dem at night."

"What's your name?"

"Werner. But Christopher callin' me Kiko."

"Is Christopher a stone man, Werner?"

Werner's direct gaze wavered in discomfiture. "Christopher my bes' frien'," he said.

Werner was right; I had to find another place to stay. Aside from his warning about theft and possible violence, there were bound to be replays of last night's obstreperous debauch and I'd been having trouble sleeping lately as it was. And anyway, I needed the perspective of an ocean view campsite. I fired up the rig and headed for the beach.

"Dónde está la ola seriosa de cual he oido aqui?" I asked Andrés Sánches, the proprietor of a little nest of oceanfront *cabinas* on Main Street. Where's the serious wave I've heard about here? Andres was in his mid-twenties, an expat surfer from Barcelona, Spain. There was a little niche by his row of *cabinas* into which my rig would fit perfectly. It was fenced and shaded, and water and plug-in electric were handy.

Andrés pointed straight offshore to the outer reef. "Es Salsa Brava," he said. *Salsa Brava.* Brave Sauce. A good name for a surf break. I'd have a direct, if distant, view of it from La Casita for the dawn patrol checkout. I made a monthly deal, pulled in, and told Shiner to get comfortable. This would be it for a while.

I liked this place I'd come to, for its physical beauty, its remoteness and the easy feel of it. If only a wave would appear on the dormant outside reef, maybe, just maybe, I'd stumbled upon my little piece of paradise.

A call to Denise was the last of a flurry I'd finally gotten around to making, from a little communications center off Main Street. I'd first called my mom, then Joe, then Tony C, the mutual friend of Christopher's and mine who'd rekindled my interest in longboarding a decade earlier and who owned a surf shop back at Montauk. I'd wanted to discuss Christopher's current situation with him. These three, plus Denise, were the last of the remaining connections I wanted to maintain with my old life.

"I've been so worried, Allan," Denise was saying. "When I didn't hear from you for so long . . . I didn't know what to think." I'd heard that quavery edge in her voice before; she was holding back tears. "It's been over a month. Are you all right? Allan?"

"I tried calling from Nicaragua, but you weren't home."

"I'm sorry." She was crying now, but trying to conceal it. I could picture the tears welling up in her eyes and then spilling over and running down her cheeks. She would be gamely trying to control herself.

"Don't be sorry," I said. "And please don't cry."

"I'm not."

"It's so hard finding a phone down here."

"Do you love me, Allan?"

I told her I did, and it was true. I also wanted to tell her that she should go ahead and live her life, that there was no future with me, in me. But I didn't.

I had abandoned her and my fear was that she would abandon me.

Shiner and I hoofed it back to the rig to find Christopher and Werner waiting by my back door. "Thought we'd drop by and see what you have cookin' for dinner," Christopher said.

"A bunch of leftover spaghetti," I said. "Should be enough."

The three of us sat at the settee, Christopher and I on the ends, Werner in the middle. The settee table came up to about his chin. Turned out that Werner was 10; he was small for his age.

I put on a Mozart tape, then served. Although Werner had never heard classical music before, he began conducting, waving both arms in very close rhythm with the symphony. After a bit, he seemed to anticipate where Mozart was going; he wasn't reacting, he was flowing.

As I was about to dig in, Werner lowered his hands and folded them on the table: "Wait! We mus' be sayin' grace." He shot me an exasperated look, then closed his eyes, blessed the table, blessed Christopher and me and thanked God for everything.

I spoke mostly to Werner, asking about his family and school and so forth. His responses were articulate and lively. "You speak Spanish, too, right?" I asked him.

"*Sí, por supuesto.*"

"And patois?" The patois of Talamanca is an amalgam of English, Spanish and various African dialects, thereby reflecting the multicultural background of the locals: the English of the era of slavery on the islands to the east (mostly Jamaica), the Spanish of Costa Rica and the African of their genetic roots.

Werner nodded, shoveled in the spaghetti.

"Tri-lingual. Not bad." I turned to Christopher. "Y tu debes hablar español muy bien después de seis años aquí."

"Huh?"

"Your Spanish must be pretty good after six years here." Christopher had always let me do the talking when Spanish was called for during our smuggling days, but I figured that now, having lived in Central America for so long, he'd mastered the language.

"I get by."

As I would realize over time, Christopher spoke almost no Spanish at all.

Werner finished his meal and asked if he could be excused; he had to get home. When I said "Sure," he started clearing the table, saying, "I clean dee dishes firs'."

"No no," I said. "Leave 'em, but thanks for the offer."

Werner thanked me for the food and left.

"What a great kid," I said.

"Sure is."

"He told me you're his best friend."

Christopher nodded.

"So listen," I said, getting serious. "I spoke to Tony a little while ago."

"Yeah?"

"I told him basically what's going on down here with you and we both agreed that you should go back up north for the summer."

Christopher laughed.

"Look. He'll fix you up with a place to stay and a summer job. You could come back here in the fall with at least five thousand dollars. With that kind of money you could really fix your place up, maybe build some *cabinas*, properly launch Hogfish Adventure Tours (he'd been talking about this). But mainly, you'll never kick this crack problem down here."

Christopher's eyes were bright with amusement at my charming but misguided naiveté.

"I'll spring for your plane ticket."

"Do you really think I'd go back there, anywhere, to *work?*"

"Just for the summer, then—"

"My life is fine here."

"You're a dead-broke crackhead, Christopher, goddammit."

"That's what you see."

"What else is there to see?"

"I'm well loved here." This particular notion would turn out to be the blindest of Christopher's many denials.

"Really? By who?"

"The local people, and the other *nortes* that live here."

"You know Mister Patterson?" He was my neighbor across Andrés Sánches's fence. A neat old local guy I'd chatted with the day before.

"Sure. We're close friends."

"He told me that crack is destroying this town. Ruining the young people. Making thieves and liars of them."

Christopher shrugged.

"I asked him about you." My voice was getting shaky with anger. "He said you are part of the problem. Part of the problem that is destroying the place he's lived for sixty years. The man does not like you."

Christopher shook his head. "You've been here a few days. You don't know anything about me. Talk to Miss Sam or Miss Dolly about me. The matriarchs."

"Okay, Christopher," I said. "You come, too."

The following afternoon, Miss Dolly squinted at Christopher from the porch of her well-kept cottage across from the Puerto Viejo Hotel as we walked up. Christopher greeted her effusively, like a favorite aunt. Miss Dolly was a wise and kind old woman, Christopher had told me. She would sit on the Hogfish Council when the world saw the wisdom of the Hogfish Way, its deep regard for children and their salubrious upbringing; its respect for the elderly; the world as benevolent extended family.

As Christopher introduced me, Miss Dolly glared at him, eyes burning angry and intent from the pulpit of her porch steps. She indicated a packet of candles in Christopher's shirt pocket. "What those fo', Christopher?" she exclaimed, "To light dee pipe gonna send your soul to hellfire?"

The banging became part of my dream—a squirrelly, nonsensical montage—shaping it until someone, somewhere was banging and banging and banging and calling out my name.

I awoke with that hollow, scattered feeling I'd lately found taking control, directing my thoughts in melancholy directions, preventing me from writing or sometimes even talking normally to people. After little more than a week in Talamanca, I'd begun to withdraw from my surroundings, as surface-beautiful as they were.

I was now sitting on my bunk in La Casita and someone was hammering on my back door. Christopher's voice whispering, "Allan. Allan!" His pounding was enough to wake the dead, let alone the insomniac I'd become, yet he found it necessary to whisper. I looked at the clock: just shy of 3 a.m. Although I knew exactly what was going on, when I stepped to the back door, I said, "Whaddyawant, Christopher?"

"I just need a thousand *colones.*"

Even in the feeble ambient light, Christopher was a sight. Having retreated to the depths of their sockets, his eyes were nevertheless so wide and unblinking as to appear lidless. His lower jaw moved side to side on its own, as if it had come unhinged from the glistening dome of his shiny pink skull, and I could plainly hear his molars grinding from two yards away.

Damn, I was thinking, he looked just like the Crypt Keeper. "Let me guess," I said. "You've run out of crack and need another hit or two."

"Listen," Christopher said, but since his lower jaw had clamped to the upper to arrest the sideways grinding, it sounded like "Lisshen." "There'sshh a woman involved." He'd stretched out the "o" in "involved" to an elongated "aahhh" and canted his head to one side, peering at me askance. Like some Groucho Marx from hell, he hoisted his eyebrows as an indication that salacious doings were afoot.

"I've been having trouble sleeping, Christopher. I told you that."

Christopher shrugged, and as if it would explain and excuse everything, said, "Crack goessh right to my dick."

"Sounds romantic." I looked around. "Where is she, by the way? Let's have a look at her."

"Come on, Allan. Please."

"Does Werner get to see you like this? You're his best friend, you know. He looks up to you."

"I just need a thousand *colones.*"

"According to the Hogfish Philosophy, children are the most important thing in the world, am I right?" Christopher just stared. "If you want the money, you better answer."

"Yessshh. Children are everything."

"If Werner follows the example of his best friend, which is likely, he'll become like you, won't he?"

"It's his decissshion."

"His what?"

"His . . . decision."

I picked up a thousand *colones* note and extended it out the door. "Don't come around here at night," I said. "Ever again. In fact, I'd prefer not to see you at all for a while."

Christopher, a man on a mission, trotted off.

Two days later the surf came up and by God did I need it, although my oblique angle of view from a burry lava outcropping by the channel was from behind the breaking part of the wave—predominantly a right-hander, it appeared—giving little indication of how big and fast and thick and hollow—in short, how *serious*—were the conditions out there.

The reefs were alive with charging lines of white water, their relentless high hiss underscored by a sonorous boom of green water breaking further outside. A fine mist of rarefied seawater wafted wraithlike over the lagoon and fringes of the town, broken water having been spewed heavenward and dissipated in a vaporous state after its downward collision with the reef. From the glimpses I caught of the drop-ins of a handful of guys already out, the swell was obviously a healthy one, head-high, maybe better. Still, I could not get a sense from where I stood of this wave called Salsa Brava.

The paddle-out was a bit unnerving. Although I'd been assured that the channel was some 30 feet deep and would not break no matter how big the swell, the chop was huge and disorienting, a result of incoming waves clashing with a current flowing seaward from the inshore lagoon. The channel was narrower than it first appeared, a scant five yards separating scabrous volcanic crags between which had formed swirling, sucking vortices; I felt their nasty pull as I stroked for the outside. But the outflowing current was strong—four knots at least—and I was quickly seaward of the channel turbulence and paddling side-shore to the lineup.

The first thing I noticed was that of 11 guys congregated in the takeoff zone, four were wearing helmets. I'd not seen a single helmeted surfer in the whole of my half-year journey along some 4,000 miles of surfable coast, so finding better than a third of those out equipped with head armor gave me contemplative pause. Just what was the problem here, fellas, noggin-wise?

There were a few familiar faces bobbing in the lineup, guys I'd seen in town, including Kurt Van Dyke, to whom Christopher had introduced me soon after my arrival. The nephew of big wave legend Fred Van Dyke, Kurt was owner of the Puerto Viejo hotel, which largely catered to visiting surfers. When we first met, Kurt had been, well, curt. As I would soon learn, the theory that my friendship with Christopher would shortcut my acceptance amongst the expat surfers in Puerto Viejo was assbackwards; such was Christopher's negative image. Kurt and I would eventually become friends, but it would be in spite of my history with Christopher, not because of it. As it was, on this, my first Salsa Brava go-out, Kurt vouchsafed me no more than a sour nod when I said "Hi."

This was a tight-knit group, I sensed; my presence was pointedly ignored. The boys were no doubt waiting to see how I'd handle myself out there, both in terms of wave riding élan and in respect owed to those already entrenched: the usual treatment of a new guy. So be it.

The first set was an eye-opener, an adrenaline pumper, a pulse quickener. Angling in from the east, it at first didn't seem like much, a head-high peak with maybe some moderate juice under it. Then, as the lead swell started to feel the drag of the shelving reef, its shoreward progress slowed dramatically. Its energy was not lost, however, only redirected into building height and in concentrating volume. (It is in fact this deceleration of a wave as it approaches shore that causes it to break. The front part reaches shallow water first and therefore slows first, causing the back part to pile up behind it. The water has nowhere to go but up, increasing the wave's height and the steepness of the face, until the whole shebang disintegrates in a forward pitch. The more precipitous the slowing—in other words, the steeper the shoaling bottom—the more pronounced this effect, and hence the bigger and more powerful the breaking wave.)

Following the pack's lead, I stroked mightily for the outside. All chatter had ceased as the set suddenly loomed then stacked, meticulously arranging itself in ascending height and increasing thickness. Someone picked off the first wave. I got a nice down-the-line view of his takeoff and quickly realized that my head-high estimate was off by about a hundred percent on the under side—and that first wave was the smallest of the set. Charging headlong out of the deep water offshore into the shallows over the reef, the wave at Salsa Brava was doubling up and pitching forward, with the verticalness then concavity of the face coming at the last possible instant before Big Blue turned herself inside out in a booming, rip-roaring, top-to-bottom, full-blown stand-up barrel the likes of which I hadn't seen since Backdoor Pipeline in Hawaii, when I was considerably younger and a whole helluva lot more out of my mind than this.

Imagine a 50-pound child doing a 40-yard dash. Imagine that under the tape at the finish line some twisted practical joker has loosely strung a big rubber band at ankle level. The kid hits the rubber, keeps going for a bit, then trips and falls forward. Not much weight behind him, plus he wasn't moving very fast to start with; and the stretching rubber has allowed him to slow down further before he falls. This is a small wave, "tripped" by a gradually sloping bottom. Not too much kinetic energy results from the falling water.

Now imagine a 300-pound-plus NFL lineman—say, William "The Refrigerator" Perry—and imagine that his severely demented team-mates have strung a drum-taut piano wire across the finish, again at ankle level. Imagine the violence of the forward pitch of the top of The Fridge's body as his feet stop short but the rest of him doesn't. This is a double-overhead wave at Salsa Brava, tripped by the suddenly shelving reef.

They just kept on coming, each bigger, fatter, steeper, meaner and ornerier than the last, with the takeoff so late that you pretty much just launched yourself over a vertical precipice of avalanching sea—which was just what that second guy was doing now, but I lost sight of him as I pushed myself through the thick, straight-up-and-down feathering lip of his wave and he free-fell into the "pit" behind me. Good luck, pal.

From everyone's mad scramble toward the horizon, this was obvi-ously a "sneaker" set—bigger than expected. Getting caught in the impact zone of one of these beasts would be no laughing matter. I veered off toward the north, making for deeper water, and noticed that a couple other guys were doing likewise . . . Whoa! there was a ballsy move, a turn-and-burn take-off, a last instant spin and launch, very late, the thick curling lip raking the guy's back as he tried to slip in under it. But again I lost sight of him behind me and didn't really give a hoot as to his fortunes anyway. I had my own problems—like deciding whether to take that next loomer or paddle over it.

I looked around. The pack had scattered, some having gotten waves already; others were further outside or down the line this way or that. No one else was in position, so the wave was mine if I wanted it.

My instinct said take it, not only because it was my, well, my *job* out there to take waves, but also out of a measure of fear: Although I could not see it for the blue-green wall bearing down on me, the next wave outside was likely still bigger and may have had designs on unloading on my sphinctering butt—the idea of hurtling shoreward therefore had a certain appeal, in the lesser-of-two-evils sense.

One thing I learned in big waves in Hawaii my younger days is that if you're going to go, go. Don't sort of go, or pretty much go, or halfway go and figure you'll decide later whether you should really go. Just fucking GO.

So I WENT, spun my board toward shore and stroked for all I was worth until I felt myself sharply rising; and then suddenly I was on my feet—a quick and flawless transition to standing is absolutely vital on a wave like this—and for a split second contemplated the view of the 12-foot drop I'd be presently making, like it or not, either standing up or somersaulting, board flying, into the impact zone.

You're pretty much weightless for the first third of the way down on a wave at Salsa Brava, and unable to make adjustments. Pursued by some ridiculous volume of cascading seawater, you stoically just hope for the best until you reach the trough, whence you project yourself in the logical direction—away from the freight-training breaking part of the wave, which, thankfully, you can't see because it's behind you.

I was more or less hoping that my first Salsa wave would be a peak, that is, a drop then a quickly petering shoulder. I could thus sort of break myself in gradually to the bodacious conditions out there. But no such luck. I quickly found myself tearing across a straight-up-and-down wall of ocean that appeared to be on the verge of closing out, dumping across itself in one mighty heave for 40, 50 yards down the line. I was in the correct position (not counting sitting on the beach with a beer in hand), halfway up the wave face or a little better, where the speed lay, so I tucked myself into a crouch and awaited further developments.

Truly, in the few seconds between when I stood up and when the wave folded over me in one gargantuan heave, extinguishing the sight of the thick, almond-shaped eye of the curl way up ahead, I rather enjoyed it. Such is the lunatic nature of an adrenaline high.

My wipeout was a minor one by Salsa Brava standards. Still, I've never been partial to collisions with sharp coral reefs and this one very definitely got my attention.

Human skin is very sensitive to touch and texture, and as my right shoulder and the upper part of my back bounced along the reef, I realized that the sea bottom in the Salsa Brava boneyard was of identical configuration to that jagged lava outcropping I'd gingerly walked out upon to get to the channel. I also knew that the holes and fissures down there were, like the outcropping, bristling with sea urchins. I tumbled shoreward like a load of laundry in a dryer, instinctively protecting my head with my hands and forearms.

I surfaced and checked myself for injuries, noticing that I'd suffered only superficial scratches on my shoulder. The logic behind the helmet phenomenon was now obvious. I'd alighted fairly softly and on a fleshy part of my body, but in the violent, disorienting turbulence I could just as easily have come down hard and on my head. A concussion, unconsciousness and subsequent drowning would then be a possibility, if not a likelihood.

A wave, like any animate entity, has a personality, frequently of some complexity. A break's appellation, which usually surfaces by unremembered, even mysto means, often reflects the dominant trait—the one most easily agreed upon. Salsa Brava. *Brava.* Brave. The other translation to English, depending on context, is *vicious.*

As I reeled in my board (half expecting it to be broken; it wasn't), the exhilaration of the ride faded. With a decision as to whether I should paddle back out my next concern, I suddenly found my stomach doing a bit of fluttering. I'd ridden waves as gnarly as this before, with just as nasty a sea bottom, but that was over a quarter century ago. I was still in good shape, no question. My weight and body fat were about the same as in those days, plus I'd spent a fair percentage of the past seven months in the water, but . . . but . . .

I looked outside to see Kurt Van Dyke tucked into the last and biggest wave of the set, an immense open-ended barrel from which he emerged unscathed onto a wonderfully flat, innocuous shoulder (my wave had no makeable shoulder), his board decelerating from some absurd velocity to a slow plane right in front of me. Falling in beside him for the paddle back out, my voice broke into an embarrassingly high squeak as I yelled, "I want one of those!"

"Go for it, bro," Kurt replied, my enthusiasm for his accomplishment breaking down the first barrier between us. "Sit in the pit and catch a fat one."

I surfed for about two hours that day and rode a dozen or so waves. After conditioning myself to the fact that everything happened exponentially faster than on a "normal" wave (which cost me two more wipeouts, along with the inevitable encounters with the reef), I found my rhythm and had a memorable session, which included two major barrels from which I escaped upright and unscathed, that malicious reef benignly below me.

The tube ride at Salsa Brava was, however, for me, a bit different from that of other breaks I surfed on my southward journey, and for many years before embarking upon it. If the essence of a meditative moment is the suspension of concern with causes and consequences—the past and the future—then my moments were technically flawed. Although causes were of no concern—I did not dwell on how I'd come to be in that remarkable hurtling niche—consequences tended to be. This had not previously been the case—not at, say, Bart's home break, nor even at Puerto Escondido, which I had caught big and mean. Puerto, Mexico's Pipeline, was as hard a breaking wave as Salsa, coming out of deep water onto a shelving, very shallow bottom with which collisions were frequent. But that bottom was sand, not sharp coral. It was the Salsa reef that put the fear of consequences into me. At the very time when my mind should have been devoid of reflection, I would find myself consciously thinking about making the wave. Really, *really* wanting to make it. To some extent this was a failure of spirit on my part, a malfunction in the arena of grace under pressure. My thoughts were a distraction and a source of internal embarrassment.

It was a problem I would work on, I told myself.

• • •

On my third day in the water at Salsa Brava, I was late getting into the lineup—I'd had a fitful night—and quickly realized the swell was peaking. The set waves were a good couple feet bigger than the day before and there were a lot more of them.

Kurt was out, lurking deep in the pit at first point to the south of the pack, just outside the swirling boils that mark the shallowest point of that jagged, treacherous sea bottom. The southern lineup point is the real deal at Salsa, where sneaker sets and unmakeable rogue walls make wave selection difficult and critical. I approached from the channel to the south, so my view was back-door—from behind the peak—as Kurt launched himself over the edge of a fat, nasty one, a near mutant. I winced, thinking no way he'll make that, but then he popped out over the shoulder 40, 50 yards down the line with a hoot and both arms raised, indicating he'd been deeply barreled. Kurt was fearless here; he had been surfing Salsa for 10 years. In fact, I found all dozen or so guys I surfed with at Salsa to be pretty much fearless, and skilled way beyond any previous group of regulars at any break I'd encountered on my journey.

For my part, I was able enough—I would get my share of deep tube rides and concomitant hoots from the pack—and I dealt with my apprehensions through conscious suppression: I pretended not to be afraid. The problem with this sort of fear management was that it diverted my concentration and hence my judgment, which at Salsa can be outright dangerous. I'd occasionally not take waves that were perfectly makeable. But on the other hand, and perhaps to offset some previous timidity, I'd sometimes stroke into some malevolent beast, too far back, too late and with near-zero chance of success, in a mental state somewhere between mindless nonchalance and petrified Zen. My last wave this day was of the latter sort, a savage piece of oceanic work that I handled improprietously.

Aside from Kurt, out that morning were Craig From San Diego on his twin-nose thruster (which looked like it should've been hanging under the wing of an F-16), Chris From Florida on a balsa beauty, Mike From Santa Cruz in a blue helmet, Mack From SoCal in a white helmet, and Big Bill From Delaware. Within an hour of my tardy arrival, one by one the rest of the boys, who had been at it since dawn, picked off their last waves and went on in. Suddenly it was just me out there.

Unbelievable. Plunk this wave down on Oahu's North Shore and there'd be 40 young international hotshots all over it, looking to build reps, the beach swarming with surf paparazzi. I still had not gotten used to the idea of this break being uncrowded, that with so many surfers in the area it was just the dozen or so expats and two or three *Ticos* (Costa Ricans) who actually surfed it.

Bobbing solo in the lineup of this world-class wave waiting out a lull, thoughts of Christopher's abysmal descent, along with the failures and fears I'd begun to see as my own life's motif, were displaced by a serene sense of accomplishment. I *had* come this far, via a route few others had the intrepidity to take, let alone solo; I *had* ridden the wave here successfully, having overcome the sort of fear others found insurmountable.

Damn, I was all right, wasn't I?

There *was* something about surfing a wave like Salsa, alone, at some obscure, far-flung corner of the globe, that was . . . significant. Right?

Isn't that what life is all about?

At that moment, Salsa Brava correctly issued a wake-up call to my somnolent, self-congratulatory musings. The set that appeared, angling in from the east as all the serious Salsa sets did, at first seemed simply big, like the others I'd dealt with for the last hour or so. But the one gathering itself out the back, probably the last, was . . . well, it had the look of something else altogether. I could have turned and taken any of the three or four initial waves. Fine, meaty suckers they were, too, but something possessed me to stroke for the outside to see what that last one had on its mind.

When you're paddling a surfboard you're very low to the water, so your view is severely limited. When a wave is in front of you, you see little or nothing of what's behind it. Until I pushed through the steepening lip of that second to last wave, all I had of the last one was a vibe . . .

But holy shit . . .

One instant I was stroking madly up the face of the biggest wave I'd seen on my journey, motivated only by the deep desire of making it to the safety of the other side; then I found I'd spun my board shoreward and done a turn-and-burn that was so late, with the wave so steep, that no paddling was necessary, or indeed, desirable. I was already too far inside for a safe entry, so to paddle further in that direction to gain board speed would only worsen my circumstance.

The problem with a no-paddle takeoff is that you have very little initial forward momentum and must rely strictly on gravity to "drop in" down the face of the wave. Sometimes gravity isn't enough to get you started down before the top of the wave goes concave and with a vengeance pitches itself plus you and your surfboard into the impact zone.

I hung there in the feathering lip of the wave for a period of time that a shoreward witness later described as "forever," unable to force my board down the face, while the wave thickened and steepened and rose up and up past double overhead to near triple, gathering itself like some humongous, oceanic version of Nolan Ryan winding up for the explosion of a fastball delivery.

At a certain point I knew I'd made a serious error in judgment—this wasn't going to work out *at all*. Seeking to get as far from my board as possible (surfboards become deadly projectiles in violent wipe-outs), with an adrenaline-assisted standing broad jump I launched myself to the right across the wave face. I skidded on the upwardly rushing wall about halfway down, then plunged into the trough.

With a wave of this size, power and top-to-bottom breaking con-figuration, it's interesting what happens next in a fuck-up of this magnitude. There is what feels like a long moment of actual tran-quility. What's happening is that the wave is fairly gently lifting you up—actually sucking you back seaward a bit—preparatory to throwing you down, along with many tons of churning white water.

I slammed onto the reef with the whole left side of my body from my shoulder to my lower leg, thus distributing the brunt of the impact over a wide area. Still, I believe I lost consciousness—I recall the dull, painless shock of the collision but nothing more until I surfaced, breathless and disoriented. The surrounding swirl of sea seemed canted at an odd angle and I was at a momentary loss as to where I was. My surfboard was within reach, which was good. I definitely needed something to hold onto, to keep me afloat while I hyperventilated to reoxygenate my blood and gather my faculties. I immediately looked to the outside; I was in no condition to bear the brunt of another wall of charging white water and sustain further contact with the reef. To my relief, the expanse of water was all but dead-flat right to the horizon, bereft of energy, as if Big Blue too were catching her breath after some enervating effort.

The paddle to shore is a long one at Salsa Brava. By the time I reached the shallows off Main Street, I had pretty much recovered from the trauma of the experience, at least mentally. Physically, I wasn't so sure.

Although I didn't sense that any bones had been broken, a dull ache in my left shoulder indicated some serious bruising. My left leg was numb and probably bleeding—upon mounting my board back in the boneyard, I'd noticed a red tinge to the surrounding foam. Thing was, I really didn't want to know how bad the lacerations were. I was squeamishly putting off a visual examination.

As soon as I stood up, the numbness in my left leg dissipated and became a throb. A swollen, purple splotch the size of an apple had bloomed on the fleshy part of my left shoulder. My leg was bleeding all right, but more from a profusion of cuts than from their depth. There were no gaping rents, no cavernous gouges, just numerous ugly scratches and contusions. What did make me wince was the sight of two sea urchin spines protruding from my calf like knitting needles. Still, I had been very lucky—I'd just experienced my worst wipeout in thirty-some-odd years of globe-trotting surfing and had come out of it relatively unscathed.

There were a half dozen surfers congregated on the waterfront overlooking the break, guys who'd come in prior to the spectacle I'd made of myself with my misconceived over-the-falls-and-onto-the-reef freefall. No one said anything as I approached; then Craig From San Diego, sitting on the hood of his pickup, shook his head. "Dude," he said, "from here that went down in slow motion."

From a distance big waves seem to break slowly, a function of the time it takes for the crest to reach the trough—or, for that matter, a falling body, such as mine.

"Fucking no-paddle takeoff." Craig shook his head again. "And on a longboard. At *Salsa.*" Since my first Salsa go-out I'd been thinking about the equipment I was using, and this incident underscored my misgivings. Salsa was very definitely a shortboard wave. I'd sold my shortboard up at Puerto Escondido.

"Hey, man," Big Bill From Delaware said, "you don't want to fool around on a wave like this."

"I figured I had a shot at making the drop," I said. "Less wind and I probably would have made it." I also probably would have made the drop had I been riding a shortboard. With less surface area to catch the wind flowing up the wave face, a shortboard likely would have dropped in before the lip-launch that had sent me flying.

"It was the wave of the day, man," Craig said. "He did the right thing, went for it."

Grunts of assent all around. Even Big Bill nodded.

I very much wanted to make friends with this crew, somehow break through their well-earned elitism. Most of these guys were serious, long-time expats, true Explorers and Homesteaders. They'd given up careers, friends, *lives*, and settled on this wild piece of foreign coast for the wave at Salsa Brava, a move you had to respect, not only for the commitment to a lifestyle it represented, but for the sheer balls it took to surf that wave day in and day out.

Over time, it became obvious that the other thing about the boys at Salsa was that most of them had . . . histories. This was nothing new; I'd run into sundry fugitive types from Baja on down. But there was a subtle intensity about these guys that was different. "There are two types of people who come here," Alan From Maui told me, once we'd gotten friendly. "The 'Wanted' and the unwanted." "If you're going to write about this place, don't use my last name," was a refrain I'd become familiar with. "As a matter of fact, don't use my first name, either," one guy added.

With the one notable exception of Christopher, all the local expat surfers had done well in Talamanca, owned hotels or cabinas or restaurants or farms. No mean feat as immigrants to a poor country with an unfamiliar culture and language. I respected them also for this.

Standing in a spreading pool of my blood, I contemplated how best to capitalize on having gotten the attention of a good portion of the Salsa crew. In theory, it was a perfect moment to shake some hands, maybe extend the surf jive to solidify the inroads I'd made. But calculatingly opting for the casual, no-big-deal approach, I shrugged and looked back out at the reef. "Tell you what," I said, with a commingling of the awe and humility I truly felt as a result of the wipeout. "This is one serious wave you guys have here."

It was the right thing to say and the right way to say it.

Carrying my longboard back to my niche off Main Street, I found myself picturing Christopher's Brewer, that racy little rounded pintail, on the January day in '92 when he came to my house in Montauk to say goodbye. I remembered hefting it for weight and balance, examining its elegant lines, caressing its transitional curves, admiring the symmetry, the art of it.

A perfect Salsa board.

I stopped in front of Andrés's cabinas and sat down on a nut palm stump by a beached *lancha*. Looked out at the distant lineup. It was empty out there now. Salsa continued to crack, a classic hair-raiser going off unmolested.

Christopher. Where was Christopher?

"I haven't had a surfboard in a few months."

My mind roared, through the past, a montage of Christopher's fearlessness, his outright lunacies in the water and out.

Surfers can do anything.

What had happened to Christopher?

What had happened *to us*?

I slept late the next morning, right through first light and dawn and beyond. Then, feeling refreshed and rested, I wandered down to the little beach in front of the *cabinas* to check conditions at the hazy specter of Salsa Brava on the outer reef.

Although the swell had dropped a bit, it was still booming. The set waves were well overhead, burnished smooth by a light offshore wind. It occurred to me how deceiving the wave at Salsa is from the distant, shoreside view. You truly had to be there, in the pit, to understand.

A fluttering in my stomach indicated what I was thinking about thinking about before I actually thought it: I was thinking about thinking about going back out. The previous afternoon, while cleaning and patching my cuts and extracting urchin spines, I'd decided to take a day or two off from surfing to let my wounds heal. But now I was remembering certain waves I'd locked into over the past three days.

I've been told that skydiving is scarier the second time than the first, the reason being that the second time you know from experience what a ridiculous, stupid act jumping out of an airplane really is. It's not just ridiculous and stupid *in theory.* You've done it, so you *know.* And you also know just how fearful you're going to be when you get up there and you're in the open door looking down.

Your fear is now a fear of fear.

Paddling out, I found a full dozen of the boys spread across the lineup. Most were down at second point, leaving vacant for the moment the lineup at first point, by which I'd have to paddle to join the group. As luck would have it, a set and myself converged on first point simultaneously; I had only to redirect my stroke shoreward to pick off the best wave of the set. First point, being adjacent to the shallowest spot in the impact zone, is considered the real pit at Salsa Brava, and the wave I took was about as mean and twisted as they came. I handled it well enough to get yodels from a guy paddling out and another in the lineup at second point who had a good view of my takeoff.

No one had been outright hostile to me in the time I'd been surfing Salsa Brava, but neither had any of the crew been solicitous with a word or even eye contact. Today, however, I got grins, waves, nods, thumbs up; one guy I'd never spoken to before stroked over to say, "Heard about your wipeout yesterday. Go for it, man."

But the real revelation came when Craig From San Diego edged over on his twin-nosed speed machine. "Some of us were wondering if you'd show up here again," he said, smiling.

So that was the deal. Flinging yourself into the maw of the beast wasn't enough. You had to go back out for potentially more of the same, presumably the sooner the better. That first wave, from deep in the pit at first point while dripping blood from my wounds of the day before had been the capper. I was now one of the guys at Salsa Brava. I was from then on included in the lineup chatter; chance meetings on the street would result in extended confabulations rather than an offhand nod or monosyllabic grunt. And after a few more sessions, I would be invited to the crew's shoreside gatherings; to their homes.

One thing I quickly came to realize about the boys who rode Salsa Brava was that none of them was involved in the local drug scene. Although joints were smoked and beer-bingeing not unheard of, white drug-taking was shunned. It just wasn't done. This, as much as their dedication to the wave, set these guys apart from the general population of Puerto Viejo. And it set them apart from Christopher.

Christopher had fallen from their ranks.

California: Fever and the First Wave
from Pure Stoke
by John Grissim

Surfer and writer John Grissim (born 1941) breezily traces the roots of California surfing back more than a century.

The late afternoon sun splashed in my eyes as I leapt over the first hedge of white water and sprint-paddled to get over a small section of shorebreak before it broke. Too late. I punched through a green wall, shook my hair, and felt a trickle of chill water leak through the neck of my wetsuit. So much for the dry-look paddle-out. Still, the mint shampoo helped wash away the past two days of canned air and cigarette smoke. The muscles in my arms and shoulders sang with anticipation of a good workout. I fell into an easy rhythm as I pointed my board toward the figure sitting outside some forty yards away. The glare prevented me from seeing who it was until I watched him paddle into a glassy four-foot peak and smoothly get to his feet for a cakewalk along a sweet clean wall. Seconds later Pat Norton, one of the best local surfers, shot by me on the nose. We hooted to each other like stoked school kids.

A smooth hump was starting to wall up just as I reached the take-off point. I spun my eight-foot Doug Haut nose-rider around and stroked into the wave. The board began its familiar hiss. I angled along the wall, set the rail high on the face and kicked out ten seconds later in a state of euphoria. The ride had been short but the wave had perfect shape and, as important, this was a crisp, windless, fall day and I was back home in northern California again—out in the water and watching the hills above the beach turn buttery gold in the late afternoon sun. I smiled as I remembered the conversation I'd had with Warren much earlier in the day just before I left Chicago. Funny, he didn't understand, didn't even have a clue.

Warren is a successful investment banker whom I'd met two years previously in connection with an expedition into the Bermuda Triangle to look for a long-lost Spanish treasure galleon. The search resulted in a bonanza of silver worth millions and an opportunity for me as a member of the dive team to write a book about the adventure. Warren, who'd helped raise the money to back the effort, also has a flair for drama so I wasn't surprised when a few days earlier he offered to fly me to Chicago to discuss another project but refused to tell me anything about it over the phone. I suspected he had another treasure hunt up his sleeve but I agreed to meet him for breakfast in the Windy City if, I added, he was prepared to hear me turn down any offers. He insisted he was.

Sure enough, when two days later we met over a sumptuous breakfast at the prestigious Chicago Club, Warren began outlining another adventure—a trek to the remote mountain regions of Colombia in search of the gold of Eldorado. Colombian scholars, he declared, had uncovered new evidence that could lead to the discovery of several treasure caches. Warren's investors would raise the money for a well-equipped expedition, the cost of which would be offset by the sale of documentary film rights even if the search turned up nothing. In return for my joining this high-altitude venture, Warren would pay all expenses and give me the book rights to the story. The pitch was impressive and when he sat back to hear my reaction he appeared sure that I would accept his offer.

I thanked him for considering me for such an exciting project—

then diplomatically turned him down. "Why?" he asked, obviously surprised.

"Because there's no surf."

Warren stared at me in unblinking silence for several seconds. Finally: "John, would you mind running that by me once again?"

I explained that I tend to get nervous when I'm away from the water for very long, that the thought of weeks or months without catching a wave was too high a price to pay. This explanation was no less baffling and I sensed that Warren was having serious trouble understanding. I bailed him out by shifting to safer ground, explaining that actually I didn't want to write a book over which I would not be allowed complete editorial control, a proviso which the expedition's underwriters would understandably not wish to relinquish. For good measure I threw in a few comments about other career moves in the works. Warren seemed disappointed but relieved. He could ignore the surfing business and concentrate on the more plausible arguments, secure for the moment that he had not made the disastrous error of having invited to Chicago at his expense a bona fide wacko.

But, of course, in a sense he had. At the conclusion of breakfast Warren told me my hotel had been reserved for another night if I wished to spend some time in the city. I thanked him for his generosity but left my plans vague. I didn't have the heart to tell him I intended to catch a cab directly for O'Hare in hopes that if I got the next plane out I could be back at the beach in time for the evening glass-off. Which, in fact, was precisely what I did.

Looking back on the Chicago encounter I had to admit that my "no surf" comment was partially motivated by a sense of mischief. On more than one occasion I have gotten myself in hot water, risking everything for the sake of a one-liner. Yet I knew, too, that my need to remain near the ocean is genuine. I *do* get nervous. Moreover, I long ago realized that surfing was a focal point in my life determining my priorities in ways that must seem incomprehensible to others. But at least I can claim kinship with fellow eccentrics such as Otis Chandler, editor and publisher of the Los Angeles *Times*.

Mr. Chandler, who has long been an avid surfer as well as a mover and shaker on the California turf, has on more than one occasion demonstrated the classic symptoms of a wave junkie. For example, one Monday morning Chandler was just sitting down to an important meeting with the entire senior editorial staff when his secretary entered the conference room and handed him a note. Chandler read it quickly, threw it in the wastebasket, then without explanation abruptly announced that the meeting was postponed until the following day. He then hastily exited, leaving a dozen staffers to wonder whether there had been a death in the family or perhaps a sudden corporate crisis. As the room emptied, one of his editors retrieved the crumpled note from the wastebasket in hopes of finding a clue. The note was from an old Chandler friend in Malibu: "Surf's up!"

And even when one is not bolting boardrooms to get to the beach, a chronic preoccupation with surfing can color one's perception of events in subtle ways that may strike others as extremely insensitive or neurotic—or both. For example, some months ago a picture appeared on the front page of the San Francisco *Chronicle* showing police exhuming from a shallow beach grave the body of a child who had been murdered by some berserk nanny. The photograph was a dramatic portrait of human sadness, and yet before I was hardly aware of it, my attention wandered from the tableau of grim faces to the wave in the background. It looked to be about four feet and peeling left with possibilities. I scanned the caption for details of the wave's location. Similarly, during the movie *Ten*, starring Dudley Moore and Bo Derek, there is a scene in which Ms. Derek is bounding along the beach in near-nude splendor, every inch a woman who rates ten on a scale of ten. During that sequence my eyes again wandered, this time to the number four beach-break behind her.

This narrow focusing of one's responses has its parallel in the realm of natural disasters. Surfers, it seems, have taken quite literally the meaning of the aphorism, "It's an ill wind that blows no good." When hurricanes strike coastal areas such as Florida, the Carolinas, or Corpus Christi, Texas, invariably in the aftermath a group of hardcore surfers will elude the National Guard street patrols and be out in the water as soon as the huge storm waves develop decent shape. Here in California, when fierce Santa Ana winds recently struck the San Bernardino and Pacific palisades causing fires that destroyed scores of homes, newscasters overlooked the silver lining: Santa Ana winds, being offshore, will turn the most unruly waves into beautiful walls that peel off with centerfold perfection. With any swell at all, particularly from the southwest, the coastline between Ventura and San Diego will briefly offer up enough exquisite surf to provide tens of thousands a taste of paradise. In fact, I sometimes get the uncomfortable feeling that the entire southern California coast could be burning to the very waterline but as long as there was a swell and a Santa Ana, the line-up would be packed with nary an eye cast shoreward.

Here at my home break along the rural coast north of San Francisco there are no seasonal offshores, but winter storm swells occasionally pull prodigious amount of sand off the beach, creating temporary sandbars. These, in turn, spawn several peaks that provide stoked locals with a shot of serious juice. During a recent winter when a dozen beachfront homes were nearly inundated by wave action, the community pitched in to build a sandbag revetment. As soon as the immediate danger had passed, a half dozen volunteers donned wetsuits and paddled out toward the virgin peaks, hell-bent for glory and total wave saturation. For the remainder of the afternoon, not even the whine of a TV news crew's helicopter could entirely drown the chorus of hoots and yells that filled the air.

And then there was the time a representative from the county's disaster planning office gave a slide lecture to a group of local residents. Inasmuch as the village rests right on top of the San Andreas fault, the official laid heavy stress on the catastrophic effects of a major earthquake (expected in the 80s). When he somberly predicted the reef at the end of the bay would subside by as much as three feet, several faces immediately brightened. A voice murmured, "All ri-i-ight." Clearly, the surfer caucus in the audience was delighted with the prospect, since waves passing over a deeper reef would lose less power, thus providing more punch to the channel entrance at the north end of the bay. It's an ill wind indeed.

The point to all of the foregoing is not that surfing is a uniquely consuming or addictive pastime but that the character of its addiction, the extent to which it can become a very important part of people's lives, is unique.

The key to surfing's immense attraction, the element that, more than anything, defines it, is the ocean. From time immemorial this watery envelope which covers three fifths of the planet's surface has inspired love, awe, and mortal fear. And since the very beginning of mankind's tentative dominion, the ocean has for some time been the world in which entire lives have been played out. Regardless of how benign or tempestuous it may be, the ocean has remained a kind of wilderness. Its waters surge up the remotest shores of uninhabited South Pacific islands, upon the crowded beaches north of Sydney, Australia, and slam against the Dana Point, California, breakwater like a vast fluid ether—mysterious, unpredictable, and immensely powerful. To leave the security of *terra firma*, to paddle a mere hundred yards away from shore on a sliver of fiberglass and foam is to quickly comprehend the reality of that wilderness.

You can be two hundred feet from Huntington Beach pier on a warm clear day with twenty thousand bathers on the beach—and perhaps two hundred other surfers hassling for waves around you—and you can still experience that wilderness, still feel the power of the sea, still engage it one on one. As important, there's something about being out there that offers an escape form the cares of the workaday world, the pressures, the crunch and confusion. At least part of that something is the wave, that paradox of nature—elemental, fluid, fickle, at once so tempting and yet utterly indifferent to the presence of man. And on that same sunny day the swell could come up fast and big, a heavy rip could develop, and you could find yourself in trouble. If conditions change in any way that puts you out of your depth, even for a few seconds, you will instantly feel very much alone in that watery wilderness.

This sense of wilderness, of its joys and terrors, is why surfers possess a kinship with fishermen, sailors, and mariners the world over—and why the more dedicated among them always have some part of their awareness focused on the sweep of the weather, the shift of the tides, and the rhythms of the sea. Considering the common bond with the brine that all sea people share, I've wondered on occasion if on some level we may possibly be precursors of a branch of *homo sapiens* that will eventually return to live in the ocean from which the first life forms emerged. Some naturalists have suggested that man carries the sea within him in the form of blood, that its salty taste is an echo of the medium that once nurtured his primordial ancestors.

Weighty stuff, this. Moreover, it may seem presumptuous to accord surfing the same dignity and status that accrue to the traditional maritime occupations. After all, one may ask, aren't we really just talking about a bunch of teenagers hassling waves at 22nd Street in Newport Beach or at Dee Why in Sydney? And isn't surfing an activity done solely for the pure fun of it? The answer is no, the kids out there are merely the most visible facet of a larger community of surfers whose ages span three generations. And yes, pure fun is the essential goal, but fun is what makes surfing one of the class acts in a world where so much emphasis is laid upon being productive and functional. As important, though surfing has a relatively scant history and tradition, that which it does have is both rich and telling. And its mavericks—pioneers, heroes, outlaws, and celebrated iconoclasts—have had a singular role in defining surfing as a sport, a subculture, a way of life, even an existential attitude. In fact, in the past, surfing has had an impact on contemporary Western culture, particularly in the U.S., that extended far beyond the water's edge. Why and how this was so is worthy of digression.

It is true that surfing very probably originated in Polynesia and was subsequently exported to the Hawaiian Islands by the Polynesian explorer/pioneers in the eleventh century. It is true that longboard surfing at Waikiki's inside break was the rage of Hawaii's royal family by the time Captain James Cook first dropped the hook off Kauai in

1778. And it is also true that Olympic swimming champion Duke Kahanamoku was one of the pioneer greats of surfing who, among many accomplishments, had Publics wired as early as 1900. Yet surfing as a social phenomenon, as an embryonic forerunner of the radical high-tech, all-rocker sport and lifestyle it has become, really began in California. And ironically, that beginning had a lot to do with the abundance of jack rabbits in the San Fernando Valley—and electric streetcars.

In 1901 the board of directors of the Pacific Electric Railway in Los Angeles were faced with a dilemma. Many of the city's residents, it seems, had developed a fondness for weekend daytrips to the San Fernando Valley, which was little more than a desert, for the express purpose of shooting jack rabbits from streetcars. Rifles and shotguns were the preferred weapons. Sandwiches and beer were optional amenities. While railway officials agreed that gunning down bunnies from streetcars was wholesome family fare, they worried about the lack of passengers on the southern line that ran to Redondo Beach. What was needed was a promotional gimmick to spark interest. They found their answer in George Freeth, an Irish-Hawaiian Redondo local who owned a 14-foot redwood longboard weighing 120 pounds, and who regularly surfed the beachbreak, even going so far as to cut across a wave ahead of the curl, a move that wasn't generally practiced until the 1930s. The railway put Freeth on the payroll, hyped his derring-do in the press, and for the next few months he put on a show several times a day on weekends, come slop or high water. The promotion worked and in a matter of weeks the passenger traffic count on rail lines to the beaches of Santa Monica Bay was up significantly. More important, George Freeth had sowed the seeds of stoke in southern California; in the decade that followed, a hard core of converts established surfing beachheads from San Diego to San Francisco. No one later determined if the Valley rabbit population ever returned to normal; however, Freeth may be the first surfer ever to turn pro.

During the Roaring Twenties surfing remained a quaint oddity in the southland, but during the Depression the beach population grew.

Many were lured to the coast by its beauty, warmth, and easy-going lifestyle. Young men without families could get by pretty cheaply, subsisting off odd jobs, and still find time to enjoy life on the beach. It was quite probably in Malibu or Venice in the 30s that America's work ethic began seriously to crumble. And it was at breaks like San Onofre, Trestles, Paddleboard Cove, and La Jolla that longboarders learned to work six- to eight-foot surf closer to the power pocket, experimenting with design, technique, and thresholds of fear. To be sure, parallel events were taking place in Hawaii and Australia, but it was California with its unique culture—young, sensual, rootless, flashy, fast, and not a little nuts—that made surfing not just a sport, but a lifestyle.

During World War II most California surfers were in uniform, leaving the waves to a smattering of beachcombers, draft dodgers, kids, gentle vagabonds, and civilian locals who worked in defense-related jobs. At war's end a great many southern California veterans went back to school on the G.I. bill, but some more or less dropped out, opting instead for life near the water. Dave Rochlen, Sr., during an interview in the early 60s, recalled the war, and his passion: "Nobody loved the ocean better than I did. All through the war I slept on top of the deck with my fins in my pack and my arm through the pack straps. I figured if the ship got blown up, at least I might have a chance. All I want is half a chance—I might be able to last longer with fins—might even be able to take a couple of guys with me. And when the war ended— Boom—we were back in the environment. It was devotion, like seeing a girl again . . . like, 'I'm never gonna leave!' We gave ourselves over to it entirely. I think it was because we had spent four or five years in the war and we had survived. And it had all been bad. Now there was no question about what had us by the throat. It was the ocean. Everything else was secondary."

What fueled Rochlen's, and others', great passion was their new independence, and an unwillingness to drop back into a regimented social system. The stance was not angry, it was go-it-alone, laissez-faire, unconsciously romantic, and a bit escapist. But that life was based on a clear, clean, passionate vision that was attainable—as were the waves.

Whenever and wherever the swell was up, there was always plenty of room. In 1954, for example, one newspaper estimated there were "as many as 1500 surfers in Southern California."

Granted, not all surfers of this era possessed Rochlen's outlook; however, a maverick spirit, combined with a commitment to having fun, pervaded the surfing community. "Surfer" suggested a natural bohemianism, an outlaw subculture that was daring, adventurous, sexy, and, if not exactly illegal, at least on occasion illicit. As important, these early veterans were tough, solid, and tested—tested by waves as much as war. And it was their nonconformist lifestyles that influenced a new generation of young Turks born around the time of Pearl Harbor and destined to become legends. To a real degree the California surfer of the late 40s and early 50s, with his baggies and huarache sandals, with his penchant for crazed "surfaris" to Mexico in search of waves, this self-made product of the tumultuous California gestalt who believed in something with an integrity that few understood, was a forerunner of major social phenomena. His rise paralleled that of the beatniks, Kerouac's and Cassady's transcontinental methedrine marathons; and predated Ayn Rand's *Atlas Shrugged*, hippies, even Tim Leary's dictum to turn on, tune in, and drop out. Ahead of the curl and ahead of the pack.

Very likely the surfer's significance in that early era has gone unrecognized because scholars of American history have always found it difficult to take seriously a subculture of mostly tanned, fit beach-dwellers who were noticeably free of existential angst, who pursued surf with great passion, and got laid a lot. They regarded surfers as having neither anything to say, nor the ability to say it. Needless to say, they'd never met Mickey Dora. Surfers, it appeared, were relegated to California's flaky fringe, along with Muscle Beach, UFO cults, and Gypsy Boots fig bars. Finally, surfing's claim to historical legitimacy was torpedoed by Hollywood.

It started in 1956 with Hollywood screenwriter Frederick Kohner's novel *Gidget*, the story of a teen surfette who hung out with the wave crowd at Malibu Cove and learned about life in the fast lane, fast. A modest but hardly lurid potboiler, the book was spun off into a feature movie (shot at Arroyo Secos, north of Trancas) and a TV series, all of which helped launch surfing as a national fad. Within a year Madison Avenue had adopted surfing themes for TV and radio commercials aimed at the youth market. In the meantime surfing movies by Bud Browne, then Bruce Brown and John Severson were drawing huge crowds at the Santa Monica Civic Auditorium and other coastal venues, helping create not only immense interest in surfing but an entire subculture with its own heroes, dress styles, language, and totems. Soon, surfing movies were drawing large audiences inland. Kids in Winslow, Arizona; Denver, Colorado; and Topeka, Kansas— many of whom had never *seen* the ocean—were affecting bushy peroxide blond hair and had adopted the lexicon of boss, bitchin', stokaboka, go for it, and stoked. There to fuel their landlocked dream was Bruce Brown's *Endless Summer*, an engaging feature-length surfing documentary released in 1962. The movie was so successful on the 16mm auditorium circuit that it was later enlarged to 35mm and distributed world-wide where it grossed an astounding $8 million. Today *Endless Summer* still stands as a remarkable document, representing the only contact that millions of older Americans have ever had with surfing.

Having even greater impact was surfing music, the pervasive California sound track that accompanied the craze as well as defined the culture. Balboa's Dick Dale and the Dell-Tones, an early Duane Eddy hybrid, was probably the first surf band. Many followed, as did a number of surfing oriented Top Ten hit singles, notably "Wipe Out" by the Surfaris, Jack Nitzsche's "Lonely Surfer," and Jan and Dean's "Sidewalk Surfin'." Towering above these classics was a string of smash hits by the Beach Boys, a group which not only captured the quintessential California coastal culture with the likes of "Surfin' Safari," "Catch a Wave," "California Girls," "Surfin' USA," and "Do It Again," but was arguably the only significant presence in American pop music during that strange hiatus between the death of Buddy Holly in 1959 and the American debut of the Beatles in 1964. And the character of that presence, the core of its imagery, was surfing—that and tanned California girls, innocent sex, waves and sunshine, little deuce coupes and woody station wagons, and fun, fun, fun. In short the whole California dream.

To be sure, the exploitation of that dream was an industry unto itself for the first half of the 60s, and found one of its more bizarre manifestations in the Beach Blanket movies with Frankie Avalon and ex-Mouseketeer Annette Funicello. Ironically, these hot-fun-in-the-summertime celluloid epics represented Hollywood's last shot at marketing the innocence and magic of that dream to a postwar baby boom audience. Acid and Vietnam would soon see to that. But for surfing the damage was done: Hollywood had insured that for the next few generations the reality of surfing would never be accurately perceived by a larger world. Perhaps it is just as well, for in these crowded times surfing is one religion that does not seek converts.

Elsewhere—and largely overlooked—in the early 60s were a crew of young men who emerged from the surfing world to achieve considerable financial success in fields often directly related to their first love. Grubbie Clark developed a technology for making foam surfboard blanks which established Clark Foam as the premier manufacturer of quality blanks worldwide, a position his firm still holds. Hobie Alter, another pioneer in foam, developed the Hobie Cat sail craft and today heads a multimillion dollar surf-sail-and-watersport empire. Jack O'Neill, who as a surfer back in San Francisco in the 50s, began experimenting with closed-cell neoprene, developed the wetsuit enabling surfers for the first time to surf in bone-chilling waters in complete comfort. These exposure suits revolutionized surfing by opening it up as a year-round activity. Today, his highly successful Santa Cruz–based O'Neill Inc. provides watersportsmen the world over with wetsuits of unsurpassed quality.

Among other successes are Tom Morey and Mike Doyle, former southern California Malibu heavyweights, who developed the Morey-Doyle softboard, which is not only great for junk surf but has a soft outer-skin, easy-paddle buoyancy that makes it ideal for beginning surfers. Among the pair's other inventions is the highly popular Boogie

Board. Another Malibu alumnus is Joey Cabell, whose brilliant style on the waves led him to Hawaiian waters, thence to a start as a restaurateur with a modest Waikiki restaurant he dubbed The Chart House. That success grew into the Chart House Restaurants, an empire of first-rate establishments in twenty states whose hallmark is dramatic architecture set amidst the most dramatic settings by the sea and in the mountains. Cabell sold most of his interest in the chain a few years ago but his imprint lingers: on the walls of many of the restaurants hang an impressive photo gallery of surfing portraits.

Lastly, no list of achievers, however short, would be complete without mention of the Brotherhood of Light. This Laguna Beach, California–based band of entrepreneurs was for some years the most successful, respected, and generally righteous provider of absolutely pure LSD, quality marijuana, hashish, and other organic psychedelics. Its founders were young surfers who, on Baja surfing trips in the early 60s, smuggled across the Mexican border kilos of Oaxacan and Michoacán under the floorboards of their woodies and Jeeps, at first as a casual lark, then later as a business. Surfing and its attendant lifestyle nurtured their success. By the late 60s the Brotherhood was a world-wide operation whose by-now-very-rich associates were no longer surfing. They owned sprawling mountaintop retreats, ranches, beach houses, and silver Porsche Targas, and lived lives intertwined with gurus, cult heroes, rock stars, and assorted Aquarian celebrities. In the end the Brotherhood collapsed, some say because all that money dimmed the Light. Someday the full fascinating story may be told. It is tempting to suggest here that failure stemmed from being out of the water too long.

In the meantime a remark made by Sam Hawk comes to mind. A California veteran and a long-time practitioner of North Shore power surfing, Hawk was asked by Australian John Witzig whatever became of the California surfers who once dominated the sport. Hawk grinned. "They're either dead, in jail, or rich—in that order."

That comment, which on one level is simplistic, nonetheless reflects an historical truth: the California surfin' dream, which for so long rode the crest of a national craze, was super-hyped to larger-than-life excess until it simply collapsed, a victim of its own hot air and a radically changing social and psychic landscape. Yet the essential stoke of surfing, not the fantasy but the reality of being out there riding waves, remained. Moreover, while the surfing population continued to grow on both coasts of the United States, world-traveling California surfers carried the torch abroad, helping kindle new flames elsewhere, notably in Europe and South Africa. Ironically, in Australia, where surfing in the 60s was already off and running, the sport was destined to flourish on a scale that would eventually dwarf California's brief but splashy dominance.

And yet there is something about California, something about the attitudes and lifestyle of its pioneer watermen, that pervades the surfing community the world over. Blessed with good weather and waves, brimming with youthful energy and possibilities, and sparked by a go-for-it gusto and optimism (not to mention the Beach Boys sound track), California set the tone for surfers everywhere.

This influence may be one of the most significant legacies the Golden State has bestowed on surfing, but it is too early to render historical judgment. California, itself perched on the continental lip of a still young nation, is riding a wave of immense possibilities.

And as always, there remains the ocean and its savage magic. Today more than half a million people surf regularly on the West Coast. Be they high school surf rats, college students, real estate brokers, doctors, graphic designers, fishermen, nurses, welders, or full-time surfers—to name just a few categories to which my surfer friends belong—each has found something in the simple act of riding waves that is immensely rewarding. And like surfers everywhere throughout the world, they well understand that sometimes not even a chance to search for the gold of Eldorado is strong enough inducement to forego the sunset gold of an evening glass-off and four-foot perfection.

Mr. Sunset Rides Again
by Rob Buchanan

Jeff Hakman was surfing's biggest superstar during the early '70s, and went on to co-found a major surfwear company. Along the way, he discovered heroin.

In 1956, the novelist and Hollywood screenwriter Peter Viertel traveled to the Basque country of southwestern France to watch location shooting for director Henry King's *The Sun Also Rises*. Viertel, a friend of Hemingway's, had written the screenplay, but it wasn't long before his attention started to wander. Standing on the promenade in Biarritz, watching the perfect rollers churn past the Villa Belza, he decided to send home for his surfboard and, as legend has it, became the first man ever to surf France.

Viertel might not recognize La Côte Basque today. There are McDonald's now, and shopping malls as hideous as any in Orange County, and an autoroute, the A63, that rumbles with trucks headed north from Spain. And of course there are surfers, so many that in the summertime you can forget about finding an uncrowded break.

As ye sow, so shall ye reap, and all that.

And yet in the fall, if you drive just south of Biarritz on the old Route Nationale, it is sometimes still possible to stumble upon the swells of yesteryear. At least that's the way it feels when I pull into the parking lot at Lafitenia, a woodsy, secluded cove with a long, hollow, right-handed point break. Back in the midseventies, Lafitenia was a mandatory stop for American and Australian surfers on the Endless Summer circuit, a hard-partying band who eventually morphed their vagabond act into today's World Championship Tour. A quarter-century later the place is, fittingly, the site of the Silver Edition Masters World Championships, a ten-day-long blowout that's part surf contest—it's the official world championships of seniors surfing—and part class reunion.

Sponsored by Quiksilver Europe, whose headquarters is nearby, the early-October event features 32 of the biggest names from surfing's storied past. The two favorites, for instance, in the 35-to-40-year-old "grommet" category ("grommet" being a mildly derisive term for an adolescent surfer) are Aussies Tom Carroll and Cheyne Horan, who not so long ago were starring on the regular circuit. (Carroll, 36, won the world title twice; Horan, 39, was a four-time runner-up.) But the real royalty here are the men competing in the over-40 division, the ones who launched pro surfing as a viable sport in the late 1960s and 1970s. They're a mostly Australian bunch that includes Wayne Lynch, the 47-year-old mystical guru whose preference for surfing on unorthodox board designs back in 1968 helped kick off the shortboard revolution; Peter Townend, 46, whose methodical compilation of contest outcomes from around the globe resulted in the crowning of the sport's first world champion (himself, by sly coincidence) in 1976; and Wayne "Rabbit" Bartholomew, 45, the brash loudmouth who led the Australian Invasion of Oahu's North Shore in the midseventies, and got most of his teeth knocked out in the process.

But if you had to pick one über-kahuna out of this august lineup, it would probably be a diminutive 51-year-old American named Jeff Hakman, otherwise known as Mr. Sunset. As a teenage surf prodigy on Oahu's North Shore in the mid-1960s, Hakman mastered the fearsome break at Sunset Beach. He eventually became one of the premier big-wave riders and a tireless competitor who pushed the sport into a new, contest-oriented era. His real legacy, though, began after he retired from professional surfing in 1977 and founded Quiksilver USA, an offshoot of the surfwear brand that originated in Australia, thereby blazing the path for the marketing juggernaut that is today's surf industry. Hakman might have ridden that wave forever, all the way to tens of millions of dollars and a big house in Del Mar. But the need for an intense physical rush stayed with him after he'd left pro surfing behind, and when heroin and the high life replaced big waves as his ride of choice, the result was a 15-year off-and-on struggle with addiction, during which he nearly lost everything, including his life. It's a very different kind of legacy—with many semipublic wipeouts—and one that is still unfolding.

The past seems both near and far away as Jeff Hakman trots down to the beach at Lafitenia, a board under each arm. His hair is gray and close-cropped now, and there are some worry lines at the corners of his eyes, but he's the same height and weight as in his prime (five-foot-seven, 150 pounds), and he's still got the flat stomach and bouncy legs of a kid. And the smile, too: a big, boyish, gummy grin.

It's a sunny, blustery afternoon on the Bay of Biscay, and the swell, though sizeable, is bumpy and confused. Hakman deliberates for a few minutes before choosing the longer of his two boards, a gun-shaped seven foot, two inches, and then launches himself through the nasty shore break. He sets up a bit outside the normal takeoff, hoping for something bigger and cleaner to roll through. After missing the first wave, and then the next, he settles for a choppy, flat one that backs off suddenly. It's a dicey takeoff, but he pops quickly to his feet, takes the step in stride, and pulls a deep, classically round bottom turn, his trademark.

"*Et voilà c'est parti!*" says the French emcee over the public-address system. "*C'est Monsieur Sunset même, Jeff Hakman.*"

A little cheer goes up in the hospitality tent, and the monster-lensed photographers down on the beach start to fire away. But Mr. Sunset doesn't do much with the wave. The judges are looking for snaps and big cutbacks, all the showy point-scoring maneuvers of professional surfing today. Hakman just swoops easily down the line, pulling more classical curves, his long arms winging wide and his hands dangling loosely.

No one in the crowd seems disappointed with this performance. Indeed, there's a smattering of applause as Hakman kicks out at the end of his ride. "He doesn't rip anymore," notes one French journalist admiringly. "He floats now. But underneath, you can still see the same style."

Masters surfing has only been around for a few years and isn't nearly as big a phenomenon as, say, the Senior PGA. In spirit, it's closer to seniors tennis—less an opportunity for a second career than a chance to do some character acting. Still, it is entertaining to watch yesterday's heroes disport themselves on the waves, and most of them can still rip. In the over-forties, Rabbit Bartholomew and Michael Ho, the quiet Hawaiian Pipeline specialist, handily win their first-round heats, as does Oahu-raised Bobby Owens, who now runs the Patagonia store in Santa Cruz (and who apparently spends a lot of time on the water, testing product). Six-foot-four Australian Simon Anderson, who was the first to market the three-finned surfboard, astonishes the crowd by throwing his legendary snaps on a board no longer than he is. Also drawing cheers is 49-year-old Reno Abellira, a former Hawaiian champion who has such a low center of gravity that he can still fit his slipper into extremely tight tubes and exit clean. Even the amiable Australian Ian Cairns, 47, a one-time big-wave star known as Kanga, who now sports an extra 30 or so pounds around his midriff, has no problem taking off in a mean beach break. Moreover, he seems to enjoy himself when he does. His wife videotapes him, and his old mates slap him on the back and offer him a "tinnie" of beer when the session's over. It's a feel-good experience all the way around.

From a spectator's point of view, however, the most interesting competition at the Masters probably takes place off the water. A lot of attendees refer to the event as a "gathering of the tribe," and the opening-night dinner, at a rustic Basque inn up in the foothills, has the feel of a giant potlatch, with old friends table-hopping, the Hawaiian contingent strumming away on their guitars, and heartfelt, boozy toasts to and by the hosts from Quiksilver Europe.

Still, as the days go by, it's hard to dismiss the idea that there are two overlapping clans within the tribe. Most conspicuous are the guys with haircuts and mortgages and good jobs, usually in the surf business. After a period of wondering what he was going to do with his life, Rabbit Bartholomew, for instance, wound up running the Association of Surfing Professionals, the sport's world body. Cairns is a surf-contest promoter who lives in southern California. Others are entrepreneurs, like Paul "Smelly" Neilsen, president of one of the biggest chains of surf shops in Australia. Then there are the apparel executives. Peter Townend is the global marketing director for Rusty, a California board and surfwear maker. Michael Tomson, a skinny 44-year-old guy who favors fatigues and T-shirts, is a former South African star who founded his own clothing company, Gotcha, 22 years ago in a rented house in Laguna Beach, California. Today, Irvine-based Gotcha is consistently ranked in the five top-selling surfwear brands internationally.

The other clan consists of the guys who are still mainly surfing, paddling, and "living the life." For the most part they're the seekers, slackers, and free spirits who tend to avoid the straight life, such as it is, for as long as they can. One day, talking to Reno Abellira, I ask him what he is planning to do after the contest. He's going to California, he says vaguely, "to clean out an apartment and maybe sell a car." Glen Winton, the notoriously reticent Australian star who became known as Mr. X, is disarmingly candid about his career ambitions. "Right now I'm working as a security guard at a shopping mall," he says, "but what I really want to do is to become a judge."

"So you're going to law school and all that?"

"No, no," Winton says, laughing. "I mean a surf judge."

Hakman is the one guy who doesn't quite fit into either category.

Between heats, he moves through the competitors' enclosure, mingling easily with members of both clans. There's a lot of smiling and shoulder slapping, remembering swells and epic parties. But you also see an extra beat of watchfulness from his fellow surfers, an uncertainty as to who exactly Hakman is today. Sure, he's now got homes in two of the world's most beautiful places (Biarritz and Kauai), a lucrative but not-too-demanding job as the marketing guru—his actual title—for Quiksilver Europe, and, even more remarkably, a reborn career as an advertising icon for the company. But you still get the sense that, for some people, Hakman may have gotten a little too far out there to ever really come back.

In the contest program, Hakman is listed not as American, but Hawaiian. Although he was born in Southern California and learned to surf in Palos Verdes, his father, an aeronautical engineer by profession but a passionate "waterman" at heart, relocated the family to Makaha, on the North Shore of Oahu, when Jeff was 12. Makaha was a rough town in those days, and *haoles* like Hakman could face a brand of hostility that made the "Valley go home" localism of Palos Verdes seem tame by comparison. "Even today," Hakman says, "the tourist board will tell you, 'Uh, don't go there.'" But Hakman had no problem mastering the vibe. "I'm not aggressive," he explains. "I always try to bend and flex around."

Within a year, Hakman was a regular in lineups up and down the North Shore. But he created his first real sensation in January 1963, when he and his father decided to paddle out at Waimea Bay on a 20-foot-plus day. Waimea is the North Shore's biggest regular break— double-high freight trains of moving water that, should you blow the takeoff or get caught inside, can hold you under for 30 seconds—and at that time only a few grown men had dared to surf it. It's impossible to overstate the raw courage of that moment: Hakman was barely 14-years-old, and small for his age to boot, weighing in at under 100 pounds and not yet five feet tall. He shakily rode one wave, and wiped out on the second. Then, with the rest of the lineup looking on in disbelief, he paddled into another one, rocketed down the face, and made the bottom turn, and then kicked out into the channel. "It really wasn't that hard," Hakman recalls nonchalantly.

The wave that truly appealed to Hakman was at Sunset Beach, a notoriously hard-to-read break halfway up the North Shore. "It intrigued me and scared the shit out of me at the same time," he says. "Things move around a lot, depending on the size and direction of the swell. It's not like Pipeline, where there's one definite takeoff spot. It's faster and steeper, and there's so much more water. You can't halfway commit. You gotta put yourself right in the guts of it." By the time he was 15, Hakman knew the wave as well as anyone; it was, he says, "my backyard."

Two years later, in 1965, Hakman was invited to compete at Sunset in the inaugural Duke Kahanamoku Invitational. Dreamed up by a Honolulu nightclub promoter, the Duke was a new kind of surfing competition. It boasted an international field consisting of the 24 best surfers in the world. There was a television crew from CBS to film the event. And there was cash—not prize money, but appearance fees—for the contestants. It was, in other words, the precursor of modern professional contests.

The surf was an unruly eight to ten feet the day of the finals. Paddling out to the point, Hakman caught the first wave and then realized that the next set was coming from much farther left, on the outside. He got there first and came away with what one of the judges would later recall as the best ride ever seen at Sunset: a screaming tube that went on and on through several different sections of the wave as Hakman crouched in a cheater-five—the toes of one foot wrapped over the nose of the board. A few waves later, he pulled a similar stunt, and the judges had no choice but to give the world's first pro tournament title to a 17-year-old kid.

Hakman was characteristically modest about the moment. "I was overwhelmed," he says in *Mr. Sunset*, a recent biography written by

Australian journalist Phil Jarrat that includes a portrait of surfing's formative era and selections from Hakman's extensive photo archives. When Hakman was pressed by his surfing pal Fred van Dyke to make a speech, Jarrat writes, he only managed to get out, "Ah, thanks everybody. I'm ah, stoked! Is that OK, Fred?"

Thus began a ten-year period when Hakman was arguably the best competitive surfer in the world. "They called him Surf Chimp because of his short legs and long arms," says Gibus de Soultrait, editor of the French magazine *Surf Session* and, as the French often are, an avid student of obscure American subcultures. "He always took a high line on the wave that gave him a lot of speed, and being so small and having a low center of gravity, he never fell. That helps when you're surfing Sunset with no leash.

"Hakman was more competitive than his main rival in those days, Gerry Lopez," de Soultrait continues. "Gerry was a soul surfer, into the mystical side. Jeff was always a guy who wanted to win. The two of them were at the heart of the old debate about surfing—is it a sport or is it an art?"

If it was a sport, it wasn't a particularly organized one at the time. There was no official circuit, no overall points title, and very little prize money. Income, such as it was, came from endorsement deals with surfboard manufacturers, travel stipends from surf filmmakers, and all the other scams that enterprising world travelers dream up. In Hakman's case, that occasionally meant small-time drug-trafficking schemes— something that seemed like little more than heart-pounding capers at the time but, in retrospect, ultimately helped grease his slide. "It was acceptable to take a couple of ounces with you and sell them when you got somewhere, to pay for the plane ticket," Hakman says matter-of-factly. "The people who were doing it weren't bad people. Now it's much more organized, and the street scenes are so hard, but back then I thought those people and that life were glamorous."

Yet as Hakman worked the "international beach scene," both partying and purveying, he was mulling more conventional business ideas. One day in 1975, at a contest in Queensland, Australia, he had to borrow a pair of board shorts at the last minute. They were of a tight-woven poplin and cut with a much wider yoke than anything he'd worn before, and they closed with Velcro and a snap instead of ties. Plus they had a cool name—Quiksilver—and a catchy logo in the shape of a wave. "I remember thinking, 'Wow, these are pretty good,'" Hakman says. "Gerry [Lopez] and I took 'em back to Hawaii and told Jack Shipley, Lopez's business partner [in a surfboard and sandal business], to import some." Shipley did, and even though he had to sell the Quiksilvers at $17 a pair—$5 more than the going rate for board shorts—he sold out all 100 pairs in two weeks.

That winter, still pondering the boardshort business, Hakman wound up at a place called Ulu Watu, in Bali, then the hot new surf spot. Drugs were a big part of the scene in Ulu Watu; the surfer who showed Hakman the place liked to quaff psilocybin mushroom milkshakes before every session in the waves. Hakman was taken aback when he found a bunch of his friends smoking heroin through foil, but by the time he left Bali, he admits in *Mr. Sunset*, he too "had a nice habit going."

Jeff Hakman's apartment in Biarritz is half a block from the Côtes des Basques, the clifftop promenade where Peter Viertel got his big idea back in 1956. It's an austere neighborhood of high walls and carefully trimmed topiary, a bit sedate, perhaps, for a surf legend and a legendary partyer. Then again, Hakman is a family man now. Six months a year he and his Australian wife of 12 years, Cherie, and their two children, Ryan, 17, and Lea, 7, live here; it's just a few minutes' drive to Hakman's office at the Quiksilver Europe headquarters. The other half of the year they're in Hanalei Bay, Kauai, where Hakman doesn't do much except surf.

The big sun-drenched apartment is empty today. Cherie and the kids have gone back to Hawaii so as not to miss the start of the school year. Hakman will rejoin them in a few days, when the contest is over, but in the meantime he's alone with a stack of surf videos, a big bowl of vitamins and food supplements in the kitchen, and on the dinner table, a copy of a book titled *Yesterday's Tomorrow: Recovery Meditations for Hard Cases.*

Hakman is a fundamentally shy man, but part of the recovery process, he knows, is being able to share one's story. And so, half-reluctantly, he begins talking. A year after that fateful stop in Bali, he explains, he made his bid for the Quiksilver name. It happened like this: Preparing for his annual Australian swing, he asked his board shaper to install an extra-thick fin, hollowed out to keep down the weight. Shortly before his departure, he filled it with three ounces of cocaine—not to use himself, but to trade for heroin, which was much cheaper than cocaine in Australia. By the time Hakman showed up for the 1976 Bells Beach Classic, the preeminent surf contest of the Australian season, he was already strung out. Yet two amazing things happened that week, although Hakman is a little shaky on the details. Not only did he win the tournament, the first time a non-Australian had done so, but he also somehow persuaded the owners of Quiksilver Australia to grant him licensing rights to their name, logo, and short-board design for the U.S. market, in exchange for 5 percent of the new U.S. company and 5 percent of its sales.

Hakman had been talking to a surfer friend he'd met in Ulu Watu, a USC business school graduate named Bob McKnight, about the Quiksilver idea. With the license secured, the two of them set about building a business. They began a series of mad drives up and down the coast between their makeshift factory in Orange County, the fabric suppliers in Los Angeles, and all the surf shops they could talk their way into. There was no time to surf, and Hakman forgot about heroin for a while, too. But then the old urge returned, and before he knew it a friend was showing him how to shoot it intravenously.

For the next couple of years, insists McKnight, now the CEO of Quiksilver USA, in Huntington Beach, California (the new location of its headquarters), he had no idea about Hakman's heroin habit. "Either I was naive," McKnight says, "or he hid it incredibly well."

Whatever the case, the company grew, slowly at first and then with startling speed. By the early eighties, annual sales were approaching five million. Hakman began to have a lot of pocket money, and his taste for heroin grew apace; at one point, he says, it was costing him $500 a day.

Hakman is surprisingly unemotional as he tells the story. There's no self-recrimination or wistfulness. Instead, there's almost a sense of wonder, as if he were describing a particularly phenomenal day on the North Shore. He doesn't look to blame his addiction on anything, and he won't take the easy way out and say it was a need for adrenaline inherited from his big-wave surfing days.

"I wouldn't go so far as to say letting go of the belt is like dropping into 30-foot Waimea," he says. "That instant of dropping down a big gnarly face—it's very close, equally potent, but not the same. On the other hand, the same thing that got me addicted definitely made me a good surfer. You know, once you get a direction, you go and commit." He pauses again. "I thought I could handle it," he says. "But every addict thinks that—that they're different."

Early on, Hakman had begun selling small numbers of shares in Quiksilver USA to pay for drugs. After 1980, though, the trickle became a deluge. "At 30, I thought I was going to live happily ever after," he says, his eyes moistening for the first time. "I still had about a 33 percent share in the company." He stops and rubs his face with his hands, regaining control. "By '82, it was all gone. The third partner in the company finally said, 'Jeff, you gotta leave. This isn't working at all.' I went, 'That's understandable.' I had a six-month-old son and about $3,000, total."

Hakman stops again, thinking it over. "The last 10 percent I sold for $100,000," he says, the barest note of regret in his voice. "It's worth at least $15 million today."

Midway through the third day of the Silver Edition competition, the swell begins to drop, from eight feet to five feet at first, and then all the way down to three. Even so, the men compete that day, and the third round turns out to be a good outing for Hakman; he finishes second to Wayne Lynch. But day four dawns sunny, calm, and flat, and the contest is postponed until further notice.

What do old surfers do when there's no surf? Pretty much the same thing young surfers do. They play video games, smoke pot, and laugh their way around the hotel golf course, and they eat, drink, and tell stories—competitively, of course.

One day after breakfast, Joey Buran, a stubble-headed Californian who became a minister about 15 years ago, regales a small but appreciative crowd with tales of an epic day at Waimea Bay when he barely escaped death by scratching his way over set after set of monster waves. Once he found himself safely outside, however, he realized there was no practical way to get back in. The sun beat down. Buran started to have sharky thoughts. Eventually he began sobbing and praying for a miracle, whereupon a lone figure on a jet ski appeared. "And you know what the guy did?" Buran says. "He came speeding up, turned and threw me a shaka"—Buran rocks his outstretched thumb and pinkie in the Hawaiian salute—"and kept right on going."

A day later, at a raucous competition dinner, Hakman, sitting midway down the table sipping mineral water, ventures a story of his own. It's about a hitchhiker he once picked up in the midseventies, driving a lonely road in the Australian countryside. The guy was, without a doubt, one of the rudest people he'd ever met; every time Hakman tried a conversational gambit, the hitchhiker came back with the same response: "None of your fucking business." Suddenly there were flashing lights and a siren—the police. Hakman pulled over. Panicking, the hitchhiker dropped his bag, jumped out of the car, and sprinted into the woods with the cop in hot pursuit. Hakman looked at the suspicious package lying on the seat next to him, considered the delicacy of the situation, and took the only reasonable course of action: He peeled out and sped off into the night.

There's a brief silence. "OK, OK," says Dave Kalama, a Hawaiian tow-in star who's been flown in by Quiksilver to do water safety for the contest. "What was in the bag?"

"None of your fucking business," Hakman says, flashing that big gummy grin.

Everyone laughs, less out of amusement than relief that Hakman isn't dropping some real-life bombshell from his past. This is, after all, a guy who got hepatitis from dirty needles in the late seventies and who was high for the birth of his son in 1982. Two of his shooting buddies subsequently died of AIDS. One day around the same time, when he was at work at his Quiksilver office in Costa Mesa, California, a Mercedes pulled up out front and six gun-packing gangsters stormed upstairs into his office, not so gently inquiring as to the whereabouts of several ounces of missing drugs. All good stories, perhaps, but not particularly funny. For some, the tales bring back memories of those in the old circle who died from drug overdoses, a not insignificant number that included several of Hakman's own friends, his brother-in-law, and, in the early seventies, two of the best young surfers in Hawaii, Rusty Star and Tomi Winkler.

There are a couple of reasons why Hakman didn't join them. "He wasn't ultimately self-destructive," says Bob McKnight. "Every time he got to the bottom, he had that instinct to straighten out. Hakman's very street-smart, instinctual, with a total survivor mentality. His dad is like that too—the guy is a frickin' aquarium diver, out in deep water every day still. Jeff was trained to be like that."

The other reason Hakman survived is that his friends and family members watched out for him. And he found a savior—or a savior found him.

Half a mile up the road from Lafitenia, just across the A63 autoroute, is the Quiksilver Europe "campus." One look at the tasteful, neomodernist lines of the new corporate offices and you know that surfing's mystical power to sell stuff has only increased by crossing the Atlantic.

For the most part, what Quiksilver sells is clothing—casual sportswear with a youthful design flair. (Its "technical" pieces, like the trademark board shorts and wetsuits, actually constitute a small fraction of its business.) According to EuroSIMA, the industry's trade association, surfwear is now a $1.2 billion business in Europe. Quiksilver Europe's share is about $150 million, which makes it about half the size of Quiksilver USA. For now.

"Europe has more surfable coastline than Australia," says Harry Hodge, the 50-year-old man who brought Quiksilver to Europe and the company's president. "There's Scotland, Ireland, Wales, France, Spain, Portugal—even Sardinia and Italy now. And I can tell you they need board shorts in Italy. Badly."

If there's one person responsible for the resurrection of Mr. Sunset, it's Harry Hodge. Born and raised outside Melbourne, "Hollywood" Hodge (he bears a passing resemblance to the actor Don Johnson) was a surfer and a journalist whose lifelong dream was to make a surf film "as good as *Endless Summer.*" In the end, he did make his movie, *Band on the Run,* but it cost him everything he owned and was, he admits, "a complete commercial failure."

Hodge fell into a yearlong depression, but he eventually rallied and found a marketing job with Quiksilver Australia. In 1984, offered a chance to launch a new license in France, Hodge did the unthinkable—he looked up Hakman, with whom he'd partied during the glory days in Costa Mesa, and asked him if he wanted a chance to start over as a one-quarter partner in a new company called Quiksilver Europe. "I had no reservations at all," Hodge says. "Hakman knew the business. And I was young."

Hakman was nearby, at Burleigh Heads on the Gold Coast of Queensland, where he and Cherie had retreated after the debacle at Quiksilver USA. He had come a long way down in the world, clerking in a surf shop and teaching Australian kids and Japanese tourists to surf on his lunch hour, and when his old peers from the pro ranks came through, they could barely look him in the eye. But Hakman wasn't unhappy.

"I loved teaching the kids," he remembers. "I'd take an eight-year-old out, and after two hours he'd be laughing and smiling and riding waves, just stoked. . . .

"So when Harry said, 'Do you want to do this Europe thing?' I didn't know. It wasn't like I was over the addiction. I was healthy and I'd cleaned up, but those little sensations were still prickling."

Armed with a war chest of $200,000 Australian that they'd raised themselves, Hodge, Hakman, Hodge's girlfriend Brigitte Darrigrand, and a fourth partner, John Winship, set off to conquer Europe. "Brigitte's parents put their house up as collateral, and then a banker here was somehow convinced and gave us a loan," Hodge says. "Two years later we had a line of credit of 70 million francs, with no tangible assets." Meanwhile, Hakman was slowly slipping off the wagon. "I was good—well, so-so—for about a year," he recalls. "Then you just run into certain people, and sooner or later you're in trouble."

In late 1986 the company accountant came to Hodge scratching his head. "I'm looking at these gas receipts of Jeff's," Hodge says, "and he's bought enough fuel in the last three months to have driven around the world a couple of times." Hakman had been putting $20 of gas in his car but charging $100 on his card and pocketing the difference. Hodge and Darrigrand, furious at the betrayal, told Hakman that if it happened again, he was finished. "I got caught with the gas cards, then I got clean," Hakman says. "It's always the same cycle."

In 1988, unable to pay off their line of credit, the four partners started looking for help. They found a bittersweet solution in a buyout offer from Quiksilver USA. "We basically sold the whole company, with an earn-out clause which we hit, for ten million," says Hakman. "We got stock options, but it's not the same as owning it. People say, 'God, you sold the company, how stupid!' But it was that close to being nothing. We had the fashion and we had the image, but none of us had a financial background."

With the sale complete, Hakman found himself with about $800,000 in the bank and not quite the same interest in running the business. Soon he was looking up old friends. "I was functioning, but it was a schedule from hell," he says. "I had to see my contact twice a day. I couldn't go to work without it, so I had to get him out of bed in the morning. Then I had to find him again at lunch. The problem wasn't when you were high. It was when you couldn't score. You're sweating, your nose is running, your voice is cracking. You're falling off your chair."

Hakman shakes his head, remembering the day the end came. "May 10, 1990," he says. "I got up, and I felt horrible. I turned to my wife and said, 'I don't think I'm in control.' I broke down and admitted it: I was scared." Cherie went to Hodge and told him Jeff was using again, and neither of them knew what to do. Rather than fire Hakman, as he'd promised, Hodge got on the phone. "I remember him yelling," Hakman says. "'Where's the place Elton John went? I want that place!'"

In his six weeks at Galsworthy Lodge, outside London, Hakman was subjected to an unsparing scrutiny and, perhaps more important, allowed to see the spectacle of other outwardly assured men and women paralyzed by their addictions. "Really elegant, refined people, guys in nice suits with good accents, who were helpless," he says. "Way worse than me."

"We both knew that we couldn't keep living like that," Cherie says. "I can't look back and say that it was easy, but we know what it is like to be human. We're lucky. A lot of people don't survive. We got through it, and the other end of all this has been great."

For close to a decade now, Hakman says, he's been clean.

The final weekend of the contest is at hand, and thanks to his decent showing in round three, Hakman now needs only a second-place finish in the last heat to make it through to the quarterfinals. The flowing, powerful Bobby Owens takes the early lead, as he has all week. Then Reno Abellira, who's been floundering at the back of the pack alongside Hakman, suddenly comes alive with a couple of nifty tube rides. But Hakman's first few waves look pretty good, too. In the spectator enclosure, the Quiksilver crew follows Hakman closely. "If he's not careful," says Hodge sarcastically, "he could wind up in the main event."

Abellira and Owens each get another wave, and Hakman slips into third place. Then, with two minutes left in the heat, a final set rolls in. Hakman almost takes off on the first wave, but it starts to break around him and then closes out entirely. He pulls back and spins to grab the second wave, but it's breaking too far to the left, and he can't quite paddle into it. The buzzer sounds, and that's it—he's out of the contest.

For Hakman, it's a victory nonetheless—one more step in the rehabbing of a legend. First, there was his job, which he describes as "sort of being Mr. Quiksilver, internationally," and which amounts to telling surfing stories at sales meetings, hanging out at trade shows, and offering an occasional design critique. Then there was the biography, which Hodge talked him into cooperating with as an act of therapy and as a way to recover his story.

Since its publication, the book has become something else—a strangely effective piece of marketing. (Though it has yet to find a U.S. distributor, *Mr. Sunset* has done surprisingly well, selling more than 20,000 copies overseas and over the Internet, and the Hollywood production company October Films has optioned it for the screen.) Just as Nike is quick to lap up anything that seems remotely cool about the NBA and The North Face leaps to outfit the next wave of mountain daredevils, Quiksilver can't help but stake out its territory. That means signing up obvious stars, like Kelly Slater, and hosting events like the Silver Edition Masters. But it also means reaching out to subversive heroes and prodigal sons like Jeff Hakman, because there's something authentic about them that no amount of white bread can match.

"We're not just some guy who looks like Jimmy Buffet with a parrot on his shoulder," says McKnight. "You get our guys together, Jeff and the other Hawaiians, and it's really real, man."

The next day, with Hakman looking on from the beach, the contest wraps up. Cheyne Horan edges out his old nemesis Tom Carroll in the under-40 finals, thereby claiming his first-ever world masters championship. (Later the same afternoon, he proposes to his girlfriend in a scene that he calls "way heavier than the final.") In the over-40 final, Rabbit Bartholomew manages to catch the wave of the tournament, a perfect, near-closeout tube ride. After what seems like ten seconds, he bursts out of the far end, pumping both fists, making the claim. The judges do what they must—they give him a perfect ten, and the victory.

The awards ceremony is held at Lafitenia, and afterward there's a pretty good party that doesn't end until past midnight. It's an idyllic scene: Hawaiian guitars, cold Buds (a delicacy in France), and the sun dipping low over the sea, just like in Southern California. One might expect Hakman to skip out on the party, especially as it gets loud, but he winds up staying, hanging out with Hodge and the Hawaiians on the deck. He even has a beer. Though Hakman never had a real problem with alcohol, you can almost hear 12-step people everywhere gnashing their teeth. A beer! It's tantamount to starting up the heroin again! To the Aussies, though, it's just funny. "Hakman's having a beer!" Hodge yells. "Someone get a camera!"

Hakman has another beer, or two. He laughs at the jokes and tells a few of his own, but it's hard to figure out if he's truly having a good time. Maybe he is. But I have my doubts. Between jokes he gets a faraway look in his eyes, and soon he's backing out of the party. It's ironic, really. The guy who started the party is the first one to leave.

Goodbye Sunshine Superman
by Matt Warshaw

Surfing history includes dozens of characters who made a splash and then more or less disappeared for decades. Matt Warshaw's (born 1960) 1994 profile of Jock Sutherland—1969's most successful surfer—found Sutherland still surfing.

There's great appeal, maybe even cosmic justice, in the idea that Jock Sutherland, master of critical positioning, rode deeper and cleaner than anybody during our-holy-year-of-gigantic-surf, 1969.

Sutherland stamped his name on '69 as hard as any surfer ever stamped a name on any year. He was tops at Pipeline as a goofy foot, among the best at Sunset and Honolua Bay as a regular foot, and the near-unanimous word among the upper ranks, as reported by Drew Kampion, was that Sutherland, in general, had simply left everyone else in the dust. He won the *Surfer* Poll. He starred in *Pacific Vibrations*, the definitive movie of the time. He had a catchy name and a nice, big smile. He even rode a red surfboard. "It's pretty simple," says Jeff Hakman, oversimplifying just a little. "1969 begins and ends with Jock."

So it's curious that Sutherland, today, has all but disappeared from the historic record. He was completely missing in 1990's *Surfers: The Movie*, and a close reading of John Grissim's *Pure Stoke*, Nick Carroll's *The Next Wave*, and Leonard Leuras' *Surfing: The Ultimate Pleasure*, combining for a total of 634 illustrated pages on surfing and surfing history, turns up zero photographs of Sutherland, and just a single, short descriptive sentence on Sutherland's contribution to the sport. He was primarily remembered in a recent issue of *Surfing Magazine* as the guy who night-surfed Waimea on acid—a true story, but awfully confining.

Why is Sutherland fading from view? One answer is simple incompetence and oversight on the part of the writers, editors and filmmakers. A more intriguing explanation is that he just doesn't fit in. Sutherland didn't win an international contest after 1967. He's never been considered part of a larger school of surfing. And by volunteering for the Army at the height of his popularity, he turned his back on surfing in what many considered the rudest possible way. Finally, the Sutherland story, if told in any kind of detail, crosses into as-yet-unsettled territory, including Vietnam and the pleasures, as well as the penalties, of drug use.

There's an irony to all of this that Sutherland must appreciate: the qualities that made him the stand-out figure of '69 have made him impossible to categorize in '94. The locus of his whole act was originality, and that can cut both ways. "He's on a different trip," Barry Kanaiaupuni said twenty-five years ago. "Jocko, he's good. He's so different and he does things that normal people wouldn't do." The idea of Sutherland as something other than normal was already well-established. In fact, he was so far removed from the rest of the surf world in the late '60s, that the rumor—which spread, for the most part, in the most complimentary tones—was that he was from outer space.

But that was a long time ago. What to do with this uncategorical person today? Ignore him. Have the Australian shortboard vanguard (Young/McTavish/Lynch) meet up with the Hawaiian power-flow crew (Hakman/Kanaiaupuni/Lopez), and skip Sutherland altogether. He's just one guy—and kind of weird. It was 1969 and he didn't grow his hair long. How to explain that?

It's hard to say if Sutherland cares about any of this. Over the past twenty-five years he's been married and separated, raised kids, spent two years in the Army and another two in prison, worked throughout as a roofer, and casually surfed two or three times a week. Virtually nothing, in other words, to support his own legend.

Still, because Sutherland's brain seems to be quietly red-lining for most of his waking hours, it's impossible to believe he doesn't pause now and then and get righteously frustrated, trying to figure out how, when and why his late-sixties reputation devolved from creative genius to psychedelic misfit.

Kiki Spangler and Jimmy Lucas first took Sutherland out at Pipeline sometime in the winter of '64–65. "It was extremely difficult," Sutherland remembers, "to get the correct angle of attack as you dropped in. You had this 10' piece of machinery with insufficient rocker, and it just didn't want to fit into that concave face." Sutherland pearled up to his neck on his first wave, pinwheeled over the falls and bounced off the bottom. Not long after, though, he got his first real Pipeline tube ride. "One of those sneak-through-the-backdoor things, totally unplanned, with a definite fear aspect. Sort of like, 'Oh, man, if I straighten out here I'm gonna get *killed*.' So I tucked in and took my chances, then popped out the other end and thought, 'Hey, wait a minute. That wasn't so difficult. Yeah, let's try it again.' "

It's not much of a Pipe story on its own merits, but interesting in the way it affects Sutherland. The memory is pleasing, and loosens his voice up. Words connect almost without effort, and some even jump out for emphasis.

The mechanics of Sutherland's conversation, usually, are wound much tighter. Each word is distinct from its neighbors. Sentences are clipped off. He talks in monotone, almost as if he were holding his breath. He'll pause, searching for a phrase, and as the muscles of his jaw bunch up slightly, he almost radiates strain—the precision he wants constantly remains just out of reach. "He's always been like that, even when he was a kid," says Roy Crump, who presided over the Long Beach Surf Club and the Harbour Surfboards team, both of which counted Sutherland as a member in the mid-sixties. "He's extremely bright, but awkward in the way he communicates; sort of hesitant, with that weird Jock-talk, where he'd always be using long, polysyllabic words—and often using them incorrectly."

Sutherland is straightforward, occasionally funny, sometimes even sly. Now and then, to good effect, he'll loosen up with a little pidgin. But as a rule, he deals in information and analysis, not emotion, and he's rarely—if ever—wistful, poetic or nostalgic. Sutherland's recollections, for example, of a year spent at a Maui junior college, in '67-68, when he roomed with Jeff Hakman, go like this: "Let's see. There was fairly consistent surf, I had good boards, classes were going well, and Jeff and I really had some great times together. We had a good surf—P.E. thing going at Honolua. Yeah, that was a really satisfying period."

Hakman's recollections, for comparison, of the same year: "Oh, man. Outrageous memories. Peaceful memories. We were eighteen or nineteen years old, both riding for Brewer, Hendrix was on the record player all the time, we could get from school to Honolua in one hour. Yeah, it was a dream! It was incredible! Out at Honolua, 8–10', fuckin' perfect, nobody else around, from three in the afternoon til dark, each of us on a really nice tab of purple Owsley. I'd be sitting outside watching Jock's silhouette go up and down this perfect wall, then I'm riding, and here comes Jock paddling back out, screaming something . . ." Hakman pauses. "Wow, you know, I guess the best moments of my surfing career have been with Jock."

An interesting embodiment of the Sutherland paradox is that Sutherland himself, as the spark for a million evocative moments, is virtually unable to bring any of those moments back to life.

Which, of course, doesn't really matter, as people have always been happy to testify on his behalf. Sutherland stories are legion. Corky Carroll recalls a sunny afternoon at Waimea Bay when he and Sutherland tried, unsuccessfully, to jump on each other's boards mid-ride. "Three times we went for it, and three times, man, we just ate it like rats."

Dan Calohan, owner of Plastic Fantastic surfboards, remembers a surf check at Waimea one evening, just past 9:00 p.m., in late '69. "We pulled up and there was this beautiful full moon, and no wind. I was with a few guys. Hakman was probably there. We'd just finished dinner in Haleiwa, I think at the Seaview, and everyone wanted to see what was happening with the surf, because it had been coming on all day, but was sloppy right up until twilight. So we were standing on the point, and it was solid 20', and I remember this feeling like electricity going through me, because all of a sudden we heard this hooting. The first thing we all thought was, 'God, somebody's out there!' And not even a second went by before we all realized it was Jock. Not just because he had a distinctive hoot, but because it couldn't have been anybody else."

Calohan considers for a moment. "The only guy, I think, who did stuff that radical," he says "was Butch Van Artsdalen. But that's not really true. Nobody did stuff as radical as Jock."

Contest results also bring up the lights on Sutherland, but the best way to get a feel for his surfing is through late-period photographs. All the precision he could ever hope for was there in his surfing by 1969, counterbalanced by great spasms of creativity, and the photos bring it all home. A two-page *Surfer* spread by Art Brewer in the March 1970 issue shows Sutherland, as a goofy foot, bottom turning around a giant ball of white water at Pipeline, with the fingertips on his back hand brush-kissing across the flats. In the previous issue, in another two-page spread, this one by Ron Stoner, Sutherland strikes in a similar position at Sunset—as a regular foot. A few more definitive Sutherland images from '69: trimming through the bowl section at Honolua; a reverse-shoulder-rotation cutback at Oceanside; side-slipping at Pupukea, Sunset and Velzyland; a super-deep-fade turn off the bottom at Haleiwa; and hidden behind the curl at Pipeline.

Another great moment comes near the end of John Severson's psilocybin-tinged *Pacific Vibrations*. As Cream's "Tales of Brave Ulysses" plays on the sound track, Sutherland is shown in the lower-right corner of the frame, paddling out as a big, glassy Pipe cylinder stands up and unloads. He sits up on his board, completely stoked, looks into the spinning eye, makes a motion of greeting with his left hand, and, it seems, begins to talk to the wave. "He's so much more comfortable in the water," says Audrey Sutherland, Jock's mother. "John Severson once said that Jock sheds his skin when he goes into the ocean, and I think that's true."

Sutherland, in other words, can't be counted on to emblaze his own history. He needs witnesses, film clips, photographs and other secondary sources. Sutherland's not reticent, and he's good with details, but he's no dramatist. He's the story, not the storyteller.

"He was really little at the time," says Drew Kampion, "so he probably doesn't remember. But Jock was in fact deposited here on earth by a spaceship."

The first version of the story is that Sutherland alone is an alien-being. The second version is that the whole family is from outer space. Sutherland thinks on it a moment, then speaks without irony. "Well, my mother's always done things her own way. She's very unique. And for us kids, I think it's just because our parents encouraged us to read and to learn. And, maybe in my case, because of the drugs."

John Carson (Jock) Sutherland Jr., the second of four children born to native Californians John and Audrey Sutherland, was delivered September 27, 1948, in Long Beach, California—a booming port city in the post-war years, a bit raw and uncultured, perhaps a little strange in places, but hardly extraterrestrial. John Sr., 29 years old, a dedicated man of the sea, was advancing through young adulthood at a smart pace. He'd learned to surf during a two-year visit to Waikiki in '37–38, and carried on as a first-generation Long Beach surfer up until his entry into the war. He served in the Coast Guard from '41–46, primarily on a sub-chaser in the Caribbean, and in the space of twelve months (in '42–43), became a husband, father and officer. For three years after the war, while the family lived in a beach house at Surfside, John fished commercially, surfed and fathered a second child.

The changes continued: John served in Korea from '50–54, and moved the family to Oahu in '52; worked one year for Fish and Wildlife, and two years as a military marine engineer; had two more children; then made a unilateral decision, in 1957, to move back to California. Audrey and the four children (ages four to fourteen) chose to say in Hawaii. The divorce was finalized that year.

John paid no child support, and for twenty years made virtually no contact with the family. He worked up to a Master's Unlimited captain's license. While in charge of a tanker in the North Pacific in 1976, he was diagnosed with lung cancer, at which point he contacted Audrey and flew to Hawaii, not telling anybody he was sick. There was a reconciliation of sorts at the Sutherland home. Six months later John died.

Audrey says that Jock has always tended to idealize his father, even though John's influence on his son's development was minimal. Disproportionately, her own influence—which Audrey doesn't comment on directly—was immense. Audrey, 73, says that "Jock sometimes knows what I'm thinking even before I do." Even that doesn't really convey how deeply connected the two are—they're more like close siblings than mother and son. They look and speak alike (Audrey with a more comfortable delivery), both are competitive, both welcome intellectual challenge (Audrey has a BA in International Relations from UCLA, and a Master's in Education from University of Hawaii), both crave solitary adventure, and both prefer ocean to land. Audrey's self-reliance is legendary. "I remember surfing Chun's in the mid-sixties," says Roy Crump, "and all of a sudden Jock's mom would pop up with a spear and a fish, getting dinner."

Audrey first swam along the uninhabited, near-vertical north coast cliffs of Mokuleia in '62, by herself, towing a waterproof bag of supplies. She returned a few years later, again by herself, but this time with a kayak, and subsequently wrote a book about her experiences. *Paddling My Own Canoe*, first published in 1978, is now in its fourth printing. All told, between '62 and '81, Audrey made 18 trips to Mokuleia, 11 of which were solo. As she wrote in 1978, perhaps confirming the family's other-worldly origins, "Water became my element.

I delight in its color, its texture, the three-dimensional freedom of movement, where buoyancy balances body weight. I stagger in an alien world of gravity's pull when first I stand upright again on shore after an hour or two [in the] water." Her expeditions over the past twelve years have been through the inner and outer coastal passages of Alaska.

Audrey worked constantly after John left, mostly as an education administrator for the Army, so the Sutherland kids often took care of themselves. By the time Jock began elementary school, he was spending almost all of his non-class time either reading or swimming. "We didn't have any TV until I was 10," he recalls. "And even then, the reception was poor. So I was reading quite a bit, even when I was young."

In 1956, the year before John left for California, Audrey took Jock out to Barber's Point and let him ride one of John's old 11′ balsa boards. He surfed alone. Nothing much happened. Baseball was Sutherland's real interest, and certainly a better outlet for his competitive drive, and his Little League team, the Cardinals, with Jock as an all-star pitcher, won their league in '58.

In '61, Audrey moved the family to a converted Army barrack just to the west of Chun's Reef, at which point Jock, age twelve, took up surfing again—this time with feeling. The following year he was known as the "Chun's Kid." Jock already was capable of making an impression. "I have this super-clear picture in my mind," says Randy Rarick, one year younger than Sutherland, "of him hanging ten at Haleiwa lefts on a 3′ day, on this metal-flake gold board. It must have been an old rental board, because it had a big number painted on it. But the thing just shined, and Jock, he was just a kid, but he was really, really hot."

Early versions of the Sutherland paradox were sprouting up during his first years at Waialua High. His manner, for example, groomed by stories of medieval chivalry (*King Arthur and the Knights of the Round Table*, Sutherland surmises) often had a rare politeness and formality. At the same time, Sutherland, the Berkemeyer brothers, the Smith brothers, the Paty brothers and a few other local boys had loosely allied themselves as the decidedly unchivalrous Chun's Reef Surf Society. "Basically," says Sutherland, "we were country rednecks. That is, we weren't particularly friendly to outsiders. Guys would drive in from Wahiawa or Pearl City, and if there were more than three people in the lineup, the Chun's boys would make a tense situation out of it."

Sutherland's surfing, too, was already showing a two-track development: studied and precise on one hand, spontaneous on the other. "When he was sixteen," says Audrey, "I said to him, 'You haven't surfed Waimea yet, Jock.' And he answered, 'Well, I'm not ready yet. I'll know when I'm good enough.' And, of course, the next year he was out there, switching stance, going left, surfing past dark, all of that." Did she ever worry about him? "No, never."

Sutherland claims not to have patterned his surfing after anybody in particular, but he must have had an eye on Butch Van Artsdalen. In '65 Van Artsdalen was overlord at Pipeline, and the world's best switch foot. Three years later, Sutherland had easily passed him on the latter count (and nobody since has come close to Sutherland as a switch foot), and was about ready to set the new standard at Pipe.

Directly after high school graduation, in '66, Sutherland flew to California and spent the summer polishing fins at the Hobie factory in Dana Point, and taking summer courses at Long Beach State. He had already had a good spot in Dick Brewer's growing stable of surfers—Sutherland says the best board he ever owned was a 10'5" gun Brewer shaped him that year—and was one of Hawaii's hot juniors, along with Jeff Hakman, Jimmy Lucas and Jackie Eberle. The previous year, in December, Sutherland had pulled off what might be the single greatest come-from-behind contest performance ever, as he missed the first 40 minutes of a 55-minute final in the junior's division of the '65 Makaha contest, paddled out with his jersey clamped in his teeth, and in just 15 minutes managed to tie David Nuuhiwa for first place—losing on a countback.

The Makaha contest helped draw the attention of *Surfer* magazine: Sutherland made the cover of the May '66 issue ("charging down the face of a Pipeline giant," read the caption), and was the subject of a short interview in the July issue, serviceable as his introduction to the surf world. The 17-year-old, with his semi-formal, pre-psychedelic language, was naive in places, prescient in others.

> **Surfer:** What is your attitude toward style, Jock?
> **Sutherland:** *I don't think I have any set style. I feel that style in surfing is really over-emphasized. I'm more interested in getting the job done . . . I just try to get as much as possible out of each wave. . . .*
> **Surfer:** Who impressed you on the North Shore this year?
> **Sutherland:** *That's easy—Jeff Hakman.*
> **Surfer:** Are you afraid in big waves?
> **Sutherland:** *Yes, but I always plan carefully before taking off. That way I reduce the chances of being wiped-out badly.*
> **Surfer:** What are your plans for the future?
> **Sutherland:** *I want to keep surfing as much as possible, especially in contests. I will be going to college next fall, however, and don't want surfing to interfere with my studies. School comes first, as far as I'm concerned.*

Sutherland had a good run in the California's WSA contests that summer, blew off college that fall, jumped from Hobie to Harbour, and qualified for the Hawaiian world contest team. One week after his 18th birthday Sutherland finished runner-up in San Diego to Nat Young. It was a mildly shocking result, obscured almost completely by the puffed-up Young/Nuuhiwa, Australia/California, "involvement"/ "high-performers" debate. Sutherland rode a lightweight 9'8" Harbour Cheater model—not as radical as Young's thinned-out 9'4", but more advanced than the rest of the field. "I thought at the time," Sutherland says, "that I should have been able to beat Nat. In retrospect, I realize he had an edge." Sutherland reflects for a moment then, perhaps automatically, comes up with a neat bit of verbal gamesmanship. "You know, I'm not even sure if I'd heard of Nat before that contest."

Two months later, in December, Sutherland made the finals of the Duke contest. In '67 he beat an international field to win the small wave event of the Peruvian Surf Championships, won the first of three consecutive Hawaiian state titles, and finished the year by winning the Duke. By '68, Sutherland was the top competitor for the powerful Kui-O-Hawaii club, which included Gerry Lopez, Reno Abellira and Tomi Winkler. He also found his greatest audience, as a distinctly hideous wipeout from his '68 Duke outing became the "agony of defeat" clip during the opening titles of ABC's *Wide World of Sports*.

Sutherland's style wasn't artistic. His stance, whether riding regular or goofy foot, was nearly symmetrical, the left side of his body mirroring the right, almost like a paper doll cutout. While Hakman, by '67, had already developed the prototype low-profile bottom turn, Sutherland obviously preferred to remain upright as much as possible—"like he had a broomstick up his ass," as Corky Carroll would put it twenty years later. Sutherland's early reputation was for doing spinners in big surf, and for switching stance at Sunset and Waimea. "Not a pretty surfer," says Dan Calohan, "but he was already doing things nobody else was doing."

In addition, Sutherland's personality was more and more often finding an outlet through surfing. Gerry Lopez describes a longboard-era afternoon at Pipeline, probably in early 1967, when a frustrated group of Pipe regulars were unable to push through the shore break, getting pounded back to the beach again and again. "Then Jock walks down with this palm-frond hat on," Lopez recalls, "throws his board in, and paddles out—without even getting touched." The crowning moment came when Sutherland, having just crested the shore break, still wearing the hat, with nothing but calm water between him and the lineup, sat up, put his feet on the rails and easily finger-paddled the rest of the way. He threw a single, smiling glance back over his shoulder. "Very subtle," says Lopez, laughing. "Very effective."

Magazine readers dug Sutherland's act, too, as he finished 5th in the '66 Surfer Poll, 3rd in '67, and 10th in '68.

Meanwhile, Sutherland was breathing deeply the winds of change, as he transferred from Long Beach State to a community college on Maui (where he made Dean's list), experienced his first LSD trips, and positioned himself in the vanguard of the shortboard movement with Dick Brewer. In '67 and '68, Hakman and Young, in general, were doing better turns than Sutherland and were certainly more polished, while Jackie Eberle and Butch Van Artsdalen were Sutherland's match at Pipeline. A number of California hot-doggers could out-perform him in tiny surf. But nobody, says Randy Rarick, could surf as well in as many different kinds of waves. "At that point, Jock was already the most versatile surfer in the world."

Gerry Lopez agrees. "Right when the boards went short, Jock was light years ahead of anyone—particularly at Waimea and Pipeline."

And, of course, Sutherland's best months were ahead of him. The '66–68 years, taken on their own, were solid enough. To Sutherland's credit, they end up looking like nothing more than a 36-month warm-up for '69.

Pacific Vibrations and *Cosmic Children*, viewed one after the other, make an excellent two-and a-half-hour diptych of surfing in 1969. True, Wayne Lynch and Nat Young are almost completely ignored, along with the rest of Australia—and the rest of the world, for that matter, except for the West Coast and Hawaii. But once the deficiencies are accounted for, a good portion of 1969, micro to macro, with all its possibilities, excesses and detours, hits the screen pretty well intact: organic food, glazed eyes, beaver-tail wetsuits, Motorskill, and surf-boards without stickers; bootlegged Rolling Stones (*Gimme Shelter*) on the *Cosmic* sound track; J Riddle on an 8' x 18" finger-fin downrailer, Nat Young (in a one-wave appearance at Malibu) on a 5'11" × 23" stub, David Nuuhiwa on a diamond-tail single-fin with a W.A.V.E. box, Mickey Dora on a semi-egg, Lance Carson on a 9' noserider; Rick Griffin's surfing eyeballs; straight-across-the-hips bikinis; Jeff Hakman doing his Charles Atlas–meets-Nureyev number on a beautiful after-noon at Haleiwa, followed directly by Barry Kanaiaupuni's abstract-expressionism; soon-to-be world champion Rolf Aurness winning at

Malibu, in the middle of his complete domination of the WSA 4A season; gutted houses on the North Shore from December's mega-swell; and new film-processing tricks, allowing surfer and surfboard to be etched in bright bands of color against a black background, leaving acid trails across the screen—art imitating hallucination.

This was the roiling landscape of 1969, and nobody walked it more freely, and with more confidence, than Jock Sutherland. His surfing, in a very short period of time, had evolved on a number of fronts. In the summer he joined up with Plastic Fantastic, a new surfboard company based in Huntington Beach, and the narrow, flat-bottomed boards—mostly shaped by Bruce Jones, some by Danny Calohan, a few by Sutherland himself—suited him perfectly. His style, never fluid, was nonetheless better lubricated than it had been the year before, and moves that had once looked slightly wooden now came off as calm and controlled. But for the most part, he'd stayed true to what he'd said as a 17-year-old, putting function above style. There wasn't any particular Sutherland characteristic equal, say, to Hakman's bow-legged trim stance, or Bill Hamilton's religious-icon hand positioning. But Sutherland loved his little flourishes, manifested usually with a quick bit of hand-jive at the end of a good ride—a kind of signature stroke, half comedy, half salute, that disappeared from the scene when Sutherland left for the Army, then resurfaced five years later in the very capable form of Wayne Bartholomew.

Jeff Hakman was perhaps the only person to keep up with Sutherland in '69. "But my trip," Hakman says, "was totally different. My style was a lot more classical. You could pretty much tell what I was going to do. With Jock, you had no idea. He'd pull stuff out of the hat that would just shock you. Everybody else, you'd say, 'Oh, he surfs sort of like Lance.' Or like Peck, or Strauch, or David, on and on. But Jock didn't do things like anybody else. And that wasn't just his surfing, it was the way he talked, the way he dressed, the way he wrote, every-thing. He was easily the most original person I've ever met."

Meanwhile, Sutherland had gained a hugely important supporter in *Surfer* editor Drew Kampion, who, like Sutherland, was hitting his creative peak in 1969. Kampion, another less-than-typical surfer (raised near Buffalo, New York; English graduate from Cal State North-ridge; utility man in the *Wall Street Journal's* West Coast production office in '67), got a staff job at *Surfer* in mid-'68 when he was 24 years old, and single-handedly turned the magazine back from its premature middle-age, into a totally with-it, experimental, colorful and intelli-gent bimonthly. Focusing on Jock Sutherland was a big part of that change. "He was the key figure of 1969," Kampion says today. "I always say that Nat was the best surfer, but Jock, more so than anyone else, defined the era. He was a little difficult to be around for too long, because he had this kind of nervousness, which I think came from having all this energy that he was always trying to keep under control. In fact, control was a big part of what Jock was all about. But he was incredibly creative and bright, his surfing was super hard-core, but still had a playful quality to it, and at times he was wonderful to talk with. So I put a lot of effort into our relationship, and did a lot to see that he was presented to the world. I wanted him to have a forum for his art and his views."

This didn't always work in Sutherland's favor. His thoughts, as expressed in the pages of *Surfer*, often skipped around from obtuse to ridiculous. In an article titled, "What is Surfing?" top surfers were asked a series of questions, one of which read: "What feeling do you get while riding in the tube?" Sutherland's response: "I do not receive a giant exudence of the senses, but rather a totality of their perceptive strivings, or a non-feeling, as it were, of some of the prismatic auras and shimmering spectrums of bright death." (Fred Hemmings' response, for comparison, to the same question: "A true sense of per-sonal accomplishment." Margo Godfrey: "Relaxed and secure, for I am being hugged by the wave's love center [like a] babe in the womb, with mother curl comforting and feeding me." Jeff Hakman: "OWOOO!")

Sutherland's "Finger English" article, and his "In the Pope's Living Room" interview with Kampion, were nearly as convoluted. But a few mitigating factors should be considered. First, according to Sutherland, Kampion embellished upon, or created outright, a good portion of

Sutherland's words. At least half of his comments from the "Pope's Living Room" article were bogus, Sutherland says, and he briefly considered, in 1970, bringing suit against Kampion and *Surfer*. (Kampion's response: "Funny he never said anything to me and *Surfer* at the time. The interview was accurate; I didn't embellish—I didn't need to embellish—Jock's words.")

Second, his comments were often made with tongue in cheek—or, as shown in the opening photograph for his article "Finger English," with tongue S-turning out of his mouth.

Third, it was '69, and Sutherland was doing a lot of drugs.

Those on the scene in the late '60s and early '70s remember Sutherland in three ways: for his surfing, for joining the Army, and as one of the great North Shore drug freaks. Sutherland doesn't react defensively to the accusation—but, at the same time, he may not have been as consistently stoned as most people thought. Pot smoking was certainly part of the daily program. But, even by today's standards among some of the world's best surfers, that's hardly remarkable. The acid trips, Sutherland maintains, happened just two or three times a month; not every other day, as some people claim. He and some friends would drive into the hills and dose themselves with whatever was going around. Sutherland knew people who were connected to the Brotherhood of Eternal Love, a California clearinghouse for LSD based in Laguna Beach, so the North Shore got its share of Windowpane, Orange Sunshine and, occasionally, some of Owsley Stanley's top-rated product. Sutherland, like most people, preferred to start tripping outdoors: "You never, never wanted to start coming on inside a building, or in a car." Eventually, after a morning hike, and maybe a swim in a nearby stream, everybody would go home, grab their boards and go surfing. Sutherland recalls going over the top on a few occasions, but his reputation for control held. "Jock's whole thing," says Randy Rarick, "was to do these massive amounts but still maintain. He'd never lose it and go berserk. He'd just get very weird."

Amphetamines, mushrooms and a variety of other hallucinogens and stimulants were mixed in. "We'd pretty much do anything we could get our hands on," Sutherland says. "Not so much the downers, of course, because that slowed up your surfing—as did drinking. It all tied in to how it affected your surfing. But, yeah, that was all a big part of my life for quite a few years."

It's easy, with Sutherland, to overplay the drug angle, particularly the "acid casualty" label that he's stuck with. The quantities he took were impressive, but it's guesswork trying to estimate any lasting effects. Dan Calohan (admittedly a fellow traveler), plays it down. "Jock was pretty strange before he started dropping acid. I never noticed all that much difference afterwards."

In a way, Sutherland's drug use argues against his uniqueness. Almost everybody in surfing was dropping acid in 1969—Sutherland, on this score, is just one of the crew. Hakman agrees, then adds a qualification. "The drugs came with the territory, so in a sense, yeah, he was doing what we were all doing. But then again, Jock could smoke more than all of us, drop more than all of us, then go out and *surf* better than all of us."

Sutherland's surfing career shot forward for the last time in the late fall and early winter of 1969. The North Shore, of course, delivered the great mother lode and Sutherland, age 21, simply matched energy with energy.

By this point, Sutherland had perfected his two-track method, and could go from carefully studied to bizarre in an instant. A 12' northwest swell at Sunset Beach, as Sutherland paddled out, seemed to be entering his mind as a field of data and power-vectors. He'd line up, almost dispassionately, then drop dead-center into a huge peak, in a right-foot-forward stance, and draw a calculated line off the bottom and up through the saddle. Then the inside section would stack up, and Sutherland's mind would jump trains. Instead of angling back down for a race around the bowl, he'd switch stance, hold a high neutral-speed line, let the wave suck vertical, then pop the fin and try to drift through the maul sideways.

But the centerpiece of Sutherland's act was tuberiding, and this is where his development, as compared to the rest of the world, went right off the chart. In December of '69, surfers were still uncomfortable or unfamiliar with the tube. Even the best would often out-run a hollow section, or, once inside, not hold a high enough trim line, or bend at the waist instead of the knees, or assume an outdated, arms-out, no-look, chin-to-the-chest head-dip position. Sutherland, meanwhile, in a practiced, nearly methodical way, was putting himself behind the curl line and staying there. He'd learned how to crouch. His ambidextrous feet and hands would turn into brake/accelerator pedals, controlling not just forward speed, but, through practical application of the side-slip—a technique Sutherland had perfected in California that summer—lateral movement as well. As a tuberider, Sutherland was on his own level in '69. Only Butch Van Artsdalen before him and Shaun Tomson after would be so far ahead of the pack. Dru Harrison, writing for *Surfing Magazine*, put it this way: "Hey Jock, why don't you lay off for a year and let the rest of the world catch up?" Harrison, later in the article, reconsiders. "Hey Jock, make that two years."

Meanwhile, John Severson was in Hawaii filming for *Pacific Vibrations*, and would put Sutherland's name above all others in the opening credits; Plastic Fantastic was giving him free boards, paying him $125 a week, and occasionally helping out with rent; and *Surfer* readers were mailing in Poll ballots showing that Sutherland had become the most popular surfer in America, if not the world.

Just as the North Shore season got underway, Sutherland's "Professionalism is Grey" article appeared in *Surfer*, as a qualified endorsement of professional surfing. In it, Sutherland wonders about the downside of professionalism. "What would the shortcomings be? For one, the subjugation of personal freedom to the corporate cause. [Also], mandatory conformation to a ruling body's decisions doesn't make for creative surfing."

It was as straightforward as Sutherland would ever be in print, making his next move all the more confounding. In a wholesale subjugation of personal freedom, not to mention an out-and-out conformation to a ruling body, Sutherland, in mid-December, without a word to anybody, drove to the local recruiting office and volunteered for immediate active duty in the U.S. Army.

The '60s, for the rest of the country, were beaten to a close over the course of three years, with the Kennedy/King assassinations, My Lai, Kent State and Manson, and the death of Hendrix and Joplin.

In surfing, Jock Sutherland entered boot camp at Fort Ord, California, in January 1970, and more or less closed the '60s out at a single stroke. "It really took the wind out of my sails," says Kampion, who stepped down as *Surfer*'s editor in mid-1970. "I was never really as interested in the whole scene after Jock left."

Sutherland's motivation for enlisting remains a mystery. Jeff Hakman never talked to him about it. Dan Calohan thought the whole thing was a put-on at first. Later, when he asked Sutherland about it on separate occasions in the early '70s, Sutherland's answers kept changing.

Randy Rarick, like everyone else, was initially amazed by Sutherland's decision, but quickly saw a kind of logic. Rarick's explanation, while maybe a little simplistic, is plausible. "Really, it was completely typical of Jock. The rest of us were doing everything we could to dodge the draft, and it was just like him to do something so radically different from everybody else." (A competing view is that Sutherland, after a drug bust, was given the option of joining the service or going to prison.)

Gerry Lopez' recollections are different from Rarick's. "The Hawaiian guys weren't as hot to get out of the draft as California guys. It wasn't like *Big Wednesday* here, with all the stunts and everything—at least not in '69. Hawaii's always had the big military presence. People just weren't as against the war here as they were on the Mainland."

Sutherland's explanation on why he enlisted, while vague in places, brings up some interesting points. First of all, he didn't enlist to beat a drug-bust prison sentence. "An understandable interpretation," he says with a smile, "but not true."

His parents, for starters, both had made careers in the military. Surf journalist Matt George, who joined the Navy in 1989—and who, like Sutherland, is the son of a military man—emphasizes the point. "When you're a little kid, and you're dad comes home in a uniform, that's huge. You can't underestimate how important that is."

Some of Sutherland's old high school friends, by '69, had enlisted, done their tour, and come home with some money and a few ideas about where to go with the rest of their lives. Sutherland's first career choice, marine biology, had meanwhile foundered when he blew the necessary math and chemistry classes at Leeward Community College in late '68 and early '69.

In addition, his surfing, Sutherland thought, had reached a plateau. "I'd already accomplished a lot. Maybe I felt a little untaxed."

Sutherland was frustrated with the biased selection lists, inconsistent judging, low prize money, and all the attendant problems with surfing's embryonic professionalism. (Sutherland's timing in the Duke was unfortunate: he earned nothing for his win in '67, while Mike Doyle, the following year, made $1,000.)

Not stated, but obvious after a quick glance through the magazines of '66–69, is that Sutherland had never really gotten it on with surfing's corporate world. Carroll, Nuuhiwa, Grigg, Martinson, Propper, Doyle, Hamilton, Kanaiaupuni, Codgen and dozens of others were mixing and matching not only with the major surfboard, wetsuit and clothing companies, but mainstream sponsors like Keds and Kawasaki. Sutherland was never a real player, even for something as basic as surfboard sponsorship. He received only token backing from Hobie during his junior years, didn't get a signature model from Harbour after the '66 world contest, and Plastic Fantastic, founded in '69, just didn't have the money to advertise regularly. When Plastic finally did take out a full-page color ad in *Surfer*, in late '69, featuring Sutherland and Hakman, it was upstaged somewhat by the Charlie Quiznel ad on the opposite page, showing Quiznel from behind, grooving somewhere up in the hills, arms raised, totally nude.

Sutherland, well-liked by his peers, was probably considered too far-out, and a little abrasive, by company decision-makers. Drew

Kampion remembers that Sutherland wasn't interested in making the traditional rounds in Southern California in order to drum up any promo work. Dan Calohan adds that Sutherland had no interest in business, was virtually non-communicative with people outside of the North Shore and parts of California, and was a complete washout as a production shaper. "He'd sit there and listen and nod his head," Calohan says, "then grab the planer and do whatever he wanted. I have no idea how many blanks I wasted trying to teach him how to shape."

In other words, for one reason or another, Sutherland wasn't going to find a career in the surf industry.

Also contributing to Sutherland's decision to enlist is that he wanted to fight. "I was pro-involvement at the time—although I don't think I fully understood what was going on. It was kind of a challenge thing for me. I figured I was a local boy, bred in the country, pretty tough, and I wanted to see how I'd do against the VC."

After basic training at Fort Ord, Sutherland was stationed at Monterey Presidio, five miles down the coast, as a company clerk. He'd been training to be a field-wire repairman, a super high-risk assignment, when a hand infection put him in the hospital, and he missed his ship-out date. Asked if he's sorry he didn't get a chance to fight, he thinks for a moment. "No, I guess not. I was relieved that I was in such a nice place [Monterey], and by that point, yeah, I guess you could say I was relieved that I wasn't going into battle. If I'd shipped out as a field-wire repairman, and been assigned to a tactical area—well, that would not have been a good thing."

The Army paid Sutherland six hundred dollars a month. He wasn't homesick. He visited the North Shore in December of '70, when he surfed in the first Expression Session, and returned for five days in the summer of '71. He kept a surfboard in Monterey (a 7'4" Plastic), and was able to surf two or three times a week, usually near the Presidio base, in Carmel or Pacific Grove—Lover's Point was his preferred spot.

Sometimes Sutherland drove up the coast for waves. In the fall of '71, 11-year-old Matt George was dropped off at Steamer Lane, while his brother Sam and a friend went to get milk and donuts. The surf was small, and the wind was cold out of the east. "I was standing with my hands in my pockets, shivering," George recalls, "and I look to my left and here comes Jock Sutherland, walking towards me, with a shaved head, wearing a long john with the ankle zippers unzipped. He stopped next to me, and looked down, and I was almost dizzy—just the full-on brush with greatness. He looked out at the surf, looked back at me and shrugged, so I shrugged, then he climbed down the cliff and paddled out. The first wave he caught was maybe shoulder high, and he did a fade, did a snap-turn off the bottom, drifted up into the pocket and did a side-slip. Then here comes the end section and he did, I swear, in 1971, the first floater I'd ever seen. It was a roller coaster that he sort of held on to for a while. His board went 'ka-thwack!' when he came down—I can still hear it.

"That was the only wave he rode. Next thing I knew he was back up the cliff and about to walk past me, and I said the only possible thing I could say, the classic Santa Cruz opening line: 'What's the water like?' He shuddered and went, 'whew,' and walked past. Two minutes later Sam came back. I said, 'Yeah, you know, I was just rapping with Jock Sutherland.' "

In November of '71, less than two years after enlistment, Sutherland's term with the Army was finished.

Today, he separates his thoughts on Vietnam from his own experience at Fort Ord and Monterey. "The war itself was a terrible waste," Sutherland says. "At first, I was upset about how disoriented the American effort was as far as methods of attack, and tactical accuracy. Later, I realized we just should have supported Ho Chi Minh and unification. Diem was nothing more than a black marketeer." Of his 22-month stay in Monterey, Sutherland says, "It was good California country, and there were some good people there. I got to surf. I enjoyed myself."

Sutherland's assessment notwithstanding, it's hard to view his enlistment in the Army as anything but a mistake. Sutherland's mother says the Army pushed him into heavier drug use. Hakman says his whole personality changed. "He went into the service as the extraterrestrial, doing everything better than anybody, and when he came out he couldn't make up his mind whether to go surfing, go back to school, or just sit in his room. I'll never, ever understand why he joined. The Army knocked him around, mentally. It took away his drive. He was so disoriented afterwards it scared me."

Sutherland's own version of his initial post-Army years isn't nearly so grim. The summer after he came home, at an Ala Moana surf contest, he met Francis Cunningham (sister to North Shore lifeguard and bodysurfer Mark Cunningham), and in July of the following year the two were married. "The old shotgun wedding," Sutherland says. "She was five months pregnant." Their first son, Matthew, was born in October of '73; a second son, Gavin, arrived two years later. Meanwhile, Sutherland surfed in a few contests (last in a six-man field in the first Pipeline Masters, in December of '71; 16th in a 30-man field in the '72 Smirnoff), and was in the middle of the action at Pipeline for Huge Monday in mid January of '71 (the most memorable day of surfing in his life), but the drive, Sutherland says, in partial agreement with Hakman, just wasn't the same. "Surfing was more of a recreational thing. I was in love, and then I had my sons, and that's where I found my happiness. There was a great deal of self-realization there, with my children."

Gerry Lopez, who hit full stride at Pipeline in Sutherland's absence, says that Sutherland was surfing as well as ever when he first came back from the Army, and that if he hadn't hit a wall of indifference from the media and manufacturers, he would have given more attention to his surfing. "He wasn't getting good boards," Lopez says, "and the magazines didn't want to know about him. But we were there on the beach. We saw him all the time, and he hadn't lost a step. He was still a fantastic surfer. I've always been a little disappointed in the way Jock was treated when he got back. He had more to offer."

In 1970, when asked, "What kind of person are you in relation to other people?" Sutherland replied, "Disrespectful at times." Today he's become circumspect, almost to a fault. He treads carefully. Sutherland's first reaction, in regards to the way he was treated by surfing after the Army, stays in character. "No, I didn't really feel ignored by the media when I got out. And, anyway, I didn't place a particularly high value on whether or not my name was in print. I wasn't that enthusiastic about a surfing career." Here he pauses, and the gears in his mind are nearly visible. He reconsiders. "I think some people in the media felt they'd made my career. So my going into the Army—that was considered traitorous." His voice now has a slight edge. "And as punishment, they chose to ignore me when I got out."

For whatever reason, the fact is Sutherland, in early '70, abruptly ceased to exist as a public figure. Lopez more filled the void (literally and figuratively) at Pipeline. Hakman, Kanaiaupuni and Abellira were all moving into their prime. Along with a handful of others, all Hawaii-based, these surfers, by virtue of their near-monopoly on the North Shore, had a near-monopoly on surfing's consciousness. The challenge to the new order wasn't going to come from the past—i.e. Jock Sutherland. It would come five years later from Richards, Bartholomew, Cairns, Townend and the Tomson cousins.

Sutherland, meanwhile, had to make a living. He and ex–Plastic Fantastic owner Dan Calohan tried and failed to sell their own line of surfboards in '71. Sutherland then worked as a roofer and carpenter, and supplemented his income with low-volume pot dealing—a sideline since the late-sixties. He moved his young family to a house in Haleiwa. His primary drug use changed from psychedelics to cocaine, which he began to sell (again, in small quantities). He separated from Francis in '77 ("not a big, horrible, messy thing"), and got a place for himself near Silver Channels in Mokuleia. In the early '80s, he began to deal larger quantities.

In 1989, after flying in from Los Angeles, Sutherland was met at the Honolulu airport by federal drug agents, who searched his bag and found a pound of cocaine. Sutherland was arrested, charged, tried and convicted, and sentenced to three years in prison. He had two previous arrests, a marijuana possession in '68 (charges dropped), and a DUI in '74. On the coke conviction, Sutherland ended up serving 26 months; the first year in Lompoc, California, the remainder in Sheridan,

Oregon. He returned to Hawaii for his younger son's 16th birthday, on October 31, 1991.

The stand-out feature of Sutherland's arrest is that he'd been warned several times, by friends with police connections, not to make the trip to Los Angeles. Sutherland went anyway. "I figured I could pull it off. I was interested in the money, plus I figured, too—and this was the influence of the drug itself; using it as much as I was—that I could outwit the cops. I'd done it before."

Telling his family that he'd been arrested, Sutherland says, was the low point of his life. "They knew what I was up to before that, and asked me, maybe six months earlier, what they could do to help, and I told them there wasn't any problem. So I was censured pretty heavily after the arrest. I spent a lot of tune wondering how I could be such a dummy for getting into so much trouble."

Sutherland's reintegration since prison has been steady, but there seem to be moments when he wonders if his position among family members and the North Shore community is secure. In general, he's down on drugs, but he stops short of a total condemnation—at least with respect to his own involvement, particularly in the late '60s. "I learned a lot from all that. I certainly had a good time. And I don't think it was detrimental to my overall physical, mental or spiritual growth." He thinks for a moment, and changes his mind. "No, there were things I would have been better off spending my time doing. I could have progressed further if, say, I'd used drugs half as much as I did, or even one-third as much. It's like my mother says, because of all that I had to start my life over at age 42."

Sutherland, at this point, opens up a second, more general, front in the conversation, and his thoughts jump to a higher plane of organization. "Using drugs, dealing drugs on the side—there's a danger to the whole thing. And not just in the obvious ways. Not just for health reasons, and not just because some guy who thinks you burned him is going to sneak over and cut the brake line on your car, or whatever. It's dangerous because you can't be yourself. You can't move around as easily as you'd like. You can't enjoy yourself in the water. It's dangerous because—" Sutherland pauses, and allows the idea to develop— "because human beings have these savage impulses which need to be controlled. Which, in fact, can even be channeled in a positive way, by setting up certain challenges. Riding big waves, for example. You tap into that savage aspect when necessary, use it now and then, and that way it doesn't pop up unexpectedly. So the danger with drugs, and dealing drugs, is that your better side isn't as strong as it should be; you're not as able to control that potentially harmful side."

Sutherland brings the conversation back to a personal level. "So you're using a power tool, or climbing a steep roof, or accelerating into some gnarly double-up section, and it might be that, for just a moment, that destructive part of you gets loose. And that can cost you."

Sutherland reviews what he's just said, and perhaps thinks it's a bit much. "You're just not as confident as you should be. That's what I'm saying."

On a clear March afternoon last spring, Sutherland walks into his house after an afternoon surf at Laniakea. Conditions were so-so: head-high sets and strong northwest trades. Sutherland rode a long-board. Three better-than-average waves came in during the sixty minutes he was in the water, and not only was Sutherland in position for all three, but he caught each at the absolutely perfect point of entry. He was hand-in-glove through the pocket on a short left, riding goofy foot. He set up the middle section on a right, riding regular foot, with a beautiful shoulder-rotation cutback. Twenty-eight years after the '66 world titles, it may be that the order hasn't changed: Nat Young is probably the best 45-year-old surfer in the world, with Sutherland second. More to his credit, Sutherland's understanding of the North Shore—including aspects; meteorological, physical, psychological, topographical and historical—is probably unequaled.

Since getting out of prison, Sutherland has lived in a small, detached bachelor's quarters behind the house he grew up in, near Chun's Reef— or, to be exact, directly in front of Jocko's, the left across the channel from Chun's. (Jocko's used to be known, in the late '50s and early '60s, as Noll's Reef, after Greg Noll. As far as Sutherland can remember, "Jocko's" took hold sometime in the mid-'70s: "I guess, by that point, I'd surfed it enough." Sutherland knows the origins of the names of most North Shore spots, and obviously likes having one named after him.) He makes a steady living as an independent roofer. The work is hard, but he seems satisfied with the idea of building, and with doing good work, and he occasionally has his two sons along to help.

Sutherland's place is small and comfortable, and not as orderly as might be expected. The bookshelves are full, and include a lot of Jack London, John Steinbeck, John D. McDonald, and books on mytho-logical legends and Hawaiian history. On top of the bookshelves are some trophies, including Sutherland's four Duke contest statuettes (a fifth is missing in action), some paddling-race plaques and a brand-new, three-foot high trophy for his win in a local longboard contest, the weekend prior, at Sunset. The rest of the room is nearly filled with a reading chair and a small table with two dining room chairs.

Two surfboards are in the rafters: a sleek 7'9" Charlie Smith, which Sutherland rides in waves up to 8', and a bulkier 8'4" Roger Hines, for bigger surf. More often than not, Sutherland rides one of these boards.

In the kitchen, Sutherland uncovers an avocado pie of his own making. A self-confessed pedant, he lectures briefly as he takes a knife from the drawer and begins to cut. The trick here, he says, lifting up a carefully-measured slice, is a thicker-than-average crust, to balance out the bottom-heavy avocado taste. He takes a bite. Satisfied, he gives a slight lift of the eyebrows. On a good surf day, Sutherland will some-times come in for a quick wedge of avocado pie and, fueled up, head right back out.

He now climbs up to the loft, changes from trunks to shorts, climbs down, makes a quick call to Debbie Travis, his girlfriend of the past three years, then begins to set a dozen banana slices inside a heating rack to be dried. At 5'10", and 145 pounds, Sutherland's build is virtu-ally identical to what it was in the late '60s. He's efficient, even graceful, as he moves through his house, the fluid body language acting as a counterpoint to his cognitive/speech functions, where the effort almost always shows. Even here, in surroundings that must be nearly womb-like, he doesn't easily relax.

Sutherland was a cipher in '69, and remains so today. The case is easily made that he's addicted to super-radical moves, whether it's fin-drifting at Sunset, or surfing Pipe on acid, or joining the Army, or trying to slide a pound of coke past the feds.

And because Sutherland is smart enough, and experienced enough, to know that super-radical moves can be costly, it could be that his persistent state of tension comes from a persistent struggle to stay in-bounds.

Some people who have known Sutherland a long time see it that way. But Sutherland himself, after agreeing that the radical impulse/control theory might be seen as covering the evidence, has a different view. He tells a story about taking off on a tremendous wave at Waimea in '66, side-by-side with Jose Angel. It was bigger than anything Sutherland had previously ridden. "I was a little nervous, but Jose looked over and said, 'Come on, come on, we can do this,' so we dropped in, turned the corner, and made the wave—and all of a sudden it seemed like the logical thing to do. It almost seemed easy."

The point is that Sutherland doesn't see any of his actions, throughout his life, as being particularly extreme. "I've never felt that the things I do are really that radical, then or now. Each one was a plausible extension of where I was at the time. Each one was feasible. In fact, I don't even know if I was being all that original. A nice fade at Outside Pipe, or bringing a package in from California—I'd seen other people do similar things, and I figured I could either do what they were doing, or do it one step better."

Sutherland, almost easily, puts this logic to work as he downplays his reputation for creative, outer-limit surfing. That came, he says, from growing up outdoors, in an environment that encouraged aggressiveness; from putting endless hours into fundamentals before pushing outward; and from watching carefully how other surfers were doing things. He was creative, but in a planned, rather than spontaneous, way.

Bringing LSD into his act, too, is seen by Sutherland as within normal range—although here he has to stretch a bit. "There was a constant potential, and more than occasional manifestation, of wildness in the late '60s. So there was actually a kind of steadiness if, now and then, you did things that would now be perceived as radical."

Sutherland's explanation for transporting and selling drugs is simple enough. He wanted the money.

And the Army? Sutherland touches on earlier-stated reasons, then opens up further the notion that surfing just wasn't filling his life the way it once had. "The tendency, especially today, with professionalism being what it is, is to see surfing as the be-all and end-all. But that wasn't the case with me. Partly because of the way I am, partly because of the time period. My direction, in '69, believe it or not, was pushing toward a family situation. And it just wasn't obvious that I'd be able to pull it off as a surfer. In other words, surfing has to be seen within a greater context. People at the time thought, 'Well, that's it, his life's over, he joined the Army, he blew it.' And I may have blown it as far as my surfing career went, but that really wasn't what it was all about. I didn't feel then as if I'd made a mistake joining up. And I still don't."

Sutherland speaks here with his usual intensity, but seems to lose conviction as he goes. He doesn't turn away from conversation about the Army, but his justification is never fully persuasive. Audrey Sutherland, who knows her son better than anyone, is probably best positioned to close out the subject. "I still don't know why Jock joined up. I don't think Jock really knows why he joined up."

Even as Sutherland, elsewhere, manages to create logic where it didn't exist before, other contradictions are recalled: the would-be man of science who sometimes entertains the idea that worsening surf conditions on the North Shore are due to supernatural phenomena; his appreciation and understanding of civility, manners and respect coupled with an appreciation and understanding for the handling characteristics of the M-16; the way he splits his ticket in the voting booth.

Drew Kampion thinks it's impossible to overestimate the duality at work in Sutherland. "Switching stance is the key to the whole thing with Jock," Kampion says. "But it's more than just ambidexterity, it's a two-sidedness. And it doesn't just define his surfing, it defines him. He goes in opposite directions—at the same time."

Back at his dining room table, Sutherland describes a day from last January, when he loaned his younger son, Gavin, his 8'4", and took him out at Waimea for the first time. Sets were 15–18', and Gavin handled himself well. As Sutherland describes one of Gavin's rides his voice takes on a becoming note of satisfaction.

He then goes on to say that this was also the day where, for the first time in his life, he'd been caught inside after going left at Waimea. "I'd gone left in the '60s and '70s, and almost got caught inside—when I sort of punched through the lip paddling back out, right next to the boil. But this time, boy, it was the full number." Sutherland straightens in his chair, and his eyes light up with the memory. "That first bugger hit me right on the head, then another one, and I'm eating soup, and all of a sudden I look over my shoulder, and the boulders are maybe 50 yards away and closing fast." After a third hold-down, Sutherland surfaced, made it to the channel, caught his breath, and paddled back out.

Without pause, Sutherland has gone from proud father to Waimea hellman revisited, and the juxtaposition is bizarre. But uncommon positioning has always been Sutherland's trademark, and it's obvious that, in this case at least, elements as disparate as paternal love and potentially serious physical risk can come together without throwing him off balance. For the moment, Sutherland looks relaxed.

Singular Achievement
from Maverick's
by Matt Warshaw

Jeff Clark discovered Maverick's, a California surf break

so intimidating that he had it to himself for 15 years.

Matt Warshaw (born 1960) profiled Clark for the Winter

1994 Surfer's Journal.

Grant Washburn opened the rusted front gate of his San Francisco beachfront apartment, guiding the key in by twilight, and entered his warm and unruly surfer's nest, a clutter of surfboards, wetsuits, leashes, and all manner of surf-related gear and paraphernalia spreading unmethodically across the garage and the vestibule, up the stairwell, into the two bedrooms, the bathroom, the living room, even the kitchen—where Washburn cleared some table space and began his daily surfing journal entry for December 21, 1994.

He printed "Big Wednesday" in block letters across the top of the page and followed with the day's buoy readings: a momentous fifteen feet at twenty-second intervals. "Unbelievable," Washburn wrote. "The ninth straight day of hugeness. Unparalleled, unprecedented, unreal." The surf was the same size as on Monday—twenty feet or more on some sets—but without the diabolically strong off-shore wind. Also, the swell angle had shifted a few degrees north, adding some slope to the bottom half of the Bowl section. Some of the wipeouts, though, were "insane . . . brutal." Jay Moriarity, Washburn noted, did it again. "I witness him flying down the face of a BIG ONE; his first wave of the morning. Then he over-rotates and gets obliterated. Déjà vu—but not as gruesome as his wipeout two days ago."

Overall, though, the number of completed rides was higher than during "the Monday Massacre," as Washburn called it. Evan Slater flat out got the largest, thickest, heaviest wave of his life. Local boy Ion Banner looked sharp. Big-wave surfer Paul Moreno had flown over from Hawaii three days earlier to ride Maverick's for the first time and had adjusted well to the long, shifting waves and the 25-degree difference in water temperature. Peter Mel from Santa Cruz was the day's standout rider—faultless in his wave selection and charging across the big faces like a gazelle, loose, fast, and rangy. The entire Cruz contingent, in fact, lit it up: Darryl Virostko, Josh Loya, Moriarity, and the Wormhoudt brothers, Zack and Jake. More photographers were perched on the cliff than Washburn had ever seen, and probably twenty surfers altogether rode between dawn and dusk.

Washburn ended his afternoon with a mildly masochistic flourish. "Here comes a fine one," he wrote, reliving the moment. "I'm late, but spin and go anyway: two strokes and up on my feet as the bottom drops out and I'm thrown into the Pit. A healthy wipeout, satisfying my need for a spill. I'd been feeling like a cheater after four sessions without any kind of serious fall."

Washburn, born and raised in Connecticut, learned to surf in the small and generally woeful breakers of central New Jersey. In 1990, at twenty-two, he moved to San Francisco to work as a carpenter, and threw himself into the powerful ebb and flow of Ocean Beach, quickly discovering an aptitude and enthusiasm for bigger waves. He first rode Maverick's in 1992, and his big-wave interest blossomed into a multidisciplinary devotion. When he wasn't surfing, he was filming other surfers, working on an outline for a Maverick's documentary, filing local oceanic data into his computer, or writing long passages in his surfing journal.

Midway through Washburn's five-page entry for December 21, he mentioned his friend and informal Maverick's mentor Jeff Clark, and his habitually effusive tone dropped to one of plain-spoken empathy. "Screwed royally once again," Washburn wrote of Clark, who'd knocked his fin loose on his first ride, forcing him to turn for shore. "Jeff just hasn't been able to get in a solid session these days."

Clark, thirty-eight, the original and dominant Maverick's surfer, was moonlighting as a Federal Express dock loader, and had been given a rotten December schedule—mostly night shifts. Also, a loose surfboard had ricocheted off his right ankle earlier in the month, and the joint was still painful and stiff. He was able to surf, but not with his usual drive and efficiency.

Washburn, earlier in the week, had even defended his friend's reputation to a Maverick's newcomer who, in passing, wondered aloud if maybe Clark had lost a step or two. "It felt weird having to vouch for him," Washburn noted in his journal. "I've caught more epic waves over the past few days than I can count, but I'm certain Jeff would have surpassed my efforts had he been feeling well. I've been hoping to help get him back into it."

Washburn did what he could that morning after Clark broke his fin, paddling over and exchanging surfboards, so that Clark might try again. An hour later, though, Clark was on the beach. He'd aced one wave, and snuffed it on another—and that was it. Better than nothing, but still below par.

Maverick's had for years been known as Clark's spot. It still was. It just wasn't his week.

Jeff Clark's claim to Maverick's has nothing to do with the fact that he has registered the word "Maverick's" with the U.S. Department of Commerce Patent and Trademark Office, and everything to do with the dizzying notion that Clark rode this fearful and beautiful big-wave break *completely alone* for fifteen years.

In 1966, Clark's father, a San Mateo County deputy sheriff, built a house for his six-member family on an oceanfront lot in Miramar, just south of Pillar Point, that had a view of the waves off the headland, two miles distant. Jeff was nine years old. That summer he began surfing, and by junior high school, after having attached himself to an older, car-driving group of surfers, he had developed a near-encyclopedic knowledge of the breaks from Santa Cruz to San Francisco. Clark learned early that the freakish big-wave reef north of his house was called Maverick's, and that it was too gnarly to ride.

Clark was a devoted young surfer but not a great natural talent, even by the provincial standards of Half Moon Bay. He had guts, though. As a high school freshman, he was known as the kid who would paddle calmly into big waves and take his knocks like a prize-fighter. Stoicism is an odd trait in a teenager, and while Clark had friends, he also made people a little nervous. "There weren't many people around here who wanted any part of big waves," he recalls in a drawling, bemused voice. "I'd go to the surfshops and say to guys there, 'Come on, let's go ride the biggest waves we can find.' But nobody wanted any part of it. So I was pushing guys past their threshold just on the beachbreaks and other [non-Maverick's] reefs around here." Clark set himself apart, too, as a seventies teenager with no interest in pot, whites, reds, or Quaaludes. "I wanted to surf. And that's pretty much all I wanted to do."

At age sixteen, he began watching Maverick's. During the winter he often surfed Ross's Cove, a break just north of Pillar Point, and when Ross's hit ten feet, he would sit on his board and cast a speculative eye toward the big, empty, shadowy peaks at Maverick's. Clark knew that kids his age in Hawaii were riding Waimea Bay and Sunset Beach; he thought he could do something like that right here, at Maverick's. It was almost as big as Waimea. Maybe as big. And just as well shaped, too. Nobody rode Maverick's, though, and Clark often wondered about that. When the *Surfing California* guidebook was published in

1973, the entry for Pillar Point said: "Huge winter walls outside Half Moon Bay harbor. Shallow reefs. Too dangerous for surfing." Plain enough. But Clark nonetheless began climbing the rim of the head-land when the surf was up, evaluating, considering.

On a warm February afternoon in 1975, Clark and his friend Brian Pinoche were slouched into their familiar west-facing position atop Pillar Point. Clark was seventeen. Pinoche, a little older, had for the past two years been the one guy to match Clark, even push him, in bigger surf. Now Pinoche began to fidget as Clark watched impas-sively. A half mile distant, the wedge-shaped Maverick's waves were peaking at ten or twelve feet, no bigger. The sun was out and the ocean surface was titanium-smooth. The bigger waves, though, were deto-nating over the reef, each blue-green wall replaced by a mushroom cloud of whitewater. Maverick's broke harder than any other wave in the area, maybe harder than anywhere else on the coast. Clark knew this better than anyone. He also knew that conditions wouldn't get any better for an introductory go-out than they were on this particular day. He turned to Pinoche and said as much. Pinoche balked. "I tried for an hour to get him to come with me," Clark remembers, "and he said something like, 'Good luck, and I'll call the Coast Guard and tell 'em where I last saw you. But I'm not going in.' "

Clark approached from the north, paddling slowly and deliberately. Maverick's, as he saw it, was a left-breaking wave. The rights were long and intricate, maybe *too* intricate, and bordered by a long stand of rocks. The lefts were shorter and more predictable, spilling into what appeared to be a rock-free channel. That was the direction he intended to ride.

If he was going to ride. Clark was on his longest board—seven feet, three inches—and the closer he moved toward the breaking surf, the more obvious it became that he was underequipped. What would he need, though? An eight-footer? Nine? Bigger, maybe, Clark thought. Seven-three, in any event, was ridiculous; it would probably wiggle and spin down the face like soap on porcelain. Clark paused. He could stand down, right now, paddle in, tell Pinoche what Maverick's looked like close-up, and try again some other time. *But look how smooth it is,* Clark argued with himself. *For sure that's going to make the waves easier to ride. And it's just a seven-three, but it's a really GOOD seven-three.* He moved a few yards closer.

Clark dropped carefully, almost chastely, down the front of his first wave, a sensible ten-footer, and was nearly paralyzed by the speed and velocity. Seven seconds later, gliding into deep water, mouth agape, Clark went prone and felt his heart thumping like a speedbag into the deck of his board. The next two waves were the same: blurry with acceleration, but safe. Wave number four was a different story. Clark had unwittingly positioned himself too far to the south, on the wrong side of the apex, on a wave that was five feet bigger than the others. Paddling hard, just before standing up, he glanced to his left and felt dread wash through him like gasoline as a long, impossible section tilted up vertically in his path. Clark was beyond the point where he could rein in and let the wave roll by. Pushing to his feet, he made a risky choice: rather than descend to the bottom, he gently initiated an elliptical line of retreat along the building crest of the wave— knowing that if he pushed too hard, his board would slip out of its track, and he'd drop like a bridge-jumper into the void. But the seven-three held fast and Clark exited down the wave's trailing slope, just as it folded over upon itself with a hydrodynamic roar.

A half hour later, Clark caught his last wave and returned to the rock-lined beach north of Maverick's. He raved to Pinoche, who, to Clark's amazement, just shrugged and looked blank at the suggestion of a follow-up Maverick's session. Visiting the local surf shops in the weeks and months to come, it was the same thing. No takers. Clark was dumbstruck. He'd *done* it. Maverick's was *surfable*. Maverick's was like—Clark hesitated at first, then got used to saying it—it was like *Sunset*. Or *Waimea*. Still, no takers.

Clark rode Maverick's alone from 1975 to 1989. He may have skipped a few seasons (in an early interview he said he rode there "pretty much" every winter; later he filled in the blanks and it was every winter), and local surfers occasionally paddled out with him to watch from the safety of the channel. But for fifteen years Clark was the only person to ride the "too dangerous for surfing" waves off Pillar Point, and it doesn't much matter if that translates to 10 sessions or 110 sessions. His solitary period at Maverick's is a stunning, unmatchable big-wave achievement.

"He's a nut, really; he's psycho," says Santa Cruz's Josh Loya, one big-wave surfer bestowing upon another the highest possible compliment. "Riding that place by yourself for all those years. . . . God, I would *never* do that. I wouldn't surf out there even *once* by myself."

Clark returned home after his first day at Maverick's and knew he had to solve his surfboard problem. The seven-three had gotten him off the mark, but he wasn't going to push his luck. Maverick's clearly required an out-and-out, fully loaded big-wave gun. Local manufacturers lacked either the interest or the expertise to produce such a board (which looks like a longer-version shortboard, but isn't; just as a cello isn't a scaled-up violin), so Clark finally bought materials and set up shop in his garage.

In this way, he apprenticed for the most venerated—maybe the *only* venerated—production job in surfing. Pat Curren, Mike Diffenderfer, Dick Brewer, Tom Parrish, Pat Rawson, and other big-wave board shapers had over the decades formed a composite mythical figure: part artist, part armament maker, part guru. These board makers each had a stable of top big-wave riders, and they often made their customers, famous and nonfamous, wait months before taking delivery on their personally designed boards. Some were autocratic and temperamental. "Brewer made me a beautiful new nine-foot, six-inch gun for Waimea in '73," North Shore master surfer Jeff Hakman remembers. "He says to me, 'Here it is, what do you think?' And I looked and said 'Nice, nice.' Then I said, 'The tail seems a little bit pulled in, don't you think?' 'A little pulled?' he asks. 'I can fix that.' And he got a saw and cut a foot off this perfect board, and the whole thing just dropped to the floor. 'How's that?' he asked me. 'Huh? Is that better for you?' "

Jeff Clark would never develop into a beatified big-wave surfboard shaper. By the mideighties, though, he was building efficient full-race guns for himself, and a decade later he was making boards for perhaps a third of the fifty-or-so regular Maverick's surfers.

Clark's boards were fundamentally the same as those built by George Downing in the early fifties: about ten feet long, twenty-one inches wide, three and a half inches thick, pointed on both ends, with the nose section fuller than the tail section, and slightly bowed. Because big waves are harder to catch than small waves (they move faster and displace more water), paddling speed was Clark's primary design concern, ahead of handling characteristics. All other design elements being equal, the longer a board is, the faster it will paddle. At about the eleven-foot mark, however, the board's weight and mass make it nearly impossible to steer once the wave is engaged. Ten feet was Downing's baseline size, and it was Clark's, too.

There were obvious differences between Downing's and Clark's big-wave boards, too. Where Downing used a homemade laminated slab of balsa with vertical redwood strips as the core material, and did most of the shaping work with a draw-knife, Clark used factory-made closed-cell polyurethane foam blanks (standard since the early sixties) and a power planer. Downing's boards had a single stabilizing fin, and weighed about thirty-five pounds. Clark's boards had either one, three, or four fins, and weighed about fifteen pounds.

As much as Clark labored in the garage, he worked even harder in the surf, teaching himself how to ride switchstance in big waves—the surfing equivalent of switch-hitting in baseball. About two-thirds of all surfers ride in a left-foot-forward "regularfoot" stance, and the rest use a right-foot-forward "goofyfoot" stance. Riding frontside means you're facing the wave as you angle across. Riding backside means your back is to the wave. Frontside is easier than backside, just as a forehand tennis stroke is easier than a backhand one, and in big surf the advantage—having the wave in your line of vision—is even greater. Nonetheless, just a handful of surfers over the past fifty years have mastered switchfoot surfing, and only two—Jock Sutherland and Butch Van Artsdalen, both famous in the sixties—were able to switchstance in big waves. Clark, a Sutherland disciple as a preteen (and, like Sutherland, a born goofyfoot), practiced riding as a regularfoot for hours at a time in the Half Moon Bay shorebreak, and ten years later, when he decided to take on the long and complex right-breaking waves at Maverick's, he was able to do so in a frontside stance. Clark was the only ambidextrous big-wave surfer in the world at the time, and remains so today. Switchfooting is his great achievement within the achievement.

On the morning of January 22, 1990, Clark drove to San Francisco's Ocean Beach—having by now given up on recruiting any local surfers, he decided to try to import a few guys from elsewhere in the Bay Area—and in the parking lot at Sloat Avenue, he began talking to Tom Powers and Dave Schmidt from Santa Cruz, and Mark Renneker from San Francisco, all of whom had some big-wave experience. Well-shaped fifteen-foot surf was pumping in steadily, but at Ocean Beach there was no paddling channel through the corrugated lines of foam. Renneker proposed that they suit up anyway and try to punch through. Clark counterproposed, saying he had a spot in mind, not too far away, that could handle the size. Schmidt and Powers were interested. Renneker waved them off.

One hour later Schmidt and Powers had joined Clark in the Maverick's lineup, and were gaping at the surf as if in the presence of an alien life form. Clark wore a little smile as he offered tips and instruction. Schmidt ended up riding six waves, and Powers got two. Clark put on a big-wave demonstration that seemed to be three-parts authoritative and one-part mad. "He just blew us away that day," Powers later said of Clark. "He was taking off super deep, charging into these big, black, hideous pits. We were worried about him. We were awestruck."

Eighteen months later, Maverick's made its feature-length debut in *Surfer*, and Clark became an instant big-wave sensation. He'd ridden those huge, cold, rock-smashing waves by himself, quietly, year after year, without photo, film, or video documentation. "Core"—short for hardcore—had long been a surf-world accolade, and Clark's solo run at Maverick's seemed to initiate a new, higher order of core.

Never before had anyone in the sport come to prominence in their midthirties, and Jeff Clark looked his years: handsome and trim, but weathered, with sun-damaged lips and thick, mannish black hair covering his workman's forearms. Everything about Clark—his soft, detached voice, the stony silences, the drill-bit blue eyes, the tight expression—suggested that this was a surfer with abundant, possibly unimaginable experience. It seemed like he'd been around for years.

In 1992 and '93, as the surfing press discovered new details about Clark, he only looked tougher, braver, cooler. He once piggybacked a drowning man to the beach, pumped water out of his stomach and lungs, waited for the ambulance to arrive, then paddled back into the surf. In 1991, he was aboard a friend's boat in the Maverick's channel after breaking two ribs during a wipeout. "I couldn't breathe too well," he told *Surfing*, "and I was really worried that I might have done some serious damage." A photographer on the boat happened to be carrying a bottle of prescription painkillers. Clark swallowed two, waited twenty minutes, then "paddled over and caught three more waves."

Clark plainly was nothing like the slick, young, media-raised, southern California surfers; for fifteen years he'd worked as a carpenter and general contractor. Though he was now also shaping surfboards professionally and earning a small monthly stipend as an industry-sponsored big-wave rider, he'd never be one to zigzag the trade show aisles, grinning professionally, slapping palms with people he didn't know and singing out "Hey bro!" But as an interview subject, he produced quotes and sound bites as easily as if he were cutting out sections of floor joist. "Maverick's is a spot that takes care of itself" was an early and oft-repeated favorite. "You have to be 100 percent committed to ride big waves," he told the *San Francisco Chronicle*. "When that set comes, your heart starts to pound, and when you take off every ounce of adrenaline in your body is pumping. It sounds like thunder when the wave crashes." When describing the hazardous aspects of Maverick's, Clark would level his icy blue-eyed gaze and lower his voice slightly. On record, he never joked about big-wave surfing.

With all of the attention, Clark soon found himself cutting a higher profile—Hawaii's Laird Hamilton excepted—than any other big-wave surfer. Intentionally or not, when Clark spoke he often did so for the entire sport, and no one blinked in 1994 when *Surfer* labeled him as one of the "world's best big-wave riders."

Clark, though, was the outlier among his big-wave peers, both geographically and experientially. His domain was proscribed and defined like nobody else's—he was the press-titled "Maverick Man." Where most other big-wave riders would resent being tied so closely to one break, it didn't seem to bother Clark. No doubt his long and unique relationship with Maverick's had created the strongest possible bond between surfer and surf break. But Clark must have recognized, too, that there would be little or no career advantage in venturing from his Maverick's dominion. To become a more cosmopolitan big-wave rider, he'd only bump shoulders with a few dozen others just as hungry and guts-up as he was. Clark rose to big-wave prominence without having ever visited Hawaii, something that had never happened before. Uniqueness became a big part of his appeal. When he finally rode Waimea, in 1994, he performed well—but so did fifteen or twenty other surfers. Clark went unnoticed.

Jeff Clark is indeed the Maverick Man, and the designation doesn't appear to strike him as limiting, or as a laurel to rest upon, but as an expression of something very close to a monogamous big-wave marriage.

Mavericks

by Lawrence Beck

Photographer Lawrence Beck's (born 1953) description of his 1993 attempt to photograph surfers at Mavericks offers something close to a seal's eye view of conditions at that notorious break.

Mavericks is located at the northernmost tip of Half Moon Bay, just southwest of Pillar Point. It is, by many accounts, a mystical place with an inner music of its own. Costanoan Indians lived and fished in the area for hundreds of years prior to the arrival of Portola in 1769. In the 1870s, Pillar Point was a whaling center for those who risked their lives in six-man single-masted boats. The 1920s saw local bootleg alcohol during prohibition. Today, the "point" is gaining notoriety for a wave that may yet set new standards for big wave riding.

Sail Rock, just inside the first reef at Mavericks, is home to colonies of seals and sea lions. One of the magical aspects of this break is the presence of these marine spectators. Sea lions watch from close range as surfers paddle out to the lineup. Following wipeouts in which a board has broken or a leash has snapped, sea lions will often dog surfers into the tidal flats inside Sail Rock. These guardians of the reef appear to sense the vulnerability of surfers, moving in close to investigate when rider and board have been separated.

On a swell under fourteen feet, the wave shape is determined to a large degree by the bottom configuration. The reefs reach out like fingers to the depths. Huge boulders are strewn around the base of the outside and inside reefs. The bottom is carpeted with large fragments of fiberglass—remnants of fishing boats which have foundered near Sail Rock.

On a medium swell the wave will often undulate like a giant serpent, heaving and rolling with a form that's anything but straight. The peak will form where the reef is most shallow—around 23 feet at the outside reef and 21 feet at the inside reef.

If the swell is over 15 feet, the peak will stretch over twenty yards and will shift without warning. The bottom will be thoroughly dredged, and a brown scum will form on the surface. On one such occasion this past April, Grant Washburn, a surfer from San Francisco, wound up with a small, disoriented shark thrashing about his groin after a monster wall raged by.

The locals who surf Mavericks whenever it breaks are as uncommon as the wave itself. They generally arrive quietly, at first light. After depositing boards and wetsuits at the base of the cliff, they hike up Pillar Point and study the swell for up to an hour. Mental notes are engraved as to the wind and the speed, size and direction of the swell. At some point the group will shuffle down to their boards to don black wetsuits and paddle out on clear, unmarked boards. Their anonymity is planned. The only color is the style with which they ride the wave.

The morning of April third started out like a dozen others during the winter of '92/93. The end of the Pacifica Pier was getting hammered by a big northwest swell, and the vibration could be felt through the floor of my apartment. The call from Jeff Clark came at 6:30 a.m. "Lawrence, I think it's time you see this wave from the water. I've arranged a boat to take us out to the channel at the south end of Mavericks . . ." Before

Jeff could finish the next sentence, I interrupted with, "See you at the café at seven."

Leicas and Kodachrome were already packed in anticipation of yet another big day. My pulse jumped as I visualized the concept of shooting this epic wave from a pitching, heaving platform. My focus was centered on a new shooting prospect . . . the water perspective.

I had seen Bob Barbour shoot Mavericks from a boat on Valentine's Day, the first day it went off this year, and I couldn't say that I really envied him. Respected, yes. (In a fishing boat: extreme motor vibration, focus, slippery deck, and keeping a level horizon, I had seen waves continue breaking into the channel, right where Barbour shot, on March 5 . . . "maverick" waves with forty foot faces that looked like mutant seismic monsters born of some benthic disturbance up in the Gulf of Alaska.) There's no such thing as a "stable platform" when shooting fifteen to twenty foot waves from a boat that bobs like a cork in a channel that's only thirty-five feet deep in places.

As I arrived at the café, Jeff introduced me to Sean Clark, an abalone/urchin diver who worked the Faralon Islands (known for its prolific great white shark population). Sean was stoked about the prospect of taking us out in his boat as he had seen Jeff surf the place alone for nearly fifteen years prior to 1990, and he was always too busy diving to watch the lunatic fringe surf on big days. (I also think Sean derived some pleasure from the thought of scaring the hell out of us on the trip out to the channel.)

Sean entertained us with stories of his daily dive trips out to the Faralones and close encounters with "the mother of all fish." I got the distinct impression that Sean, like Jeff, was one of those people whose pulse didn't climb above sixty unless he was involved in a life threatening situation. We could see the fog begin to lift in the harbor, so Jeff downed his "power breakfast" of mocha java and Ibuprophen and we crossed the highway to Pillar Point Harbor.

Within minutes, we cast off and motored out of the calm and into what felt like a seiche, a standing wave, much like the inside of a pig's stomach after a binge at the trough. Rather than motoring south from the breakwater, and around the buoys marking "safe passage," Sean chose to run along the breakwater . . . just to make things a little more interesting. As we proceeded to "beat" northwest, taking each wave on the nose, we crested a large swell and Sean throttled back to minimize the impact of our landing. The boat slammed into the trough and the anchor flew off the deck, pulling chain with it. Waves were lined up, coming straight at the bow, as Sean sprinted out of the heaving cabin onto the foredeck and pulled up chain and anchor as if they weighed nothing. Jeff steered into the swell, I said ten Hail Mary's and looked with wanton lust at Jeff's surfboard laying on the deck. The cameras weren't even a consideration. (I would soon find out if my renter's insurance policy was worth the paper it was printed on!)

Sean lashed the anchor to the deck with amazing speed and jumped back into the cabin, pushing the throttle forward as he braced for the next wave. The boat coughed, sputtered and stalled. I was grey, Jeff was white and Sean muttered something like, "Aaah, this motor's kind of tired . . . it needs to be blown out . . . I need to run it flat out for a while."

After unplugging two air intake ports on the deck, the 327 finally came alive. We motored outside the breakwater and Jeff climbed into his wetsuit in what must have been record time. I tried to remain calm as I asked Sean, "What's the top end of this boat?" He replied, "12 knots, on a good day." I then asked how fast the swell was running, to which he calmly answered, "About 22 knots . . ." Jeff was overboard and paddling for the horizon before I had a chance to turn and gauge his expression.

I racked my brain in an effort to find a way to suggest that we return to the harbor. Much as I wanted some good shots from the water, my instinct for self preservation was taking control. At the same time, I couldn't let Sean know I was ready to walk on water. After all, this was just routine fun in his eyes. (I would discover a week later that Sean had blown his engine and was looking for a bigger replacement.)

Jeff wheeled and caught his first wave. It was triple overhead and barreling as he came straight at me. My immediate fears were put aside as I focused on the ride in front of me. As Clark dropped into the double up, the wave seemed to gain speed, pushing him faster and faster until he climbed out of the tube and coasted over the top, shaking both fists and howling. Sean looked at me and asked, "Wanna get closer?" Adrenaline was pumping all around, so I said, "Yeah, just don't get shallower than 25 feet."

By now, Matt Ambrose, Shawn Rhodes, Mike Kimsey and Jim Tjogas were paddling into the channel, followed by Grant Washburn with a video camera. The swell was getting bigger by the minute. I remember someone saying that Mavericks looked like a house coming at you at 20 knots. Today, it looked more like a four story hotel stretching for a city block, coming at you at 22 knots. Clark had it wired . . . he'd make the drop, crank a hard bottom turn and climb back up the face just as the wave pitched, enclosing him in an elliptical barrel.

About that time, Sean received a call from someone who wanted to use the boat, so we motored back to port. I decided to head back up to the cliffs to shoot from a more stable perspective, so I grabbed my equipment and ran out to the point to set up.

As I fastened my camera to the tripod, I watched Clark dive off his board just before it closed out. What follows are Jeff's thoughts and words, in quotes, as to what has to be his closest ever brush with death.

"I dropped into one bowl, and then there was another bowl across the crease in the wave, so I pulled up into it. I could see that it was going to clam shell, so I dove off. I came up, pulled my board back and began paddling left as I was still in front of the bowl and this was the beginning of a set.

"The next double-up broke my board, and the turbulence was unreal. I was thinking: I've got half a board and it's dragging me towards the rocks . . . this leash has got to come off. I tried to get under the next wall of white water as it passed overhead, dredging everything in its path. The bottom was shallower with each passing second and the water seemed to accelerate as it hit the shallows. I remember seeing the rocks getting closer, and I tried to reach down and pull off the leash with my webs and I couldn't find the strap! At that moment I was hit by another wave and I was upside down and fighting to stay on the surface in all this turbulence. I struggled to stay afloat while trying to get the leash out from under my wetsuit and I was burning air while being rolled wave after wave. The next thing I knew, I was 20 feet from the face of the big rock and there's lots of white water coming right behind me: I knew I had no control over this situation. I was at the mercy of Poseidon's washing machine and it was locked on "spin cycle." A lot of things would have to happen right in order for me to make it, and I didn't have any control over this. What scared me most was the possibility of my board hanging up on a rock and me being attached to it, with no possibility of escape.

"The next wave pushed me into the rock wall and I could feel the back pressure of the water off the wall while under water. I was swirling around and was shoved through a gap between two large rocks. As I swept through I was able to reach up and grab a handhold. The water level began to drop as it pulled and tried to dislodge me from the rock. My hands were two feet from the top of the rock and my feet were out of the water as the current sucked out to sea.

"Within seconds, the next wave hit, covering the rock with water as I hung by my fingers. The broken board, still attached to my leash, pulled at my ankle as the wave swept over and around the rock through the narrow channel. All I could think of was the rock climbers hanging by their fingers in the video *Blood, Sweat and Glory*; rock climbers totally suspended by their fingers. I didn't have a good handhold . . . I was suspended on the face of that rock by my fingers. I was fortunate to have gloves on as the rock was encrusted with big mussels and barnacles.

"The third wave covered me over, and as it started to recede, I pulled myself up the face and over the top of the rock and got rid of the leash. I was so relieved to be on the rock that I took a moment to reflect on the situation.

"So I'm standing on the rock, after getting rid of my board, and I'm thinking about what I had just gone through when this massive wall of white water came roaring in. I lay down on the rock and held on while the wave rolled over me. I realized that I was going to be here for a while. I could see off the back side of the jagged rock that the current would suck all the water out from around the rocks during the sets, leaving nothing to swim in to get out of there. The chance of me swimming back out through white water was not a good option. Luckily there was a good handhold across the top of the rock. There were also cracks that I could wedge my right arm and knees into. I just held on for wave after wave.

"I was hanging on so tight that after ten minutes my arms were shaking and I was getting really cold. I had shut down circulation to my arms and legs while I played abalone, keeping a death grip on the rock. I knew my longevity would be severely limited if I got hypothermia or fatigued my muscles to such an extent that they were useless. I started shaking and moving my arms to get the circulation going between waves.

"I kept looking in to see if anybody was going to come out to the rocks because I was pinned down. Then I heard this voice shouting, 'What are you doing?' I looked up to see Jim, with this crazy smile on his face, standing on another rock not 25 feet away. He had scrambled to the top of a fifteen foot rock, barely escaping being swept off by a wave. He asked if I was all right and if I needed a helicopter. I told him I was okay.

"For the next half hour, Jim kept me informed as to when to brace myself for a big swell and when to get up and rest for a moment. The danger was not so much the big sets, as their energy would dissipate from the outside reef through the impact zone and finally through the inside section to the rocks. Waves too small to break on the outside reef would gather energy as they rolled into the shallows, eventually focusing their energy on the rocks where I was stranded.

"Matt Ambrose and Mike Kimsey had paddled in to see if they could help. They could see Jim on one of the larger rocks just inside the one I was pinned down on. Just as they climbed up the face of another rock on the inside, Jim shouted. 'Look out!' An unusually large inside wave had just broken and after burying me with several feet of water, it rushed over and around the inside rocks, sweeping Matt and Mike off into a narrow channel where they were smashed into the surrounding rocks. I couldn't see them from my vantage point, but I knew they were getting worked. Within seconds, Jim shouted, 'Jeff, jump now!' I didn't hesitate. I trusted Jim's judgement as I knew he'd be conservative in a situation like this. I swam the thirty or so yards of swirling, boiling white water to the edge of the tidal flat just as another set started to roll in. Jim, Matt and Mike appeared as I walked onto the flat. Matt looked to be in a great deal of pain as he limped on one leg while Mike helped him to shore. Mike was bleeding from the top of his head and limping from a knee injury.

"As we approached each other, Mike started laughing and said, 'Boy . . . some kind of rescue team we turned out to be!' "

Jeff smiled and with characteristic calm replied, "Oh well . . . another day at the office."

Life Among the Swells
by William Finnegan

William Finnegan (born 1952) grew up surfing, and went on to write about subjects ranging from war in Mozambique to teenage gangs in America. This is his 1997 report on the Pipeline Masters, a stop on the professional tour.

The professional surfing circuit ends each year at the Pipeline Masters. Here the would-be, the has-been, and the already-are hero boys of the sport come to be swallowed up—and possibly anointed—by the hungry waves of Oahu's North Shore.

I found a peak, a no-name wave just west of Off-the-Wall. A lifeguard told me an unusual sandbar had formed there after a recent storm and would probably be gone after the next storm. When a set caught it right, the bar produced a steep takeoff with long tapering lefts and short, quick rights. Over the course of a week I surfed the place three times, each time alone or nearly alone. The waves weren't very big, but they were mostly clean and deeply pleasing. What I couldn't decide was whether the light edge of ecstasy I felt while riding this evanescent spot was radiating from the experience itself or from my awareness that it was happening on the holy North Shore.

If the surfing world has a shared mythology, then the North Shore of Oahu is its Olympus. For those who surf, it doesn't matter where one lives—I live in New York City—the place takes up an alarming amount of one's fantasy life. High-resolution images of waves at the Banzai Pipeline, Sunset Beach, Waimea Bay, Backdoor, and Off-the-Wall fill the collective surfing unconscious with mesmerizing caverns, pitching silver lips, and impossibly deep, dreamlike rides.

What happens there is straightforward: Winter storms in the North Pacific generate large swells that strike the coast of Hawaii, their force undiminished by a continental shelf. A fortuitous concentration of reefs and channels on the North Shore turns those swells into ridable waves, and great surfers come from all over the world to ride them. A critical mass of photographers and cameramen gathers to immortalize—and commodify—it all for the entertainment of the rest of us. The imagery produced has, at least for surfers, a power, a fascination, a *glamour* of complex transcendence.

From November to February the North Shore teems with visiting surfers. They come from Brazil and Europe and Florida and Japan and, most numerously, southern California. This seasonal migration began in the 1950s, when a handful of California surfers first ventured over from Makaha, a West Shore spot then considered the last word in big waves. Nowadays the seasonal influx numbers in the thousands.

For the most part, it's a hard-core crowd—young, male, low-budget, dead serious about surfing. An elaborate dominance hierarchy, both in and out of the water, is constantly under construction. Hot locals and famous pros occupy the heights, but bold, talented newcomers are forever on the rise. Different surfers excel in different conditions, and each spot has its own pecking order, adjusted daily. Given the intensity of the competition, the absence of formal rules, the great cultural diversity of the players, and the sheer quantities of adrenaline being pumped, it all goes off pretty peaceably.

A few young women, some of whom surf, make the pilgrimage these days. Local nightlife, however, is nonexistent. Even in December, the peak month for visitors, the scene is decidedly tame. Short-timers stay in cramped rental cottages, eight and ten to a house. Parties tend to be muted, pot-themed affairs, ending early. A night out is pizza at D'Amicos, a no-frills joint near Sunset Point.

Surfers come for the waves. They also come to get their ticket punched: North Shore experience is indispensable on any ambitious surfer's resume. And if they're planning to make a career in surfing (an option reserved for only the hottest of the hot), they come to perform in this, the main arena—and to be photographed doing so as often as possible.

The highest concentration of cameras usually occurs in December, at the Pipeline Masters (or the Chiemsee Gerry Lopez Pipeline Masters, as it's currently known). Held since 1971, the Pipe Masters is probably the world's best-known surf contest and is the final event of the year on the nine-country professional World Championship Tour. Insofar as most surfers take an interest in any contest, they take an interest in the Pipe Masters. When the waves are good, it can be a spectacular show.

But that's a big "insofar." I was at the 1996 Pipe Masters as part of the media mob. Though the contest was on hold for more than a week while its promoters prayed for Pipeline to break, the North Shore surf community didn't seem to be holding its collective breath. Out at Sunset one balmy, brilliant morning, I asked a local surfer about the Pipe Masters and its various affiliated events. "Next year they're going to put up a Ferris wheel," he said, jerking a thumb back toward the beach.

His tart dismissal of the pro scene captured nicely, I thought, the attitude of most surfers toward the organized, commercialized version of the sport: rumpled apathy, contempt, a whiff of envy. Contests are a scam, a distraction from more important things: the ocean, the weather, and of course that weightiest of matters, one's own surfing.

I largely shared this attitude. Indeed, just being in Hawaii heightened my ingrained suspicion of everything that seeks to package and sell surfing. I lived in Honolulu as a kid—I went to junior high school there—and it now makes me physically ill to revisit certain South Shore spots, obscure breaks where a few friends and I used to surf, and find 100 boards in the water. The sport's salesmen have done their job too well. And the World Championship Tour is, naturally, their favorite marketing tool.

This was my first trip to the North Shore since 1978, and it too was dramatically more crowded than I remembered it. There were traffic jams and parking hassles. Surfers on bicycles, boards under arms, patrolled the coast constantly, keeping a close watch on the dozens of spots. Whenever a break got halfway ridable, people were on it, battling for waves. If the surf was actually good, it was crowded from dawn till dark.

Still, I was wildly happy to be there. Out at Sunset that morning, long, sparkling sets moved in from the north, their broad faces buffed by a light south wind. I could see Army C-130s flying lazy, low-altitude circles offshore and a big green sea turtle swimming near my takeoff spot. I lucked into a solid wave alone and rode it from a big-shouldered, sapphire-blue outside wall through a jacking inside bowl. On the paddle back out I was grinning like an idiot.

As I sniffed around the North Shore, I kept catching small glimpses of myself as a young dog haunting these same neighborhoods, in scenes long forgotten: riding a beloved board at a fast, shallow break known as Gas Chambers; staying in a creepy, celibate Baha'i household up at Waialee; surfing Pipeline for the first time on my 19th birthday; getting drubbed within an inch of my life by a ten-wave set at Sunset.

While the surf on the North Shore may be Olympian, the place itself is another matter. Beyond the cropped edges of the exquisite photos, it's a damp, semirural, rather ordinary-looking stretch of tropical coast, 12 miles long, between the old sugar towns of Haleiwa and Kahuku. Military installations and pineapple fields occupy the rolling terraces behind the coastal bluffs, and horse farms take up the verdant flats where the bluffs swing inland. There's a small harbor at Haleiwa. Otherwise, the only significant notch in the coast is the U-shaped, cliff-lined, river-mouth bay at Waimea. Beach houses, both modest and posh, fill the narrow, intermittent strip between the ocean and the only through road.

The year-round residents are native-born islanders, ex-Californians, and a scantling of transplants from farther away. Some surf, though most don't. Ethnically, it's Hawaiians, Chinese, Japanese, Filipinos, haoles (whites), Koreans, and every conceivable combination thereof. Some people commute to Honolulu, 30 miles away on the South Shore, or to one of the island's military bases, but local jobs are scarce, particularly since the sugar mill at Haleiwa closed last year. There's only one hotel, a Hilton near Kahuku, which seems to be struggling.

Tourism reaches the North Shore mainly in the form of charter buses, which stop in Haleiwa, where curio shops and "art galleries" lie in wait for them, or on the roadside at Sunset Beach, where they exhale packs of camera swingers in front of the famous wave every few minutes, inhale them back, and proceed.

Surfers on the North Shore, like surfers most everywhere, are often broke, or nearly so. And the winter pilgrims have tended to bring with them a motley flock of hangers-on, not all of whom leave when the winter swells end. A transient layer of nouveau poverty thus lies uneasily alongside the community's older rural Hawaiian poverty, the two worlds sharing, among other things, an underground economy specializing in crack, heroin, speed, stolen property, and above all, marijuana.

This is the non-glam North Shore, and you can scarcely be here a day without noticing it. Its denizens trip along the roadside, trade food stamps at tiny cinder-block groceries, settle domestic disputes in grubby laundromats at night. Just east of Sunset Point, near a surf spot known as Velzyland, the road passes a long row of low beige houses that could be in backwater Alabama: rotting carports, muddy trucks on blocks, chained pit bulls, large men drinking beer on a weekday morning, barefoot children in dirty shorts.

So while a Ferris wheel on the beach at Sunset obviously won't happen—that was just a metaphor—there is this other perspective on the pro surfing circus that passes through Hawaii each winter: that of the kids who live here, many of them poor.

I think it's safe to say that they're unlikely to share my bourgeois purist's distaste for crass commercialism. In fact, the local boys who've made it as pro surfers are heroes to such kids, who would no doubt be happy to join the circus and see the world themselves. And this poor-boy's perspective was really more interesting, I later decided, than my own.

But I only saw that after spending a week, waiting for the Pipe Masters to start, with one of the homeboy heroes, a young pro named Conan Hayes.

He's not one of the professional surfing tour's poster boys yet. He had a great year, though, rising from number 35 on the 44-man tour to number ten going into this, the year's final event. In an August meet in Lacanau, France, he defeated, in successive heats, Kelly Slater, Sunny Garcia, and Shane Beschen, who were then ranked number one, two, and three in the world, respectively. Perhaps, I think, that's why everywhere we go on the North Shore—to the beach, out surfing, into Haleiwa for breakfast—people greet him with peace signs, double-clutch handshakes, cryptic jokes. They're drawn to him, sensing he may be the Next Big Thing. "Nah," says Conan. "It's because I cut my hair."

Just yesterday he had a burgundy-tinted Afro. Now, suddenly, he has a burgundy tennis ball. He's obviously into abrupt revamps—in surfing magazine photos past, he had blond braids and then blond cornrows. "Experiments," he says, when I ask him about other self-adornments—a pierced nose, a pierced tongue. (His half-dozen tattoos must fall under another category.)

Conan is strangely self-possessed for a kid of 22, with a quiet, watchful manner that crosscuts suavely with his flamboyance. Although he's a haole, he's got a streetwise, multicultural air. With his long arms and powerful torso, he looks like a boxer, some junior welterweight brawler from the Bronx. At five-foot-seven and 145 pounds, he's one of the smaller men on the pro tour.

Conan really doesn't seem to see the North Shore through the prism of his own success—a sports-mad campus on which he is a popular jock. His humility can be quite disarming. One day we're crawling down a narrow road near Pipeline in my rental car, easing past a battered sedan going the other way. Conan waves to the other driver, a shirtless old Filipino, who waves back. "You know him?" I ask, a little surprised.

"Nah," Conan says. "But you gotta wave to people in Hawaii. It's like super-mandatory. I was just covering for you."

Conan learned his rural Hawaiian manners on the Kona Coast of the Big Island, where he grew up and, when he is not out on tour, still lives. His parents were country hippies, his father a marijuana farmer. For a haole kid, Hawaiian public schools can be tough places. "Yeah, they had a Kill Haole Day at my school," Conan recalls. "But all my boys were the gnarliest Hawaiian guys, and by junior high I was known for surfing, so I was cool. I never fazed."

The Big Island doesn't have a reputation for good surf, but Conan's parents gave him a used board when he was ten, and his talent was noticed immediately, even at his mediocre home break. A local surf shop and a Honolulu board company began to sponsor him when he was only 11, flying him to Oahu for amateur contests, which he soon began to win.

John Carper, a board shaper on the Big Island at the time (he's now on the North Shore and shapes boards for Conan), remembers a whole crop of hot local kids, from which only Conan and his best friend, Shane Dorian, also now a top pro and Carper team rider, emerged. "There were so many drugs around," Carper says. "And all these other kids were turning into little jelly piles—no motivation. Shane and Conan were different. They were dead-set against drugs. They were like ghetto kids. They had that kind of determination."

When Conan was 14, his father got busted for growing pot. His sentence: ten years in federal prison. Conan had been largely raising himself already—"He was sleeping on people's floors, hanging with adults," according to Carper—and developing his trademark equanimity. "He was never angry or hyperactive, like a lot of kids coming out of the drug culture," Carper said. "He could always entertain himself."

After his father went to jail, Conan began raising himself for real. "My mom had no money, and she had my little sister," he says. Conan, barely five feet tall at the time, moved to the North Shore, where he scraped by on whatever his local sponsors gave him, lived off friends, became a strict vegetarian, and won every state amateur title in sight. One year he and Shane Dorian lived together in a walk-in closet. Somehow Conan managed to graduate from high school.

The adult he most credits with helping him through this hand-to-mouth adolescence is Ben Aipa, a legendary Hawaiian surfer and board maker who became his coach. "Conan was really very independent," Aipa recalls. "But I took him everywhere with me, trying to keep him busy. I was coaching Brad Gerlach"—a world-tour pro—"and I used to take Conan along. Conan already saw where he wanted to go."

Against his sponsor's advice, Conan turned professional and soon found himself with an unorthodox new sponsor: Chris Lassen, a painter from Maui who had parlayed his work—garish, tropical-fantasy fare—into a multinational schlock-art business with revenues last year of more than $20 million. Lassen, who surfs, wanted a surf team with his name on it. Conan ended up sharing a palatial North Shore beach house, just down the road from his old walk-in closet, with other Lassen beneficiaries. Lassen bankrolled his travels to contests on the World Qualifying Series, where top finishers graduate to the World Championship Tour.

Conan was in awe of Lassen's custom-car collection—Cobras, Lamborghinis—and remembers, with a rich chuckle, cruising Waikiki with Lassen's team manager in the boss's Porsche 911. This idyll ended when Lassen's corporation reorganized and disbanded the team.

By the end of 1994, Conan had qualified for the World Championship Tour. He had a board sponsor, a wetsuit sponsor, a sandals sponsor, a sunglasses sponsor—and the fees they paid him to promote their products far outpaced the prize money he won in 1995, which came to less than $30,000. Tour life was not luxurious for surfers at his level, who doubled up on hotel rooms and rental cars. Still, his income allowed him to make down payments on a house in Kona for his mother and, just down the mountain and across from the beach, a modest condo for himself.

His 1996 results were sharply better, making Conan an increasingly hot commodity. But rather than cash in on his promotional value with a clothing sponsor—the main source of most pros' income—Conan started, with several partners, his own clothing line, called Seventeen Apparel. "It's so much better than having a sponsor breathing down your neck," he says.

Conan's commitment to the company is intense. He has SEVENTEEN tattooed in large letters across his back, and "17" inside a star on one calf. He recently turned down an endorsement offer from another clothing outfit that would have paid him $450,000 over three years. "I believe in my company," he says. "And I won't always be on tour."

This odd combination of forward-looking prudence—rare, to say the least, on the pro tour—and go-for-broke recklessness (making one's body a lifelong billboard for a fledgling enterprise in a high-risk business like the rag trade) struck me as essential Conan. While his job at Seventeen is, as one of his partners put it, "to surf"—to appear in ads, to win contests with the firm's logo on his board—he is passionate about its designs as well.

"Our clothes are, like, *all basketball*," he told me, indicating the sweatpants, jersey, and sneakers he was wearing, which were, I guess, pretty basketball. He pointed to a Seventeen ad in a surf magazine, which featured a photo of him doing a spectacular snapback. "We're going for a super-clean look," he said, studying the ad. The avant-garde athlete as entrepreneur, I thought—part performer, part promoter. They had named their company Seventeen, one of his partners told me, because "that's the age when a surfer comes into his own, when the little grommet grows up, when he stops following and starts wanting his own image. Kids that age love Conan."

Although Conan rejected the idea, when I mentioned it, that selling surf-related products ultimately exacerbates, by glamorizing the sport, the problem of crowds in the water, he is not insensitive to the ambiguities of what people in his world, like people in the film business, call simply "the industry." He is very protective of the anonymity of surf spots on the Big Island, for instance, actively opposing any coverage of them in the magazines. When the publicity machine meets his ordinary surfer's preference for solitude, commercialism loses.

Indeed, he surprised me by saying that he had been training for the Pipe Masters not at Pipeline, the obvious place, but back on the Big Island: lifting weights, mountain biking, surfing. Why? "I hate the North Shore," Conan said. "Too many people, too much hype."

Conan and I paddled out at Pipeline one morning during the Pipe Masters waiting period. The surf was about two feet and exceedingly gentle. The swell was too small and too north for Pipeline—a spectacular, ultra-hollow left—to be breaking. And yet there were 20 guys in the water at the famous patch of reef that morning. When Pipeline is breaking, the crowd there is the most dangerous on the North Shore. Today it was just the most annoying.

My eye kept drifting down the beach to my no-name peak, on the other side of Off-the-Wall. It looked empty, as usual, and it seemed to be working. But Conan pointed out a photographer on the beach and said, "Taylor's guy's here, so I should stay here." He meant Taylor Steele, a well-known surf-video producer.

"But these waves are too small," I whined. "The pictures won't be any good."

"You'd be surprised," Conan said, with a little grimace. I guessed what he meant: The surf mags are full of shots of guys doing aerials against a blue sky with nothing in sight but a spray of saltwater to indicate that there was even a wave outside the frame. And the other guys in the water with us were, I noticed, indeed launching some incredible maneuvers—"slutting out," as the pros say, meaning that the cameras present were turning them into "photo sluts."

While Conan went to work for the cameras (later, when I asked Taylor Steele about his professional relationship with Conan, he said, "I need Conan, Conan needs me"), I paddled outside and went for a swim in the clear water among the fissures and rocks of the Pipeline reef. The jagged bottom, with its holes and caves and overhanging ledges, was terrifying when one pictured ten-foot waves exploding into the thin cushion of water above it. There were so many places for a falling body to slam against or get stuffed under.

A little later, Conan, having grown bored with milking knee-high waves, joined me. He also studied the bottom. "All this sand in the gullies and inside," he said. "That all has to wash away before Pipeline will go off. We need a big west swell."

I found an area of reef that looked like it might form the head of the peak—the first place where a wave starts to break—on a good-size day. I asked if it was the takeoff zone. Conan turned and studied the shore. "Yeah, it is," he said. "But I like a boil over there better. It's a little more deep." He pointed some yards west, and I realized I had seen him take off over there, from a spot frighteningly far behind the peak, in a surf video. In that piece of footage, Conan had been rewarded for his daring with a huge backdoor barrel. It was rides like that one that had earned him his reputation for surfing Pipeline with abandon.

For the Masters, Conan was hoping that Pipeline would assume its full form. Even among the top 44, having to surf big Pipe would sharply narrow the field of serious contenders. And Conan, who loves big waves, would be in that winnowed group. (The women's WCT, which normally holds contests alongside the men's tour, doesn't have an event at Pipeline. The wave, when it's happening, is considered just too hairy.)

I noticed that Conan had started shivering. I couldn't see why. The air and water were wonderfully warm. "I don't have any body fat," he explained.

We were joined by a couple of young Brazilian women on bodyboards. Like half the surfers on the North Shore, they seemed to know Conan well. Both were darkly tanned and were completely naked. Drifting and chatting with them, Conan seemed to forget about being cold. They hung on his words and laughed at his jokes. In the ocean, even without waves to ride, Conan, his shoulders rippling, lolled like an alpha-male dolphin.

With waves to ride, he was something else again. A few days later, the swell was bigger—though still not big enough for the contest's purposes—and he and I were surfing Off-the-Wall. It was fairly crowded, but the waves were worth competing for, so a pecking order was in place. Conan shot to the top of it without seeming to consider any other possibility. He paddled for position faster than anybody else, seemed to read the swells sooner, caught every wave that interested him, and then tore it apart. There were several other excellent surfers out, but Conan's turns, snapbacks, lip bashes, gouges, floaters, and re-entries were all a solid notch sharper and more startling.

While his intensity was presumably only a fraction of what it would be in serious waves or in a contest, it was formidable. The look on his face when he dug for a wave bore a distinct resemblance to fury.

And his virtuosity, his superiority to an ordinary surfer like me, was not, I realized, simply a matter of degree. There were also basic category shifts. When I consider a wave, I ask first if I can catch it and second if I can make it (that is, stay ahead of its breaking section). Conan, it seemed, wasn't asking the same questions. Catchability, for instance, is less of an issue when you can paddle as fast as he and other pros can. You can catch almost any wave you want. Conan had been trying to explain certain tactics in three-man heats to me, and they hadn't really made much sense, but now I saw that they did make sense if the normal limits of wave-catchability were simply repealed. Clever dodges of all sorts suddenly became possible.

I noticed Conan giving me blank looks more than once when I asked him, of an approaching swell, something like, "Do you think this right looks makable?" To me this was a normal question—he knew the break well, after all, and I didn't; a lot of waves were closing out hard on the inside bar. Eventually, from some mumbled replies about "open face," I gathered that he didn't really care if a wave was makable. He wasn't looking to ride waves the longest possible distance and pull out of them cleanly before they broke—the traditional definition of a successful ride—as I was. He was just looking for some "open face" to shred, maybe a lip to bash, maybe a barrel to pull into. A wave that closed out was not, in his book, necessarily to be avoided.

His gravity-defying floaters and monster re-entries were in fact designed for making the most of close-outs. Indeed, such maneuvers were essential to success in contests, when you often couldn't wait around for "makable" waves.

I rode in feeling old.

One reason most surfers don't care about contests is that they're usually held in mediocre surf, which even the best surfers cannot make interesting. Another is that surfing is simply not, at bottom, a competitive activity—there is no objective standard available to rate performance. Contests, furthermore, "promote the sport" at a time when the biggest problem in surfing is crowds in the water and the last thing most of us want is for more people to get turned on to our chosen obsession.

Then there are the locals at the spots where contests are held, who are often unhappy about having their home breaks rented out and closed off. Protests by what pro tour officials are pleased to call "recreational surfers" have been growing all along the WCT trail—in Australia, South Africa, Rëunion, California—over contest permits and public access.

On the North Shore, enforcement of a contest's exclusion zone has traditionally fallen to a crew of local heavies who used to be known as the Black Shorts and are now called Hui O He'e Nalu ("Group of Wave Sliders") or simply the Hui. Ostensibly a Hawaiian cultural self-help group, the Hui is widely feared among both visiting and resident surfers. The Hui's franchise on contest security has been eroded by local lifeguards, only some of them Hui members, who've formed something called Water Patrol Inc., complete with Jet Skis. But this lucrative little business only underscores the tension between the contest scene and the rest of the surfing world.

Rob Machado gives this dynamic an extra twist. A brilliant surfer, Machado finished 1995 ranked second in the world after losing to Kelly Slater in what many people think was the greatest Pipe Masters heat ever. (Mediocre waves were not a problem that year.) Afterward, Machado said that the most exciting thing about the contest wasn't the prize money or the glory, but simply the opportunity to ride immaculate Pipeline for 25 minutes with only one other surfer. It was a peculiar form of purism, but it resonated, I think, with the masses.

Slater for his part could probably afford to rent any break he liked. Easily the biggest name in surfing, he is said to get a million dollars a year from his sponsor, Quiksilver, and to have been offered two million to sign with Nike. Coming into this contest, he had won the Pipe Masters three of the previous four years and had already sewn up his fourth world title in five years. While anything could happen in any given heat, Slater stood firmly as the primary obstacle between hopefuls like Conan and the Pipe Masters crown.

Conan was crashing in an empty room at the Sunset Point house of another young pro named Jun Jo. "We're all professional time-consumers," Conan said. He meant pro surfers, who spend half their lives waiting around for contests to start. Conan amused himself during the Pipe Masters waiting period by playing basketball, golf, and Hang Time, the video game of choice at Jun's place. Weight lifting and other serious training were on hold—Conan didn't want to be sore if the contest suddenly started. He listened, as always, to a lot of rap—especially Tupac Shakur—and played a lot of guitar.

One day we sat on the deck of a beach house that Rob Machado had rented for the contest. The surf had come up, finally, but so had an onshore wind. Pipeline was a foaming mess—still no lefts in sight. A fitful traffic of young pros, coaches, shapers, and photographers drifted across Machado's deck. High-performance surfboards filled the small yard. (A couple of these would later get broken in moments of pique by their owners after unsuccessful Pipe Masters heats.) In the space of an hour, the entire cast of some of Taylor Steele's surf videos wandered past—including the soft-spoken, Afro-haired Machado, a rangy Hawaiian phenom named Kalani Robb, and Conan's friend Shane Dorian, whose clean-cut charm has also landed him a leading role in a forthcoming Hollywood feature film, *In God's Hands*. Steele's videos, with their punk soundtracks, have become cult objects.

"It's weird," Conan says. "These kids in Japan and Europe and wherever know every wave, every note of every song, on Taylor's videos."

Conan and his friends are, in other words, the coolest of the cool in a large patch of youthworld. Certainly, I thought, watching them come and go, the pros—with their deep tans, their amazing physiques—carried themselves like young gods.

The way they speak about surfing is a peculiar combination of sports talk and art talk. On the one hand, there are wave conditions and training regimens and heat tactics, and on the other there are hopeless efforts to describe the indescribable: what moves them in surfing, what they love. Many young pros, I found, including Conan and Dorian, grew up idolizing an unorthodox Australian goofyfoot named Mark Occhilupo, who flourished in the mid-1980s, disappeared from the surfing scene for seven years, and recently resurfaced on the pro tour, again surfing wondrously. Occy, as he is known, was ahead of his time, his acolytes say, but when pressed to elaborate they flail, sounding a bit like art majors.

"He had no weird influences," Dorian finally told me.

Conan agreed.

But what did that mean, I asked—no weird influences?

"He came from nowhere," Dorian said. "He didn't look like he had studied anybody else's style. The way he looks at a wave is just genius."

Conan agreed. Genius.

Conan and his buddies also talk a lot of regular surf talk—with some differences. I once asked Conan about peak experiences, and he mentioned surfing in East Java last year at a remote break called Grajagan. A WCT contest was being held there, but what he seemed to treasure was simply the great waves they found. He got what was probably the longest tube ride of his life, he said, and he saw the most amazing tube ride ever. I knew the ride he meant, because I had seen it on video: Kelly Slater, insanely deep for insanely long.

"I was on the shoulder, paddling out," Conan said. "And I could see Kelly back in there, just so far back in this big, sucking-out, overhead barrel. He was actually skidding around on the foam ball. I really thought he'd never come out. And then I looked back, and—" Conan thrust his arms upward in imitation of Slater's brief, ecstatic gesture as he escaped the great tube. Conan, shaking his head, gave a vivid groan, eloquent in the pre-verbal language spoken by all surfers about surfing. It was notable to me that he, busy making his living from the sport, still obviously shared the basic stoke of it.

The Pipe Masters finally got under way on the ninth day of the 12-day waiting period. You sometimes hear the Pipe Masters described by nonsurfers as the Super Bowl of surfing. The opening-day crowd for this Super Bowl numbered about 150. A few surfers—mainly friends of the contestants. A few Japanese girls, hoping to get Kelly Slater's autograph. Some confused-looking tourists. And a few clumps of idle North Shore scenesters—shaved heads and wraparound shades, ponytails and big pirate earrings, nobody stinting on tattoos.

Otherwise, it was all cameras. They lined the water's edge, practically outnumbering the spectators. The Pipe Masters is, as pro tour officials say, a "media-driven event." It lives by its TV coverage, its syndication sales. The Jet Skis of Water Patrol Inc. cruised the lineup, keeping the throngs of "recreational surfers" out of the contest site.

Unfortunately, for the start of the 1996 Pipe Masters, there was no Pipeline. There were good-size, clean waves at the place called Pipeline, but they were walled-up rights, not ultra-hollow lefts. The swell still wasn't west enough, people said. There was still too much sand on the reef. The trialists, who competed in the morning, surfed well, but many Pipe specialists got nowhere. Even Mark Occhilupo didn't make it through.

In the afternoon, as the main event commenced, though, a superb left began to fire just down the beach, at Off-the-Wall. Shawn Briley, a rotund local tube-riding wizard who had failed to survive the trials that morning, paddled out at Off-the-Wall, where he snagged barrel after barrel. I watched his performance from the judges' platform overlooking Pipeline. Nothing much was happening in the heats out front, so all eyes (and binoculars) were on Briley, with the usual chorus of screams and groans rising each time he made one of his miraculous, casual escapes. "Ten! Ten!" a judge would shout. The judges were all old surfers, clearly still not oblivious to ordinary stoke.

Only one surfer was being eliminated in the three-man, first-round heats. Still, Pipe aces were dying like flies in the chunky rights. Rob Machado and Kalani Robb, two of the contest favorites, were unceremoniously bounced. Conan's first heat wasn't scheduled until the next day.

As there was still plenty of light left when the day's competition ended, I hurried down to Sunset. The waves were bigger and much better there than they had been at Pipeline, and I ended up surfing until dark. There was a daunting array of pros in the water—I counted three former world champions—which made it difficult to get waves to oneself. So I tried to see the session as a chance to study, at close range, the moves of the masters. I even succeeded, in part.

And that's when I realized that the North Shore, the pro scene, had seduced me. My aggressive skepticism about the upper reaches of surfing—that hazy area where hot surfers turned into commercial icons and magnificent waves became some huckster's profit margin—had been undone by ten days at the circus. I was actually interested in something other than the ocean and my own surfing.

I was fascinated especially by Mark Occhilupo. He seemed unaffected by his loss at Pipeline earlier in the day. He was surfing exuberantly, anyway, with great concentration. I can't say I understood everything he was doing—his moves were so quick, so fearless, that I found them strange and hard to follow. Maybe, I thought, "no weird influences" was the best description.

Conan's opening-round heat was held in head-high, inconsistent rights. His opponents were a fellow Hawaiian named John Shimooka and a Brazilian goofyfoot, Flavio Padaratz. Both were tour veterans whom Conan had passed in the rankings over the course of the year.

All three started with a couple of low-scoring rides. Then Conan caught a bigger, longer wave and reeled off a series of wild lip bashes that scored an 8.25 and put him in the lead. He caught a second, fairly good wave, a 6.4. He needed one more decent score to be sure of advancing (heats are decided on each surfer's three best waves). Shimooka got a nice barrel for a 9, putting him in the lead and Conan in second.

Then things got interesting.

Conan and Shimooka started shadowing Padaratz. To avoid elimination, Padaratz needed a good wave. But Conan and Shimooka, working together, could prevent him, I realized, from catching one. They could do this, under the rules of the three-man heat, simply by taking off on either side of him. The way it worked was diabolical: Once Padaratz caught a wave and committed himself to riding it in one direction or the other, the Hawaiian in front of him would pull back, as if to give him the wave, but the Hawaiian in back of him would drop in. Since, in surfing, the rider in front is always wrong, Padaratz would be cited for interference—a penalty that would kill his chances of advancing.

I thought this seemed like dirty pool, and some of the Brazilians on the beach seemed to agree. But, I was informed by a contest official, it was a not-uncommon tactic. In fact, only the opening round of the Pipe Masters used three-man heats. After that, it would be man-on-man, and that, I was told, was when the serious hassling would start.

Padaratz paddled furiously up and down the beach, looking for a wave. Conan and Shimooka paddled gaily along with him. Very few waves came through. Nobody took off.

But then, with perhaps five minutes left in the heat, Conan and Shimooka seemed to relax—seemed, actually, to be absorbed in conversation—and Padaratz slipped away, getting just far enough to catch, alone, a small wave that suddenly stood up nicely. He rode it fiercely across the Backdoor sandbar and scored a 7.15, enough to move him into second place.

Now Conan needed a wave, any wave, immediately. And Padaratz was shadowing him. They charged back and forth. Padaratz's plan was brutally simple. Any wave Conan caught, he would catch, too, and surf right at him, earning Conan an interference.

There were several hundred people on the beach today, and they were starting to yell—in Conan's favor, I thought. Conan was a faster paddler, but not so much faster that he could completely elude Padaratz in the confined space of the contest site. Whether he could outrace him by a margin large enough to catch a wave by himself began to seem, in any case, like a moot question, because no waves at all were coming through now. Shimooka seemed to be watching the whole drama passively.

It was the worst, most graphic hassling the contest had seen so far. And I found it really unsettling to watch—mainly because, if any "recreational surfer" were to do for 15 seconds to another surfer what Padaratz was doing to Conan for minutes on end, a fight would break out. As crowd behavior, it was beyond outrageous. As contest behavior, however, it was apparently normal. So much, I thought, for contests as a respite from crowds.

And that was how the heat ended. No waves came, and Conan was out of the contest in the first round.

Pipeline never did break that week, but the Pipe Masters limped on. The beach crowd grew toward the end of the contest, though surfers on the whole seemed to stay away—other spots, after all, were getting better waves. Padaratz made it through his second heat but then lost to Shimooka man-on-man in the third round. Shimooka ended up tied for fifth. Shane Dorian, who was surfing brilliantly, made it to the third round, where he ran into Kelly Slater, who was quite unstoppable. Slater went on to win the contest for the fourth time. Of the 14 WCT contests held in 1996, he won seven.

Watching Slater, I kept thinking about things that Conan and Shane had said about him earlier in the week. "Other guys surf incredible," Conan said. "But all that stuff *came* from Kelly."

He didn't mean specific maneuvers necessarily, he said, but a sensibility that put them together in startling, beautiful new ways, an original understanding of where certain things might be done on a wave, and the rare, even unprecedented athletic ability to realize his ideas. He made the perhaps inevitable comparison to Michael Jordan.

Shane said, "I don't know how Kelly does it. He can't look to anybody else for inspiration. He can't look to us. We have to look to him." This, coming from one of the best surfers on earth, was heavy praise.

But it seemed to me clearly warranted, as Slater burned through the

Pipe Masters, surfing on a distinctly higher plane than anyone else. His turns were bigger, cleaner, more gasp-inducing, his floaters more prolonged and dazzling, his tube rides longer and more agile, his down-the-line speed measurably greater.

And within this overwhelming repertoire was a presence of mind, too, a wit that saw subtle opportunities for unexpected moves, moves that drew screams of surprise and even laughter from the crowd. I had seen Slater in many photographs and a few videos, and while he was obviously a great surfer, I had usually found his style rather odd and even ugly. Now I saw how his surfing adapted to conditions, how breathtakingly spontaneous it was. What had seemed odd to me was simply original. What had seemed ugly was simply new. And a contest situation brightly showcased his raw superiority.

One incident in the final serves as an example of that superiority. It was Slater against Sunny Garcia, a powerful Hawaiian who has the second-best record in pro surfing over the last five years. Garcia surfed well, but Slater surfed supernaturally, scoring a 10, a 9.5, and an 8.25 in waves that weren't particularly good.

As the heat wound down and Garcia lost all hope of catching Slater, a beautiful wave came through, with Slater in position. Garcia stunned the crowd by taking off in front of Slater, thus incurring an interference penalty and effectively conceding the heat. It was a kamikaze move, a measure of Garcia's frustration, but both surfers, recognizing that the contest was over, chose to surf the wave hard, for the hell of it.

They charged down the line, Slater on Garcia's tail. The wave threw out, both ducked, both disappeared. The crowd was screaming itself hoarse. Two surfers getting barreled together is extremely rare. Both of them making it out is far rarer. As the wave roared along, faint traces of the surfers inside could be seen through the curtain. Then somebody fell, and a board went over the falls. And then Slater emerged from the tube, standing tall. Garcia, surfing in front, hadn't made it. But Slater, riding behind, had.

It made no sense. But there it was.

After his first-round loss in the Pipe Masters, Conan went back to

Jun Jo's house, took a nap, and shaved his head. When I saw him later and asked him why, he shrugged. Because he felt like it. His scalp was white as bone. He stuck it out the window as we drove down the road. It needed sun, he said. People we passed who recognized him howled.

Conan wanted to go home to the Big Island, but he was obliged to stick around for the pro tour's year-end banquet in Honolulu. Slater would be crowned world champ again. Conan would receive the Most Improved award. If he missed the banquet, he could be fined.

So he passed his days surfing, golfing, Christmas shopping, going to the movies—*Jerry Maguire* twice, a midnight premiere of *Beavis and Butt-Head Do America*—watching a few Pipe Masters heats, and visiting with his dad in Honolulu.

His father had just been released from federal prison, after seven and a half years. The terms of his release confined him for now to Honolulu. I spoke to him on the phone, and he told me that one of the nicer moments of his incarceration occurred in 1995 while watching television. A Hawaiian surf contest unexpectedly came on. It was the men's finals of the Town and Country Pro. And there was Conan, ripping it apart and winning the contest.

"That was a really pleasant surprise," he said. But his prison years had been made bearable, he said, mainly by the fact that he is a dedicated Buddhist. And in his calm and careful way of speaking I thought I heard the wellsprings of Conan's signature sangfroid.

Toward the end of the week, Conan finally talked to me about his lousy Pipe Masters showing. "The bad part is that because Kalani [Robb] and Rob [Machado] were already out, all I had to do was get through a couple of heats, and I'd have finished the year at number seven." As it was, he would fall to number 13.

We were sitting on the beach at Pipeline, squeezed into a small patch of palm-tree shade in deference to Conan's pale melon. "What can I do?" Conan asked mildly. "I can't make the waves come." He bent forward, shut his eyes, put his fingers on his shaved head, and tried to beam telepathic orders at the ocean. We both laughed. Then he added, "All you can control is yourself."

A middle-aged photographer came padding across the beach toward us. He nodded to Conan, who nodded back. The photographer gestured toward Off-the-Wall. "The light's getting better," he said. "If you could just go out and get a couple . . ."

Conan sighed. "Sure," he said. And he grabbed a board and went surfing.

Life Isn't Fair
by Rob Story

*Some surfers frown on competitions—and even some
competitors worry that surfing for pay will diminish the joy
that made them surfers in the first place. Rob Story (born
1962) covered the 2000 Ocean Pacific Pro/Surfer Boat Trip
Challenge for* Outside.

W e the people who commonly wear long pants appreciate a
sheltered rear end. That is, we prefer to keep our assorted
rumps, cabooses, booties, and derrieres fully clothed
when outdoors or engaged in public activities. Regret-
tably, such modesty is not shared by those aboard the *Mangalui Ndulu*,
an 82-foot sloop crawling with all-but-bare-assed surfers. Like most
surfers these days, they're wearing long, loose trunks tied low on the
hips. Whenever one of them bends to wax his board or climb below-
decks, his shorts slip inexorably, indecently south. At this very
moment, 28-year-old Shane Beschen of Hawaii, ranked tenth on the
international pro circuit, is leaning over a rail to scope the water, his
exposed bottom shining white in the equatorial sun.

Beschen's bald tush is a metaphor of sorts, a jarring reminder that
surfing's not what it used to be. Once steeped in tradition and

romance, the sport has been suffering cultural amnesia of late, at least on the competitive level. Surfers have adopted the same big-mouthed, baggy-pantsed, bastardized hip-hop attitude of snow- and skateboarders. Waves are their half-pipes, the means by which they score their gnarly rides. The aesthetics of the sea, of pristine beaches and exotic locales, don't seem as big a part of the equation anymore.

Case in point: Beschen and his comrades aboard the *Mangalui*. They've come to Indonesia for most of June to compete in something called the OP Pro/Surfer Boat Trip Challenge. As surfing events go, it's the first of its kind, most significantly because it doesn't take place on a beach. Rather, competitors travel by boat from surf break to surf break, eliminating entirely the need to set foot on land, paddle out to a wave, or otherwise waste time that could be spent riding. There are no shrieking PA systems, 20-foot-tall inflatable Hawaiian Tropic bottles, or bleachers full of cheering surf rats. Fans can catch it all on the Internet, but the live audience is limited to a few fishermen and several thousand coconuts.

And unlike other surfing competitions, the field is tiny. Only ten surfers have been invited, six men and four women, chosen for their professional stature and wave-riding creativity. In addition to Beschen, there's reigning world champ Mark Occhilupo, 34, of Australia; burly Hawaiian vet Sunny Garcia, 31; American Timmy Curran, 23, ranked sixth in the world; and the Irons brothers, Andy, 21, and Bruce, 20, also from the States, whose signature aerial maneuvers are being hailed as surfing's Next Big Thing. The women's contest includes Australians Serena Brooke, 24, and Layne Beachley, 27, the world's top-ranked female surfer, and Rochelle Ballard, 29, and Megan Abubo, 22, of Hawaii. All of them will be duking it out for one of two winner-take-all purses. The top woman gets $37,500, while the winning man takes home the fattest payout in competitive surfing history: $65,000. (Despite stabs at egalitarianism, the sport remains as economically sexist as ever.) And here's the clincher: All ten surfers, along with 45 assorted photographers, event organizers, judges, and crew, live together aboard four boats. For two weeks, or however long it takes to find rideable waves and complete the competition, they will troll the Mentawai Islands, a cluster of 70 atolls, reefs, and palm-choked isles about a hundred miles west of Sumatra in the Indian Ocean. This quest for perfect surf, while fine in theory, means that the pros must bunk next to their rivals in very narrow cabins. Things could turn nasty. "It can be a feral pack on a boat trip if the recipe is right," says Australian surfing photographer Martin Tullemans. "People are at each other's throats. One doesn't like another's politics. Someone else farts too much."

The boats are all filled past capacity. The female competitors share a cramped room with a photographer, the captain, his seven-months-pregnant wife, and a delirious, shivering crewman suffering from a bad case of malaria. Over on the boys' boat, eight beach towels and 19 pairs of trunks hang on the rails, and surfboards lay scattered about. Dinghies with outboard motors rattle back and forth, ferrying surfers, judges, satellite phones, and cases of Bintang beer.

Naturally, the organizers are hoping this inaugural Boat Trip Challenge will set a new standard for competitive surfing. "The future of competition is now taking a small cadre of super-hot surfers to cutting-edge surf," says Matt George, a former pro who designed the contest format. "This isn't some half-assed all-star game."

And here, as testament, is Shane Beschen, leaning farther over the rail, revealing another inch of surfer's crack. A hundred yards out, a few of his competitors are practicing, carving elegant parabolas across the green waves. Beschen gazes at them with the casual interest of a tourist at SeaWorld. He seems unaware that he's part of a sports revolution. "I'm cruising," he says laconically. "I'm just here to have fun."

The contest armada departed from Padang, a port city on mainland Sumatra. At the harbor, the group split up according to status and boarded the four boats. The judges and organizers beelined for the *Indies Trader II*, the lead yacht and unquestionably the cushiest, with two-person cabins and a 40-inch TV. The female pros got the *Nusa Dewata*, the smallest boat, even dinkier than the media boat housing several photographers and the event's Web site manager. Serena

Brooke's bunk was right next to the WC. "I'll always know when someone's gotta go," she said ruefully.

Despite the seaworthiness of the *Mangalui*, the men were not pleased. All six were accustomed to the luxury hotel rooms typically doled out during land-based contests. By contrast, their single cabin looked like a basement rec room: four narrow bunks alongside a conversation pit with foam cushions that folded over to form another few beds for the three-man film crew covering the event. "When they saw that we'd be sleeping in a hold as tight as the *Amistad*, the pros freaked," says Matt George.

Before the boats had even left Padang Harbor, the lads had lodged a protest, informing officials on the *Indies Trader II* that they wanted to switch boats. Martin Daly, the Australian captain who oversaw the fleet, said he wouldn't consider the request until the next day, then ordered the boats to set sail. The verdict was in. George plopped his head on his shaving kit, while Timmy Curran curled up beneath his guitar case to block out the others' snores.

There was a time when top-drawer surfers reveled in squalor. In the sixties and seventies, you attained stoke by following your gypsy soul to the ends of the earth, chasing down remote waves as the seeker dudes did in *The Endless Summer*. Since moving water remains nature's ultimate ephemera, the search yielded both soaring triumphs and deep disappointments. Still, surfers always came back with stories to tell around the bonfire on Huntington Beach.

But that was when surfing thrived only on the beach, on the literal fringe of American culture. The sport went mainstream long ago. Since the early eighties, marketers have eagerly exploited surfing's coolness quotient. California icon Corky Carroll, the first surfer ever to receive endorsements, got the ball rolling by appearing in a series of popular Miller Lite ads. Ocean Pacific corduroy shorts and Hawaiian-print "jams" (the "OP" in the OP Pro/Surfer Boat Trip Challenge) may have seemed like short-term fads, but they actually laid the foundation for America's ongoing appetite for beach culture. With every pimply teenager from Des Moines to Woonsocket sporting shiny Billabong board shorts and a Quiksilver guayabera shirt, it's all too clear that surfing is no longer a cult activity. The surf-fashion industry earns a staggering $1 billion in annual revenue, the royalties getting cycled to the pros in California and Hawaii. "When you're a millionaire at 22 like [some of] these guys are," says George, "you relate more to Puffy Combs than to your waterman predecessors. The result is that judges have to kowtow to young guys with 'fuck-you' money." Guys like Sunny Garcia, who won $80,000 in a three-week period in 2000 and who holds the record in the Association of Surfing Professionals for most fines levied for flipping-off judges.

Older surf competitors call the current generation "the Walkman pros," for their habit of donning headphones, cranking Korn, and all but ignoring the foreign cultures they're exposed to on the contest circuit. "Before they can fully mature, these physically dynamic people get influenced by a surf culture that's relentlessly trying to turn them into simpletons," says George. "They're sold on ease, ease, ease."

And now, dammit, they wanted a better boat. When the flotilla regrouped at dawn, word of the *Mangalui* quasi mutiny spread fast. Two of the judges, esteemed surf veterans Mark Richards and Chris Malloy, were, in the words of event organizer Paul Taublieb, "offended at spoiled athletes exercising their desire to get pampered." Serena Brooke just shrugged. "Whatever," she said. "The men are used to getting the best of everything, so they want the best boat. Girls don't get paid as much, so we're used to roughing it." Megan Abubo, ranked seventh on the women's circuit, succinctly sums up the feelings of the majority by calling her male counterparts "fuckin' pussies."

Contest judge Mark Richards, a lanky 43-year-old four-time world champion from New South Wales, tapes a ceiling-to-floor mosquito net around his bed on the *Indies Trader II*. Despite 95-degree temperatures and dripping humidity, he spends every waking moment in a long-sleeved T-shirt and long pants tucked into his socks, striking a radically different fashion stance from the droopy board-shorts crowd. When he finds a mosquito, Richards smashes it as "revenge" for attempting to bite him.

No one else takes such precautions, though malarial mosquitoes blanket the Mentawais so thickly that contest director Bernie Baker guarantees that someday "you're gonna hear of surfers dying there." In addition to malaria, the Mentawais are plagued by a host of other diseases, including cholera, typhoid, tuberculosis, and various worm-borne infections. Very few contest folk bother to hop a dinghy to the islands, and those who do don't stay for long. "Surfing here is more about the waves than a cultural experience," says Taublieb. "Maybe it's better to leave the Mentawaians alone. They don't need to be running around in cutesy Orange County T-shirts."

The highly publicized Boat Trip Challenge, however, will only encourage more visits from the First World's leisure class. Such surf imperialism occurs wherever a developing nation butts up against prime oceanfront. It started in the sixties, when California surfers "discovered" Baja. The Australians followed suit, laying claim to surf breaks in the South Seas. Now in both Mexico and much of Indonesia, the sight of white folks with surfboards elicits a Pavlovian response in local children, who run up begging for money and candy. A recent letter to the Australian surfing magazine *Tracks* proposed invading Indonesia and making it Australia's seventh state: "We'll start a rumor amongst the Indos that an Aussie tourist dropped a 50,000 rupiah note [about $5 U.S.] somewhere on Borneo and let their rabid lust for cash do the rest," suggested the less than politically correct writer.

One night Chris Malloy is sitting on the deck of the *Indies Trader II*, gazing at a beachside cooking fire tended by islanders he can't see and will never meet. Malloy, a 29-year-old native Californian whose two brothers, Keith and Dan, are also well-known surfers, now works as a surf filmmaker. He's pensive—his idea of a good tropics read is *Crime and Punishment*—and almost nonplussed by the luxury of the yacht. "I don't know about this deal," he says, waving his hand to indicate the boat's wet bar, nicely appointed cabins, and three-member kitchen staff. "It's kind of a perversion. I just got back from a primitive boat in the Maldives where we shivered on the deck, trying to sleep in the rain. That's kind of how it should be." Malloy has just begun to relax after being rattled by a series of loud explosions that rocked the boat a few minutes earlier. He thought the generator was backfiring. It turns out it was just the DVD player blaring the final shootout scene from *L.A. Confidential*.

On the deck of the *Nusa Dewata*, Rochelle Ballard finishes her daily yoga routine and makes her way to the hatch. "'Scuse me, darling," she says to Serena Brooke, who's waxing her board alongside cherub-faced Megan Abubo. None of the three women—Abubo, Brooke, or Ballard—is favored to win. Odds are on 31-year-old Layne Beachley, winner of the World Championship Tour for two years running. Once nicknamed Gidget, she's now called Beast. Beachley, who's listening to techno music on her MiniDisc player, removes her headphones for a moment. Picking up Ballard's energy drink, a yellowish Powerade, she cries, "Who peed in your bottle?"

It's the fourth day in the Mentawais, and the competition has yet to begin. Everywhere the fleet has gone, the surf has been adequate, but not towering. Today, at long last, satellite forecasts indicate an oncoming swell. Competition will begin tomorrow, but you wouldn't guess it aboard the *Nusa Dewata*. The girls, as everyone calls the female pros, appear as antagonistic as friends at a slumber party. They tell serial bedtime stories. They share pineapple slices, nail polish, and an astonishing array of personal-care emollients. They giggle a lot.

Whither the dissonance, the roiling cauldron of tension and claustrophobia stoked by the competitive fire of mighty surf warriors?

Not on the *Mangalui*. The men are just returning from a euphoric "expression session" in the best practice waves yet. They grab icy cans of Bintang from a giant cooler and change into dry board shorts. Andy and Bruce Irons start a game of backgammon. Two others vanish behind closed doors to smoke a joint. Sunny Garcia, in search of a little decompression-time reading material, reaches over both *Time* and *Playboy* to pick up a copy of *Surfer*. The conversation takes a brief detour involving the IRS, accountants, and agents, and then quickly returns to surfing.

The men, ashamed of their petulant demand to switch boats, have since apologized and are settling into the ease of their Indian Ocean boondoggle. Only Garcia, who's 31 and ranked number one on the WCT tour, seizes the rich mind-game opportunities afforded by the close quarters of the flotilla. "Picking the bunks was interesting," says George. "Sunny basically told us where we were going to sleep, and we obeyed." When others begin praising the Boat Trip Challenge as a floating party, Garcia responds, "Bring your combat boots—we ain't here to dance." His favorite target is 23-year-old Timmy Curran, a quiet, devout Christian consistently ranked in the top ten. Garcia taunts him with singsong chants of "Tim-EEEE!" and steals food off his plate. Curran just turns the other cheek (the face kind). "At a normal contest, you surf your heat and then leave," he says somewhat morosely. "Here, you're always around."

It's a living. Shortly before sitting down to a dinner of grilled wahoo with lime and dill, the guys assemble on deck to watch the sun descend behind a palm-fringed isle, the underbellies of puffy cumulus clouds streaked with shades of crimson, lavender, and orange. Expressing the moment's reverence as only a surfer can, Andy Irons gushes, "The whole sky is mental."

After five days, competition has finally begun, and the tubes are totally slabular. The Mentawais may not receive the freakish, skyscraper-size waves of northern California or Hawaii, but, unlike shifting sand breaks, their unflinching reefs rarely fail to send up crisp sets. Surfers rave about glassy, six-foot barrels that they can ride for as long as 15 seconds.

The judges, watching from a nearby dinghy or with binoculars from the wheelhouse of the *Indies Trader II*, have thrown away the original rules drawn up by Matt George. It seems the pros didn't care for a stipulation that certain heats would be judged on a maximum of 20 rides, including flubs. Instead, they wanted every wave in their heats to be considered, and the judges relented. "For the contestants to change the rules like that is akin to football players showing up at the Super Bowl saying, 'OK, there'll be eight quarters and fumbles don't count,'" says a bemused George.

The contest takes place over ten days. The men surf in four two-hour heats; the women surf three. The boats pull close to the bobbing lineup of surfers waiting to take their turns. The show is dramatic. Everyone leans over the rails, gasping as Beachley breaks two boards on two consecutive waves. Curran notches an amazing 11-second tube ride. Bruce Irons's aerials blow the group's collective brainpan. "It's like Brucie's from another planet," raves Paul Taublieb, "and he's trying to launch off the wave and rocket home."

Despite Irons's otherwordly flights, he loses the competition by one point to Mark Occhilupo, who is in the midst of one of pro surfing's greatest comebacks after dropping from 245 to 170 pounds on a diet of smoothies. Occhilupo surfs so powerfully at this event that he repeatedly snaps his board's fins. In the women's division, Beachley is upset by Ballard, who catches barrel after thundering barrel. "Rochelle just went for it," says contest director Bernie Baker. "She didn't have a bad heat."

As it happens, the awards ceremony falls on Occhilupo's 34th birthday. Standing in front of the vanquished lounging and drinking on the deck of the *Mangalui*, he and Ballard join hands and announce that they're going to divvy up their $102,500 purse with the other eight contestants. The men hoot and drain their Bintangs. The women burst into tears and hug each other, looking, says Taublieb, "like sorority girls when a sister gets pinned."

The ensuing party keeps dinghies shuttling off to fetch booze from other boats late into the night. As Serena Brooke later explains, "The whole BTC was like a glorified pool party—hanging out in the tropics in sarongs and bare feet, people doing backflips off the boat. We all were having such a good time that we didn't want this weird competitive vibe spoiling it." So all agreed days before the finals to split the proceeds.

The old seeker dudes huddled around the bonfires would be proud.

Something Wicked This Way Comes
by Daniel Duane

This 1998 Outside *article by Daniel Duane (born 1967) offers a sense of why the best big-wave surfers risk their lives on the water.*

Unlike any other athlete, a big-wave surfer never knows when, exactly, his marquee game will come. Keeping packed bags by the door and an open plane ticket ready to go, he might wait months—even years—for that once-in-a-lifetime moment. And when it happens, he has to drop everything and move. On a Thursday late last January, Evan Slater, a surfer from Encinitas, California, heard that a howling North Pacific storm had just blown the biggest waves in ages through Hawaii's Waimea Bay and that they were due on the West Coast by morning. More big surf had already hit in the last two weeks than in most years; SurFax, a service that crunches Pacific weather data to provide clients with a daily wave forecast, had recently quipped, "We're reminded of the *Simpsons* episode, where Homer goes to Hell and he's strapped to a machine that continuously force feeds him donuts. He liked it." But this new swell was something else altogether.

Outside Hawaii, only two places in the world reliably turn waves like these into high-quality big surf—"rhino waves," as they're known—and choosing between them requires both water knowledge and good judgment. The westerly direction of the swell that Thursday coupled with a sloppy local storm seemed to rule out the first, Maverick's, a deepwater reef near Half Moon Bay in northern California, so the smart money was headed for Killers, at Baja's Todos Santos Island. Some of the best big-wave riders in the world were already waxing boards, canceling appointments, and preparing to travel through the night. Which is the way it goes: These breaks all fire during the winter, are relatively far apart, and don't even perform their normal magic (much less the rare juju on its way that day) more than a few times in a normal year. A committed rush disciple just might have to face the ocean's wildest offerings in less than peak condition: jet-lagged, sleep-deprived, and all-around disoriented.

The tom-toms usually start with someone like San Francisco's Mark Renneker, a 46-year-old big-wave-riding oncologist and surf-meteorology obsessive. Calculating wind speed and direction for the far-off storms that generate waves (the one behind this swell, for example, got started off Japan), and then factoring in wave heights gleaned from ship reports and buoy readings, Renneker might come up with the right numbers on a Friday afternoon and begin working the phones. Maybe let the guys down south know that tomorrow looks like a Maverick's day. Or perhaps, like this time, that Killers was the only sane choice: clear skies likely all day off Ensenada, and the tide dropping just in time for the estimated noon arrival of the 4,000-mile swell.

In surf parlance, the term "big wave" means a wave of at least 20 feet. The word "feet" in this usage, however, bears only a mystical and as yet unrevealed relationship to dozens of inches. Developed in Hawaii as a way of sandbagging visiting haoles, this traditional wave-measurement scale rigorously underestimates actual surf dimensions—such that "20-foot" actually means waves with faces of at least 30 feet.

The more reliable method simply measures body lengths: knee-high, head-high, double overhead, triple overhead.

But however you look at it, the surf generated by that Thursday's swell was enormous. Even as it began to build, professional surfers were flying into Hawaii for the invitation-only Quiksilver big-wave contest, held at Waimea Bay in memory of Eddie Aikau, a Native Hawaiian surfer who drowned in 1978 while sailing in a storm. The event requires at least 20-foot surf; by Tuesday night, the Hawaii wave buoys had jumped from 11 feet to 23.

By Wednesday morning, 40-foot waves were overwhelming Waimea every ten minutes, prompting comparisons to the legendary swells of surf history—most tellingly, to the Swell of '69. That was the year Greg "da Bull" Noll, a big-wave pioneer, caught what everyone was content to call the largest wave ever ridden, in spite of (or perhaps because of) the lack of photographic evidence. Regardless, the Swell of '69 was the biggest of the sport's first Golden Age, the moment when surfing's Neil Armstrong planted its first extraterrestrial flag. Big-wave riding has arguably entered a second Golden Age now, with aggressive young talent and new techniques stretching the limits of both wave size and performance—not just surviving monster waves, but riding them in high style. This swell, like that of '69, ranked as the biggest that a new generation had yet seen.

The contest organizers held the surfers at bay all morning, waiting for the waves to get *small* enough for this, the world's premier big-surf event. Aside from the sheer power of the swell, something else may have been weighing on their minds. For years, big-wave surfing had seemed curiously safe; despite its aura of lethality, nobody had died since the 1943 drowning of Dickie Cross right there at Waimea. But then, in December 1994, Mark Foo, the famous Hawaiian big-wave rider, surfed giant waves at Waimea and then caught a red-eye to face the very same swell at Maverick's the next day. Taking off on a big—though not monstrous—wave, Foo lost balance and fell. His body and shattered board were found an hour later, floating south of the break. A year later to the day, a veteran surfer named Donnie Solomon tried to push through a big wave's lip at Waimea only to get pulled back "over the falls" and drown. And finally, just last year, a fit and experienced surfer named Todd Chesser got caught shoreward of a big breaking set on Oahu. Held under repeatedly, he lost consciousness and eventually died.

In the end, the organizers called off the Quiksilver at midday Wednesday. Walls of whitewater were rolling across Hawaiian highways, uprooting palm trees, and blowing furniture into backyards, sending Oahu's Civil Defense to Code Black. Haleiwa Harbor and all North Shore beaches closed. But before the clampdown, a few surfers jumped on jet-skis and headed for distant offshore reefs. One pair, going full speed on their 700cc Wave Runner, got run over and nearly drowned in a 30-foot wall of foam. Another team that included Ken Bradshaw, the foremost big-wave rider of his generation and Foo's companion the day Foo died, made it out to a break called Outside Log Cabins. The size of the swell ruled out traditional paddle-in surfing, but Bradshaw made a kind of history that day by getting towed like a water-skier into a wave he later "conservatively" called 40 feet. By this he probably meant that it had a 70-foot face and a barrel big enough to hold a small savings and loan. The surf-world buzz repeatedly described Bradshaw's wave as "cartoon," even "beyond cartoon," and a growing consensus was calling it the largest wave ever ridden on the North Shore.

Now buoy and ship reports showed that same swell roaring across the Pacific, holding speed and size unusually well and promising what Thursday's SurFax called "a rhino stampede."

At dawn Friday morning, huge waves poured over Ensenada's mile-long harbor jetty. Fishermen—who knew well that rich gringo surfers would need boats—crowded the docks shouting, "Big boat! Big, fast boat! Come with me!"

Crawling out of a white, surfboard-loaded Suburban, we breathed urine, fish, and desert grasses riding the morning breeze. In addition to their almost comical taciturnity, there's a loose humility to young big-wave surfers, their eyes more quietly distant than aggressive. There was big, blond, easygoing Keith Malloy, a 24-year-old professional surfer and friend of the late Todd Chesser; Santa Cruz's Josh Loya, a quiet Maverick's regular who'd caught a late flight into San Diego; and blond Evan Slater himself, who was building a career as an editor at *Surfer* magazine but still chased big waves at every opportunity. Stretching like cats, they pulled muscles into readiness, didn't talk much about the fear they must have been feeling—just a little chatter about how many boards to bring, which wetsuit.

An open fiberglass outboard puttered into the dock, and the nine- to ten-foot boards went in first. Rounding the end of the huge black jetty, the boat began to skip and pound, bouncing off chop and climbing open-ocean ground swells. From the wave peaks, Todos Santos Island appeared hazy on the horizon. Running well outside the island's shoals, we motored into sight of Killers, a submerged reef that breaks giant waves into rideable shapes. There, a blue mountain rolled under several speck-figures lying on long surfboards.

"Hey, that's Taylor," Slater said quietly, referring to Taylor Knox, a successful pro from Carlsbad, California, "and Snips," meaning Mike Parsons, the unofficial mayor of Todos. Mike Stewart, the best body-boarder in the world, was out there, too.

A good-size wave rolled over the reef then, but never quite broke. "Tide's still kind of fat, huh?" Malloy said.

"Yeah," Loya responded. "Wind's offshore, though."

A jet-ski driver circled, ready to pull guys out if they got in trouble.

"I like seeing him here," Malloy muttered. Foo, Solomon, and Chesser had all died in conditions no more dangerous than those before us.

Slater peeled off his sweatshirt and pants, pulled on his wetsuit. Loya checked the knot on his ankle leash and touched up his wax job, not wanting to risk the slip of a foot.

As they got ready to go, I brought up the K2 Challenge. Late last year, K2, the ski and snowboard manufacturer, offered $50,000 to the surfer who got photographed riding the season's largest wave, wherever that might be. I was wondering where these surfers stood on the matter, how much it motivated them. After all, the Challenge forbade jet-ski tow-ins, and if ever there was a day to paddle into the biggest wave of the season, this was it.

Malloy just dropped his huge spear in the water and jumped after it—no comment. Slater tried to be polite, but was too focused on following Malloy. Only Loya had anything to say. "I'd rather move to Oregon and grow dope for a summer," he offered. "The odds are a lot better."

The topic seemed to make all of them squirm, and as they paddled off, I thought about why. For one thing, the Challenge, due to end March 15, had the potential to lure unqualified surfers out of their depth. But probably more troubling to guys like these was the way it clarified the blurry lines between the purity of the surfer's pursuit and less noble aspirations. In other words, the $50,000 potentially waiting in the trough of every big wave undermined the dearly held belief that real surfers never do it for money.

Soon after Slater, Malloy, and Loya reached the other surfers, the wind at Killers went completely slack, and the surface took on the character of royal-blue oil. Parsons caught a "smallish" 15-foot wave, but mostly the guys just floated in a small pod, waiting. Looking out to sea. Perhaps wondering what was happening at Maverick's, wondering if they'd picked the right spot.

As it turned out, about 20 surfers were paddling in circles at Maverick's at the time, trying not to get killed. Offshore wind usually improves waves, but Maverick's heaves over so brutally that wind coming up the front slows down your entry, stalling you right where you least want to be: in the lip, which can drive you to the rocky bottom 25 feet under. A westerly swell like this one also produces both a current drawing you into the impact zone and waves that, when they catch you there, blast you toward a hideous cluster of rocks. Mark Renneker later reported that either two or three consecutive waves—nobody was quite sure—spun one surfer around like a propeller and denied him air for over half a minute. A Brazilian named Deniks Fischer wiped out so badly he tore every ligament in his knee, burst an eardrum, and was left temporarily numb from the waist down. Screaming for help, he got rescued only by a boat crew throwing him a life preserver.

Conditions at Todos looked much better, though when the tide finally began to drop at noon, I felt a faint onshore breeze. Nothing spoils surf faster. It picked up even more in the next few minutes, and I could feel the tension in the water: If the swell didn't hit sometime soon, and if that wind kept building, this whole mission would end up a colossal waste of time.

Suddenly, Killers turned on. Loya lay on his board and paddled for the horizon as two outsize sine curves bent out of the benthos and bore down on the crowd. The others followed. Malloy wheeled first and caught one, absolutely free-falling for perhaps ten feet, somehow landing on his board. Loya took a high line on the next, cutting fast along the wave's summit ridge. The tide had begun to run out now, and for 30 or 40 minutes waves broke with cannonlike booms. Slater, flying in front of one, seemed a tiny doll skipping before a flash flood. Terrance McNulty, an underground big-wave hero from San Clemente, caught several genuine monsters. Now that the huge stuff had arrived, drowning became a very real possibility; someone—from the boat, we couldn't see who—got blown toward the island by successive rows of foam, then dragged himself back onto his board only to be blown off again. The jet-ski prowled the impact zone for long seconds before it could get to him. But the surfers kept at it, riding 20-foot waves to their dying shoulders and then sprint-paddling back for more. The sun kept shining, the wind held its breath, and one massive blue wall after another drained a foregoing pit and poured forward.

And then the biggest set yet appeared, and something extraordinary happened. Slater turned and paddled with one wave. The bottom kept dropping below him, blackening into a wall of shadows as Slater pulled and pulled, trying to get his board sliding down the thing's face. Just as a thick lip bounced into being, Slater hopped to his feet in one motion. Halfway down, as the floor vanished, his legs straightened and he began to free-fall, down and down as the mouth of the wave spread wide. Then he landed square and his knees compressed. Laying his board over on a rail, Slater carved to the right, sending out a spray of foam as the jaw clamped shut with a shocking detonation. It was the largest wave I'd ever seen surfed.

But the moment soon passed. First, a beast broke far outside the crowd and blew everyone off their boards, putting them through a serious rinse-cycle and dragging them 50 yards deeper into the impact zone. When they'd all clawed back up to daylight, a ripple of fear came off the foam. The wind had kicked up yet another notch, cross-chopping the surface in a way that can buck you off a wave and make paddling to safety impossible. The window of optimal conditions had closed.

That's when a wave of another order of size appeared and did something quite different. Instead of breaking in the usual place and peeling to the right, it broke like an avalanching cornice and rumbled left, which meant that as our boatman yanked frantically at the engine cord, the guys in the water had some serious thinking to do. This kind of reversal—a wave normally a right becoming a left—can be terrifying, upending all the knowledge you've been counting on to keep you safe. You thought you were only flirting in danger's way, and it turns out you're lying on its train tracks.

As that backward mountain of foam rolled toward the already tired men in the water, our boat's engine engaged. We shoved up the face of an incoming berm, down its back, and then over another one. When the waves had passed, the surfers fought their way back to the surface, panting. Lying on their boards, they breathed awhile, shook it off, noticed that the wind had turned on strong again and that whitecaps already flecked the outer waters. Loya appeared beside the boat first, and then Slater and Malloy. They hauled themselves in, dripping, coughing, and flushed with pleasure, and we headed for shore.

In the end, you just have to trust that there's nothing else in the world like pushing your board off the edge of a heaving 30-foot wall of water, harnessing all that titanic impetus, and doing something beautiful and pointless with it. Far from a man-versus-nature show-down, it's an utterly wild kind of play. Timothy Leary once said that in the far future humans would attain a state of purely aesthetic existence; surfers, he felt, had already arrived.

When all their boards were piled in the boat and we had started for home, the guys sat down and actually talked for once. About what? Maybe the fact that they had just done everything Solomon, Foo, and Chesser had died trying to do, and had come away unscathed? To the contrary. In fact, the chief issue was whether they should change back into their clothes now or leave their wetsuits on for the ride back to the harbor.

Wondering if this could really be it—the total occupancy of their minds after several brushes with death—I remembered something a friend once said to me. I'd remarked at the unflappability of a partic-ular big-wave rider on a similar day. With a knowing smirk, my friend had said, "Just ask how he slept last night."

So I did.

Slater smiled his egoless smile. "You want to know the truth?" he asked. "I thought I was driving to my death this morning."

And then he turned to Malloy. "You really leaving your wetsuit on? Won't that be kind of clammy?"

Polynesian Surfing

by Ben R. Finney and James D. Houston

Archaeologist Ben R. Finney (born 1933) and writer James D. Houston (born 1933) collaborated on this piece for Natural History *magazine back in 1969. The article describes the early development of surfing.*

Riding the breaking face of an ocean wave has become an international sport enjoyed along surfable shores throughout the world. Surfers number in the hundreds of thousands and crowd the beaches from San Francisco to Biarritz, from Capetown to the North Atlantic coasts of Cornwall and Devon. Two hundred years ago this was almost exclusively a Polynesian sport, and among Polynesians the surfers of early Hawaii were clearly its masters. Today's worldwide surfing movement stems from the ancient Hawaiian sport, which in turn developed from a more rudimentary wave-riding tradition brought to Hawaii by the first Polynesian settlers of a thousand or more years ago.

All surfers, ancient and modern, have had at least one thing in common: the waves they ride. And whether or not a wave is ridable depends on the right combination of ocean swell and shoreline configuration. A gradually sloping beach, an underwater reef close to shore, and the interference of a jutting headland usually produce the best waves—those that rise steeply, but break with a regular curl and leave an open shoulder in front of the moving break so a surfer can ride free of white water.

Three main ways have been developed to ride such a wave: by swimming to catch it, then body-surfing down the slope; by paddling a canoe so that it slides in front of the breaking wave; and by using a surfboard. Surfboarding is the most popular, spectacular, and exhilarating, and is the form we're most concerned with here. Kneeling or lying prone, the surfer uses his hands to paddle into position. Just before it breaks, he paddles with the moving wave until he has enough speed and the wave's slope is critical enough for him to slide free. The surfer then stands and maneuvers his board with body weight and footwork, holding to the wave's breaking edge or darting in and out of its foamy shoulder as he rides toward shore.

The first step in the development of this form of surfing was probably the discovery that a stray plank and an ocean wave made a handy way for a swimmer to get back to shore. This in turn may have led to the simplest form of surfing—belly boarding—using a short board held against the belly or chest to ride a wave prone. This form was well known on many Pacific Islands, from New Guinea to Easter. It was also developed by water-loving people along the coast of West Africa, from Senegal to Nigeria, in the only example we have of wave riding as a popular recreation anywhere beyond Oceania before the nineteenth century.

In most of Oceania it remained a simple sport. In Micronesia and Melanesia, for example, it has been mainly a children's pastime. It was among the major islands of East Polynesia—New Zealand, Tahiti, the Marquesas, and Hawaii—that surfing became something more than a casual recreation. Among these islands longer boards were developed and adults did much of the surfing. And among the surfers of eastern Polynesia, the Hawaiians led the way. There the finest boards were built, the riding of waves was a highly respected skill, and the sport itself was a vital element in Hawaiian culture—which helps to explain why the sport survived there, though barely, while it died out in other Pacific Island groups during the nineteenth century.

Why surfing blossomed in Hawaii is open to conjecture. The islands have some of the finest surfing conditions in the world. Many surfers would say *the* finest. They are directly in the path of strong ocean swells from both the north and south Pacific, so that good waves break there year-round, fanning south from northern storm centers during winter months, rolling up from southern storms from June to October. The coastlines, moreover, are dotted with beaches, coral reefs, and headlands that focus these swells into ideally surfable waves of every shape and size. Perhaps this in itself explains why the early Hawaiians channeled so much of their energy into wave riding.

In any event, having arrived in these islands from the Marquesas about A.D. 750, they had developed a sport that was in full flower when Captain Cook first sailed up the Kona coast in 1778. Hawaiians were then using surfboards of several kinds. They rode them prone, kneeling, or standing up, and moved with ease across the slopes of waves, turning and twisting to get the best possible ride. Their skill moved Lt. James King, of Cook's expedition, to exclaim in the first published account of Hawaiian surfing, "The boldness and address with which I saw them perform these difficult and dangerous maneuvers was altogether astonishing and is scarcely to be believed."

Other early observers were equally impressed by what they called the Hawaiians' "favorite amusement," "national pastime," and "national sport." According to one missionary, their love of it was such that when the ocean offered a sudden run of good surf, "daily tasks such as farming, fishing, and tapa making were left undone while an entire community—men, women, and children—enjoyed themselves in the rising surf and rushing white water."

The finely made Hawaiian boards, a few of which survive in museums, were shaped from the trunks of local trees with stone adzes, coral scrapers, and other pre–Iron Age tools. Koa wood, from which canoe hulls also were made, and the lighter wiliwili wood, used in making canoe outriggers, were favored for surfboard construction.

The boards were divided into two main types: the *alaia* and the *olo*. *Olo* boards were long, thick, and buoyant, while *alaia* boards were shorter, much thinner, and probably could not fully support a rider until the board was planing on a wave. An average *alaia* board would have been about eight feet long, eighteen inches wide, and an inch or so thick. The nose was wide and rounded, and the side rails tapered to a squared-off tail. Although some observers reported *olo* boards twenty-four feet long, most were probably in the fourteen- to eighteen-foot range. The board surfed during the 1830's at Waikiki by the Hawaiian chief Paki, and now on display at the Bishop Museum in Honolulu, is probably a representative *olo* type. It is nearly sixteen feet long, over eighteen inches wide, six inches thick, and weighs about one hundred sixty pounds. Like the *alaia*, both decks are convex, but its thickness and length give the *olo* a long cigar shape, compared to the planklike *alaia*.

Highly maneuverable, *alaia* boards were good for catching steep, fast-breaking waves. Even though they lacked the tail fin considered essential on modern boards, the *alaia* boards could be easily turned and ridden at an angle across the wave. An eyewitness to a Hawaiian surfing a seven-foot board at Hilo in 1878 describes a typical *alaia* ride: "One instantly dashed in, in front of and at the lowest declivity of the advancing wave, and with a few strokes of the hands and feet established his position; then without further effort shot along the base of the wave eastward with incredible velocity . . . his course was along the foot of the wave, and parallel to it . . . so as soon as the bather had secured his position he gave a spring and stood on his knees upon the board, and just as he was passing us . . . he gave another spring and stood upon his feet, now folding his arms on his breast, and now swinging them about in wild ecstasy in his exhilarating ride."

Olo boards were designed for massive but slower-breaking surf and for getting long rides. Their length, narrowness, and buoyancy enabled a rider to paddle fast and catch a wave well before it became critical enough to break, and to ride it all the way to shore even though it may have crested and lost most of its force. *Olo* boards were thus ideal for the long-breaking surf at Waikiki Beach. But their bulk made quick turns and maneuvers difficult, so they were not suited to rocky beaches and fast-breaking waves. Since most of the Hawaiian surfing areas were of this latter type, it is not surprising that *alaia* surfing dominates early accounts of the sport, and that most of the ancient boards remaining—ten of thirteen in the Bishop Museum collection—are of the *alaia* type.

This distinction between *olo* and *alaia* also figures in Hawaiian social structure. Commoners (*maka' ainana*) and chiefs (*ali'i*) were rigidly divided, and it appears that the *olo* boards were exclusively reserved for the chiefly class. In addition, there is evidence that chiefs could reserve waves for their own pleasure and taboo a surfing beach to commoners. *Alaia* boards, on the other hand, were used by chiefs and commoners.

Chiefly privileges in surfing were accompanied by expertise, for chiefs were known for their surfing prowess. King Kamehameha, the high chief who conquered all of Hawaii and founded a dynasty in the early years of European contact, was particularly famed for his ability as a surfer. Instruction in surfing was part of a young chief's upbringing, and the strength and stamina derived from this and other aristocratic sports, such as canoe racing and spear handling, was undoubtedly one of the objects of the training. In addition to their own type of board, their own surfing instructors and expert board makers, Hawaiian chiefs also had special chants in which their surfing exploits were celebrated. Even King Kalakaua, the last king of Hawaii, had his own surf chant, one he appropriated from the chants of an earlier high chief who had surfed Hawaii's waves long before Captain Cook arrived.

Another measure of surfing's role in the life of these islands is its frequent mention in the legends that make up Hawaii's rich heritage of oral literature. These provide one more source of information to supplement the reports by early visitors and mission-trained Hawaiian scholars who wrote about their culture. That Hawaiian women were active surfers is confirmed by the many legends mentioning female exploits in the surf. The role of surfing in courtship also stands out in these tales. The legends tell of many a chief who is first attracted to his wife through watching her perform in the surf, and frequently a young surfer shows off in front of his favorite, hoping to win her hand.

Legends reveal the importance of competition among Hawaii's surfing chiefs. Contests, in fact, were a large part of the game. And the wagering on such matches, by contestants as well as spectators, was a favorite and often fanatic pastime that could overshadow the sport itself. Hawaiians were inveterate gamblers, known to bet everything, down to the last article they possessed. Overcome by the excitement of a surfing contest, a chief might wager canoes, fishing nets and lines, tapa cloth, and sometimes his own life or personal freedom on the outcome of the match.

The seriousness of this kind of competition is illustrated by the legendary match between Umi-la-liloa, a chief of ancient Hawaii, and Paiea, a lesser chief. As a young man Umi attended a surfing match where Paiea challenged him. The wager was so small that Umi refused, so Paiea raised the bet to four double hulled canoes. Umi accepted, handily defeated Paiea, and won the canoes. But during the match Paiea's board clipped Umi's shoulder, scratching off some skin. At the time Umi did nothing about it. Later, though, when he came to power as high chief, he had Paiea sacrificed to his god.

Like just about everything else in ancient Hawaii, surfing also had its sacred aspect. The making of a board, from the felling of the tree to the initial launching, required appropriate rituals to placate or invoke certain spirits and deities. Among the roots of a felled tree, for instance, a board builder would place a red fish, with a prayer, as an offering to the gods in return for the tree he was about to shape into a surfboard.

There is even evidence that surfing had its own *heiaus*, or stone temples. Two of these were still standing in the early 1960's, the *Kuemanu* and *Keolonahihi heiaus* on the south Kona coast of the island of Hawaii. Although how these temples were associated with surfing is not entirely clear, it is notable that both structures stand opposite well-known surfing breaks and were probably fine sites for observing the surf, for resting after surfing, or even for invoking the waves. *Kuemanu heiau* consists mainly of an upper stone terrace on a larger foundation. A deep, stone-lined water pool is sunk into one side of the foundation terrace, ideal for bathing or for rinsing off salt water. The terraces themselves are so aligned that from the upper level, which is like a bleacher, spectators might easily watch surfers riding waves less than a hundred yards away.

Although it is not specifically associated with these *heiaus*, one Hawaiian surf invocation has survived in the literature. When the ocean was flat, surfers waded in carrying strands of the *pohuehue* vine (beach morning glory), and striking the water with them, they would try to call up some ridable waves by delivering this chant:

> Arise! Arise! Great surfs from Kahiki,
> Powerful curling waves, arise with the Pohuehue,
> Well up, long-raging surf.

Such was surfing's position in Hawaii when the first explorers came, but by the end of the nineteenth century, the sport had almost completely disappeared. The reasons for this are of a piece with the decline of Hawaiian culture as a whole: the general impact of Western civilization, which seduced the islanders away from traditional habits; the drastic drop in Hawaiian population—from 300,000 to 40,000 in one hundred years—due to disease and social disruption; the arrival of Christianity to replace the old religion; and the repressive dictates of missionaries who discouraged gambling, men and women swimming together, exposing one's body in public, and the general frivolity and time wasting that went along with popular pleasures like surfing.

By the 1890's observers were mourning the sport's decline. "There are those living," said one, "who remember the time when almost the entire population of a village would at certain hours resort to the seaside to indulge in, or to witness, this magnificent accomplishment. . . .

But this too has felt the touch of civilization, and today it is hard to find a surfboard outside of our museums and private collections."

Surfboards did take their place in museum collections, alongside other Hawaiian artifacts of activities now forgotten. But surfing didn't die. Of all the traditional sports and pastimes, it fared best. Most of the others quickly disappeared early in the period of foreign contact. As the twentieth century began, surfers could still be found in the Waikiki area of Oahu. But almost none of the former style and plumage remained. Gone were the chants, the contests, the wagering, and the chiefly privileges. The regal *olos* were no longer being constructed. The boards in use were crude copies, about six feet long, of the old *alaia* boards; many were hardly more than roughhewn planks. And only a handful of surfers remained to ride them.

During the nineteenth century few outsiders had learned how to handle a surfboard. Mark Twain, while visiting Hawaii in the 1860's, remarked, "None but the natives ever master the art of surfing thoroughly." A popular myth held that only a Hawaiian could ever stand and balance successfully on a moving board. The first sign of surfing's revival came when, soon after 1900, a group of Honolulu residents, including several eager schoolboys, challenged this myth. They rediscovered the waves at Waikiki, generating new interest in the ancient sport.

Among these new surfers was George Freeth, the Irish-Hawaiian who later brought surfing to America. Also prominent was Alexander Hume Ford, a mainlander so taken with the sport he became its key promoter. Ford conducted surfing classes at Waikiki, where his most famous pupil was Jack London. In 1907, during his cruise on *The Snark*, London spent several weeks in Hawaii and camped for a while in a tent on Waikiki Beach. He became one of surfing's most outspoken boosters.

Just as this revival was getting under way, it was threatened by hotels and new private residences along Waikiki Beach, which began to close off the beach front to surfers. Under Ford's leadership several enthusiasts formed a group to protect surfers and to promote the sport as a pastime and as a tourist attraction. About this time, Jack London's

impassioned article, "The Royal Sport," in a national American magazine, heightened interest in surfing, not only in Hawaii but on the
mainland as well. Aided by this and other publicity, Ford's group
acquired an acre of beach-front property in 1908 and founded the
Outrigger Canoe Club, for the purpose of "preserving surfing on
boards and in outrigger canoes." It was an unprecedented move. The
club became the world's first organization whose stated mission was
the perpetuation of wave riding. A Hawaiian surfing club, the *Hui Nalu*
(literally Surf Club) was founded soon thereafter, and rivalry between
the two helped foster the revival. By 1911 as many as a hundred surfboards could be seen at Waikiki on a weekend.

Once revived at Waikiki, surfing thrived not only in Hawaii but along
other Pacific coastlines visited by Hawaiian surfers. In 1907 George Freeth
came to southern California as part of a promotion venture sponsored by
a railroad company to introduce water sports to a public whose interest in
ocean recreation was just starting to grow. Freeth gave wave-riding
demonstrations, offered classes, and began the exchange between Hawaii
and California that has in recent years become the greatest source of
energy in the sport's rapid postwar expansion.

Five years after Freeth, Duke Kahanamoku passed through California on his way to the 1912 Olympics. At the time Duke was one of
the world's fastest swimmers and, like Freeth, a leading Waikiki surfer.
His performances at such now familiar surfing spots as Santa Monica
and Corona del Mar greatly encouraged the growing body of surfers
there. With ridable waves coming from the north and south Pacific,
numerous beaches and headlands to shape inviting surf, and a blos-
soming interest in outdoor living, California provided the ideal environment for the first successful transplant of Hawaiian surfing.

Meanwhile, down below the Equator another world of surfing was
coming to life. In the late 1800's a South Sea islander had taught some
Australians how to body-surf waves without a board. Soon after the
turn of the century tales of Hawaiian surfboarding trickled south to
Australian shores. Stimulated by this notion, several body-surfers

around Sydney tried to make their own boards, but with little success. Their crude planks were failures. Even a surfboard imported from Hawaii in 1912 proved impossible to ride. Australian surfers needed an example. They soon found one in Duke Kahanamoku, who arrived in 1915 to give swimming exhibitions. While there he built a board from local wood and gave Australians their first look at Hawaiian surfing. And from there the sport soon began to spread in Australia, much as it did in California. But with a major difference. It quickly became integrated with a lively organization later to be called The Surf Life Saving Association of Australia. And during the past fifty years, as the SLSA spread to other countries in the British Commonwealth, surfing has gone with it—to South Africa, to England, and, ironically, back to New Zealand, to revive a long-dead pastime there.

The subsequent spread of surfing around the world has generated from these three areas—Hawaii, California, and Australia—most of it during the past ten years. Improved world travel and communication, increased leisure time, and a growing worldwide interest in water sports all help to account for this growth. But perhaps the most important factor has been the development of the light, mass-produced surfboard made of plastic foam and covered with fiber glass.

Prior to the 1950's surfboards were heavy, cumbersome "planks." They were made of redwood or redwood and balsa strips, or they were "hollow boards" made with watertight compartments of plywood. Both these types derived from ancient Hawaiian boards, but differed in design features as well as in performance. The plank was descended from the crude *alaia* copies being used at Waikiki at the beginning of surfing's revival. By the 1940's, after several design changes, the plank had lost most of the fine features that distinguished the *alaia*. Measuring eleven to twelve feet in length, some two feet wide, and three to four inches thick, the plank had become a massive board, resembling the *alaia* only in its basic outline.

In an attempt to re-create the fast paddling and long-wave riding features of the ancient *olo*, hollow boards were developed during the

1930's. These boards survive today as lifesaving aids at lakes and ocean beaches. They were usually fourteen to sixteen feet long, at least four inches thick, and close to two feet wide. They differed from the planks most radically in their tail design, which tapered to a point, making them fast paddlers. Both boards were heavy, weighing from sixty to one hundred twenty pounds or more, and hard to handle. Learning to surf with one of these boards usually took months or even years, which discouraged many prospective surfers.

In the late 1940's Californians began experimenting with surf-boards made of light balsa wood covered with a protective layer of fiber glass and resin, and they added a tail fin to improve stability and turning. The result was a board about ten feet long, weighing only twenty to thirty pounds. It revolutionized surfing. It was light, buoyant, easy to learn on, and allowed surfers to perform maneuvers never imagined with the ponderous planks and hollow boards. California surfers introduced these new boards to Hawaii, Australia, and New Zealand, where they were labeled "Malibu boards," after the famous southern California surfing beach. The balsa board soon became readily available from surfboard shops that sprang up around the major surfing areas, and it greatly popularized the sport. Within a few years old-time surfers were complaining of the "log jams" at their favorite breaks. They had more to complain about when, after surfing was featured in several Hollywood films, it became a fad sport for teenagers, and beaches from Malibu to Sydney were invaded by thousands of young, rambunctious surfers and surf-followers.

In the late 1950's, as the rising demand for boards made balsa more and more scarce, builders began fashioning boards from ultralight, solidified plastic foam, called polyurethane. Easy to obtain and easy to mold, this material brought mass production to surfing. New, larger firms entered the field. National advertising and installment and mail-order buying became regular features of a business once dominated by a few garage shops where boards were handcrafted for each customer. The resultant flood of foam boards were eagerly bought by veteran and novice surfers alike.

In the early 1960's these easily exportable foam boards, and the surfing techniques developed by a new generation of surfers, spread from California and Hawaii to overseas surfing centers, and then to areas where surfing had previously been unknown. Within a few years the coast of France around Biarritz had become a major new surfing area, together with hundreds of other spots scattered along both coasts of North and South America, Europe's Atlantic and Mediterranean shores, parts of Africa's coastlines, and new island surfing meccas like Maritius and Puerto Rico. Even frigid waters have not completely limited surfing's spread to temperate latitudes. With the assistance of neoprene diving shirts and suits, surfers ride waves year-round off the coasts of Japan, Oregon and Washington, and the British Isles.

The sport has not stopped growing. New surfing areas are discovered every season. Builders continue to experiment with board shapes and surfers with riding techniques. Yet for all its expansion surfing remains inseparably linked to the islands where it first thrived. Hawaiian surfers themselves still hold an important place in their ancestral sport, and many have international standing. The Kahanamokus and Freeths of sixty years ago have their modern counterparts in such skilled instructors as Rabbit Kekai, and in overseas experts like David Nuuhiwa, who makes his home in California where he is a reigning champion.

Geographically, no one has yet found a coastline to match Hawaii's blend of balmy climate, comfortable water, exotic beauty, and year-round selection of favorable waves. Surfers everywhere look to Hawaii and save their money to travel there, arriving each year by the thousands—from places like Los Angeles, Melbourne, Lima. Some try the gentlest rollers at Waikiki, others test themselves against the raging winter storm surf on Oahu's north shore—awesome twenty-five footers that present the ultimate challenge in wave riding.

With its deep ties to the island's early culture, surfing was one of the few elements of Hawaiian life to survive into modern times. From Hawaii the sport has spread, in this century, around the globe. Today Hawaii continues to be not only the historical source but the vital center of an international surfing world.

Kaku

by Bruce Jenkins

Mark Cunningham made his name surfing without a board. Sportswriter Bruce Jenkins's (born 1948) profile of Cunningham appeared in the fall 1994 issue of The Surfer's Journal.

Gerry Lopez often said they should clear the water on a vintage day at Pipeline at least once a winter, just to give Cunningham his due. "Let him have the place to himself," said Gerry. "And everybody could watch."

With Cunningham, it's never too late. As a lifeguard and bodysurfer, he is a timeless presence at the world's most famous break. He's been saving lives and preventing catastrophes since 1976, and he has shared the lineup with everyone from Butch Van Artsdalen to Shawn Briley. Rail-thin at 6'4" and 170 pounds—then, now and forever—he is Cunningham, the one constant over the years. To the North Shore's general populace, his is Pipeline.

How do you bodysurf Pipeline? How could such an absurd notion even occur to someone? "Sure as hell beats me," Noll said recently. "I remember all of us standing there in the sixties, wondering if anybody could ride that shit with a board. Then you try it, get thrashed a few times, and from that point on you get your ears all taped back, grab your nuts and hope for the best. Look what it's come to, a guy like Cunningham out there bodysurfing at 12-foot plus. Just the idea of that is incredible to me. I have so much respect for him, the way he travels, the way he sees the waves and comes through those barrels. The guy's fuckin' magic. It's like he's from some other dimension."

North Shore pioneers recall the likes of Bill Coleman, Fran Heath, Bob Shepherd and John Kelly bodysurfing Pipeline during the days of tankers and single fins. Many have done it well, right up to the contemporary crop including Don King, Fred Asmus, Larry Russo, Alec Cooke and a number of local lifeguards. But nobody has ridden the place quite like Cunningham. He'll go down in history like Lopez on a Lightning Bolt, Sean Ross on a paipo, Mike Stewart on a sponge. A singular, dominating presence whose style will never quite be matched.

On takeoff, Cunningham's initial kick-drive is almost frightening in its power. As the savage drop unfolds, he finds the perfect line with his patented "iron cross," lifting his trail arm to the sky and gliding beautifully through the pit. In a proning position (both arms back), his speed and grace are unmatched. And while most bodysurfers perform with frantic-looking spinners, Cunningham has the uncanny ability to make functional climbs, drops and turns—a true surfer's approach—as the wave dictates. His goal is to *make* the wave, right there at Pipeline, and he pulls it off with amazing regularity.

"A few winters back, he got one of the best rides I ever saw by anyone," says longtime North Shore photographer Pete Hodgson. "He got a complete ride from the second reef all the way through, start to finish. Imagine trying to get into the wave out there, then coming through the steep inside section and flying out of the tube. He just rode that thing all the way to the sand and stepped right onto the beach. This guy is a hero to me."

Bottom line: Nobody—Lopez, Rory Russell, Derek Ho, even the relentless Stewart, an incredible bodysurfer in his own right—has spent more time in the Pipeline tube than Cunningham. He'll try to downplay that, saying he's merely been around longer than anyone else. But it's an indisputable fact, forever establishing Cunningham's place in surfing lore.

When a magazine approached Randy Rarick a couple of winters ago, asking him to list the ten best surfers at Pipeline, Rarick included Cunningham without the slightest hesitation. "It goes a lot deeper than his riding ability," Rarick says now. "This is a guy who truly becomes one with the wave, setting him so far apart from the average weekend body-slammer. And the way he carries himself . . . it reminds me of Lopez. It's just not in Mark's nature to boast or seek the limelight. For example, I don't think most of the young lions would be out at Pipeline if nobody was there to watch them. Cunningham would be delighted if nobody was there. That shows you someone dedicated to his personal pursuit."

Some of the old hands on Ke Nui Road, established watermen like Jeff Johnson and Warren Harlow, saw the essential Cunningham on countless mornings in the late '70s and early '80s, with nobody else in the water. "It was just like a casual swim for Mark, even at real size," says Johnson. "He lived in the neighborhood for years, right next to us, and he'd just charge out there alone, like there was nothing to it."

Even today, there's a mystique to Pipeline at dawn. "Morning sickness," they call it. The sunshine and trade winds don't really kick in until 10 or 11 a.m., and when the place is really firing, few have the courage or determination to break the ice. As an example, on the day Bill Delaney shot the priceless closing footage for his film *Free Ride*, Shaun Tomson and Rabbit Bartholomew studied the place for nearly two hours before hitting the water. One of the local hell men, Tony Roy, had a brief solo session before the big names took over. For all anyone knows, Cunningham had toweled off much earlier.

"I had countless sessions out there that nobody even knows about," Cunningham says. "Early morning, late evening, in the middle of a thunderstorm, when everyone else was huddled around their cocoa and color TV, I'd have big, wild-ass Pipeline with lightning goin' off, just loving it to death."

Today, from his familiar spot at Tower 26, Cunningham settles for the memories, the rescues, the beach camaraderie and the occasional miracle session, free of hostile super stars, clueless foreigners and the almost absurd proliferation of bodyboarders. He lives near Honolulu now, sharing a spectacular piece of Nuuanu Valley property with his wife, Linny, and her family. The crack-of-dawn days are over, and for Mark, it's not even an issue.

"I've found that I almost enjoy being away from it," he says. "I had a pretty bad injury last September that took me out of the picture [boarding up the house for Hurricane Iniki, he took a heavy fall that broke his left ankle]. Sometimes it's nice to leave the whole scene behind for a while."

Just when you think the man might be getting a tad creaky—he just turned 38—the old reality hits home. There's Cunningham, pulling a drowning tourist to safety in the churning trenches of Pupukea. Heading out on Water Patrol to monitor a contest in heaving, 15-foot Pipeline. Or just getting a few waves to himself along the 200-yard stretch of Ehukai Beach Park, looking exactly as always. And the North Shore seems fine and comfortable right then, an eternal paradise once more.

> "Mark Cunningham is the missing link between homo sapiens and cetaceans (aquatic mammals). If Darwin were alive today, Mark would have blown his mind and sent him back to the drawing board."
> —Rory Russell, 1993

In those few words, Russell may have captured the magic of Cunningham, and how he is perceived in Hawaii. His big-wave artistry is so startling, yet so effortless, he appears to transcend the limits of humanity. A number of observers have caught Cunningham's act, then simply dismissed it, figuring it was some type of illusion.

"It's something that God gave him," says Russell. "You ask me to recall a certain wave he got, or one memorable tube, and it's very difficult. Mark was—and still is—like a creature of the ocean out there, just in his own world, not hassling or trying to impress anybody. He just blended in. Like, I'm out at Pipe, and there's Cunningham. After a while, you hardly even took notice.

"Here's the whole thing," Russell went on. "A few years back, I was paddling out with a bunch of younger kids next to me, and here comes this 8-foot beast, a triple suck-out, one of those waves you could never ride with a board. And Mark's right there, just stroking into this massive energy. I mean, he comes skittering down the face, and man, this is a major thing. But the kids just kept paddling out, oblivious to the phenomenon that was taking place, right in front of their eyes."

All of which is fine with Cunningham. He is a complex man, not easily deciphered, but his bodysurfing boils down to the purest simplicity. He has spent the better part of his life in search of harmony, far removed from the spotlight, and as such, he has joined the likes of Lopez, Keone Downing, Terry Ahue, Brian Keaulana and Clyde Aikau among the truly respected, tuned-in watermen of Hawaii.

He certainly doesn't look or sound the part, the way Greg Noll so richly embodies the big-wave pioneer, or Darrick Doerner epitomizes the mainland surfer fully assimilated into Hawaiian culture. Cunningham has the look of high class—perhaps a ship's captain in a sparkling white uniform—and his precise, deliberate speech reflects his proper New England heritage (his parents moved the family to Oahu from Massachusetts, when Mark was two months old). The lines were clearly drawn: his father pure Irish, his mother pure Lithuanian. From this unusual blend came a true original, a singular figure on the surfing scene.

He grew up neighbors with Lopez, Rarick and Dennis Pang in Niu Valley, bodysurfing East Side spots like Makapuu and Sandy Beach at every opportunity. That was the easy part—just hitting the water and cutting loose. The rest of the scene got a bit cloudy at times.

"His life at home wasn't so good, there was a lot of unhealthiness," says Linny. "Both of his parents [now deceased] were alcoholics, and there just wasn't much support behind Mark or his two sisters. For him, being in the ocean every day was a way to stay healthy and sane, to offset the festering situation at home. And it eventually provided his livelihood."

Cunningham is rather guarded about his home life, saying, "It wasn't like I was getting any physical or even mental abuse, and I've never complained about those days. But there wasn't a lot of support. It was never, 'let's pack the picnic bags and go watch Mark compete.'"

Cunningham found another brand of resistance at Punahou, the most prestigious school in the Hawaiian islands. "He was a good student there, and in that setting, you're supposed to move on into business or some high-paying profession," says Fred Van Dyke, who taught at Punahou for many years. "Mark could have done a number of things. He was a great swimmer, for that matter. Probably had Olympic potential. But the surf was beckoning, and he heard it—just like Lopez, Jimmy Blears, Paul Gebauer, Kimo Hollinger; a number of Punahou guys.

"It's so damn frustrating, because North Shore lifeguards don't get anything close to the salary they deserve," says Van Dyke. "It's not even two-thirds of what they make in California. But with Mark, it was a matter of choosing a value. He's like a living sculpture of the person who bypasses great rewards to do what he really loves."

Cunningham was in the ninth grade at Punahou when he first bodysurfed Pipeline, and by the time he graduated in 1974, he had built a formidable reputation on the Hawaiian contest circuit. "I couldn't tell you what I've won, or where," he says. "But if the waves were any good, I'd be there, just to get that uncrowded water time. I hate to sound egotistical, but I pretty well hands-down dominated. Sandy's, Makapuu, Point Panic and finally over at Pipeline."

For a period spanning some fifteen years, Cunningham never lost a contest in the big, pumping waves that constitute real Hawaii. Not that he or anyone else can recall, anyway. "If you picked up the paper and saw he didn't win," says Asmus, "you figure he either didn't show up or the waves were so shitty it didn't matter."

In the ever-cynical world of North Shore beach life, Cunningham takes endless ribbing about his build. Roger Erickson, for instance, calls him Eel. "My partners always give me shit about wearing Speedos," he says. "I just say it's too bad you guys are too fat to wear 'em. I've been wearing the things since high school, and they're functional as hell, and that's pretty much the end of the argument."

In fact, no less an authority than Lopez feels that Cunningham's body is the essence of his art. "Mark's built like a Pipeline gun," says Lopez, laughing warmly at the notion. "Long and narrow with real thin, hard rails, capable of generating tremendous speed. And he uses his body like a surfboard, actually changing his shape to conform to whatever part of the wave he's riding. I always thought if he could take off with me on his back, I could have stood up and done something really good."

Cunningham hauls out conventional boards occasionally, "but you wouldn't really call it stand-up surfing," he says. "I call it my stand-up comedy act. I've just never been quick or agile enough to get into these Hawaiian waves early. Just last spring I was out at Backdoor at about 6–7 feet and a rising swell. Fool that I am, I picked up one of the smaller ones and kicked out, feeling pretty stoked, and here comes this huge north-west set. I was right in that zone: Do I turn tail or try to bully it out, like most people do? I went for it, just in time to put myself in the impact zone. Just got the bejesus beat out of me. There had to be a big trail of brown behind me in my wake (laughs). The next wave snaps my board, so here I am with real trunks on and a wetsuit, just getting thrashed, and I'm thinking, 'How do these guys do it? Give me my fins and my Speedos *now*.' "

Just as friends are surprised to see Cunningham on a board, they are comforted by his presence as a bodysurfer. Lopez says he can't count the times he high-fived Mark at Pipeline, as one or the other came streaking onto the shoulder. Some of the true hell men of the late '70s and early '80s—surfers like Brian Bulkley, Bruce Hansel, Bob Fram, Jim Ingham, Mark Wildman and Adam Salvio—recall him as an essential part of the scene. "Mark's the only one who would be out there after dark with me," says Salvio. "He'd go on waves I wouldn't go on. I surfed Pipeline with Jose Angel, and I surfed it with Lopez. Cunningham is in that category. It gets chaotic when they aren't around."

One of Cunningham's unforgettable moments came on the night of his bachelor party at Kawela Bay. "Fram pulled me aside and said, 'Mark, I just want to tell you we really appreciate the fact that you're out there. You're sort of a guardian angel. We know you're kind of looking over your shoulder after those nasty wipeouts, and it's a little extra layer of security for us.' That was just the greatest thing. Little things like that keep me out in the lineup, too."

Cunningham has always found it difficult putting his performance into words. But it is something all first-rate bodysurfers understand. There is no sensation quite like tackling big waves with your body, a pair of fins and your wits (Cunningham scoffs at the notion of gloves, handboards or other gimmicks). Only a poor swimmer worries about getting run over, and Cunningham has witnessed epic tube rides by Lopez, Jackie Dunn, Jeff Crawford, Johnny Boy Gomes, the whole 20-year procession of characters, from point-blank range. Caught inside? Rarely a problem. There isn't a duck-dive in captivity that can match a bodysurfer's carefree trip to the bottom.

"It's just so wonderful to be totally immersed in it," Cunningham says. "That's what's so invigorating, satisfying, soothing to me. God, just that sensation of water flying by, rushing like a fire hose against my chest. The sense of speed, which is phenomenal. Just threading the needle through those white liquid hurricanes, spinnin' down trying to get you. Swimming through the shore break, diving under the close-outs, being there face-to-face with a closed-out wave, and just submerging at the last possible second as the lip goes right over your head. Just the whole dance out there. Maybe it sounds corny, but it really is like a dance."

Every time Cunningham enters a contest, he finds a few kindred spirits, like King and Asmus, with a smooth and distinctive style. He also finds competitors in a wild, maneuver-crazed effort to attract attention. "To me, tricks are for kids," says Mark. "It's just common sense. When you start doing spinners and bellyrolls, you usually lose the wave and wipe out. Hey, the wave is too precious a commodity. I want to ride and enjoy this thing, just as long as I can."

It is somewhat remarkable that Cunningham hasn't had a really bad experience at Pipeline since high school. "And that was at Backdoor, actually. It's like a terrible childhood memory you try to put out of your mind . . . maybe I need professional help on this one (laughs). But I got stuck in one of the caverns out there, got a little panicky, and came up just in time to get impacted by the next wave. I was just rolling around the parking lot down there; I remember seeing stars and being very shook up. To see Dane Kealoha and those guys riding Backdoor with such abandon, that just blows my mind. That's the most insane wave that I know of.

"They've never carried me off the beach at Pipe, knock on wood," he says. "No board up the ass, no heavy lacerations, no Bruce Hansel, who we carried up on a stretcher a number of times. I've had my fair share of torques, abrasions and stuns, but never a trip to the hospital. Not that I don't think about it. A couple of years ago, first big swell of the season, a kneeboarder got knocked out and dragged underwater for maybe 150 yards. Basically, the kid was dead. He walked out of here because the jet ski got to him, and because he was attached to his leash. The board was just bobbing around like a cork. That kind of scares me, because I'm not attached to anything. If I ever get my bell rung out there, nobody's gonna find me. It's just gonna be a whim that somebody paddling out catches a glimpse. You get a little older, you think about those things. You get a little more cautious."

Not that Cunningham has ever represented the insane, go-for-it-at-all-costs surfing mentality. In fact, he is given credit for triggering theories of prevention among North Shore lifeguards, dating back to his first shifts in the Winter of 1975–76.

He had taken a stab at college, enrolling at UC Santa Barbara and joining the water polo team. But when he returned to Hawaii for the Christmas holidays in his sophomore year, his father was gravely ill with cancer. Mark decided to stay home and help out the family, and when his father died two months later, Cunningham saw no point in returning to California. "I wasn't cutting it scholastically, to be honest. I don't see how people can be full-fledged, semi-pro athletes at a major college and get an education at the same time. It just baffles me. Let's face it, I was an Island boy. I'd had my California experience, and damned if I didn't want to get back home to this."

Cunningham moved to the North Shore, where he would live at various locations for 15 memorable years. When he joined the Hawaiian lifeguard department, Butch Van Artsdalen was still manning the tower at Ehukai Beach Park. Terry Ahue, who would become Cunningham's long-time partner, was Butch's right-hand man. "I was almost unaware of what was happening with Butch," Cunningham says. "I do remember he'd be sucking 'em up on duty. He'd come to work carrying a carton of milk with his pastries in the morning, and I'm thinking, gosh, Butch is getting healthy again—until Terry told me there was vodka in the carton. I can only imagine the depths of depression that puts a man at that stage. But I remember feeling a lot of pressure, that I had some mighty fuckin' big trunks to fill (laughs). It's like, good God, I'm a North Shore lifeguard. There's Butch and Eddie Aikau, and I'm some 20-year-old, snot-nosed gremmie, trying to be one of them?"

Cunningham's most critical connection was with lifeguard Sean Ross, who rode huge Pipeline on a paipo board long before Daniel Kaimi and Jack Lindholm pioneered the bodyboarding era. "Sean liked to bodysurf, too," Mark says, "and he wanted a partner who was young, strong and fit. When the shit hits the fan at Pipeline, you want some backup, baby, someone you can count on. Sean tagged me to work with him in the fall of '76, and I've been here ever since."

The North Shore has always been a deadly place for tourists. It's so horribly simple: After a couple of sun baked hours, you figure, what the heck, time for a swim. Suddenly you're knocked off your feet. Then you're sucked into the shore break zone. Big set coming outside. Can't get in, can't get out. Each wave thrashes you a little more, until you're dead. Simply. It has happened countless times, particularly along those stretches without lifeguard protection.

"I worked with the old-timers," says Ahue, "and we had a macho, stud image back then. That's the image we wanted to give the public. With Butch and Eddie it was like, 'Hey, we'll go get 'em if they get in trouble.' You know, maybe teach 'em a lesson before we get on the case. Cunningham came in and said, hey, prevention is the best way. He has a way of talking to people, making them understand. He'd spot some guy trying to impress his girl or something, and he'd just *know* the guy was in big trouble if he hit the water. He'd sit down with the guy and try to explain everything that goes on out there. Some guys felt Mark was overdoing it, but they didn't know what's really happening. Thanks to Mark, we're not the stud guards we used to be. Prevention is what we stress now."

At the mention of Ahue, Cunningham just shakes his head in admiration. "This guy's one of the real unsung heroes of the North Shore—now, and for nearly 20 years. He's moved on to the jet ski program, and I miss him dearly. Terry's a great surfer and a big-time hero from all the lives he has saved, but he's such a quiet, humble guy, you don't really hear about him. We had a wonderful relationship. I dealt with the haoles, Terry took care of the locals—that's always how it was. If things got heavy, one look from Terry was more effective than anything I could have said. Just a furrow of his brow, a turned-down corner of his mouth, and you knew you didn't want to mess with Terry.

"I'm so gratified at how safe we kept Pipeline, the two of us, over the years. All the bad wipeouts that went down, all the people we prevented from going out—you can count on two hands the people that died here, and that's counting the off-duty hours. I mean, way less than a dozen fatalities for the 12–15 years we worked together."

"Yeah, I got a lot of respect for Mark," Ahue says. "Except for his diet. I mean, this guy's gotta put on some weight (laughs)."

"A great deal of publicity has been given to Hawaiian swimmers riding waves with surfboards. Without a doubt it is

great sport, but in my estimation it cannot compare with
the thrills, pleasure and exercise of bodysurfing."

—Ron Drummond
in his book, *The Art of Wave Riding*, 1931.

There is a wonderful innocence to Drummond's classic, out-of-print work. It is dedicated entirely to the art of bodysurfing a wave straight to the beach. Fins did not exist then, nor did the notion of "angling" on the shoulder. As Drummond wrote, "The object is to fall with the wave as it curls over. And there are vintage snapshots of Roaring Twenties athletes taking the plunge, striking noble poses on the way down, arms pinned to their sides.

The history of bodysurfing is a bit sketchy, to say the least. Many credit Wally O'Connor, a U. S. Olympic swimmer in 1924 and '28, for popularizing the sport in Southern California during the post–World War I era. To the amazement of beach onlookers, O'Connor would dive underwater on his way out, do a push-turn off the sand, then appear fully immersed in a wall of onrushing white water.

In a 1972 book entitled *The Art of Body Surfing*, Robert Gardner acknowledged USC football stars Morley Drury and Jeff Cravath as avid bodysurfers in the mid-20s, along with a lesser-known tackle named Marion Michael Morrison. "On a sunny August afternoon in 1926," wrote Gardner, "the lanky 19-year-old came from his home in Long Beach to surf at the Balboa Pier. He took off on a big one, made a mistake, landed on his shoulder, tore the ligaments and ruined a promising football career." Rebounding nicely, Morrison headed straight for Hollywood, where he would become John Wayne.

As legend has it, California surfer Owen Churchill went to Hawaii in 1932 and saw locals dipping palm fronds in tar, then attaching them to their feet to get more speed. Churchill came back to California, refined the theory, and unveiled rubber fins for the public in 1940. He remains a vital name in the sport of bodysurfing, where it's a simple choice for world-class fins: Churchill or Duck Feet.

"Fins were great for transportation—to get out of the trough—but the surfer still went straight off," wrote Gardner. "Then some genius discovered that by using the speed generated by fins, he could cut to the left or the right and thus increase his speed, as board surfers had been doing for years."

As it turns out, that "genius" might have arrived much earlier, and he wasn't wearing fins. California old-timers identify him as Cal Porter—the same man revealed in *The Surfer's Journal* as the first life-guard at Malibu Pier, back in June of '59.

"I used to bodysurf the old Sunset Pier, just south of Venice, in the late 1930s," says Porter, who is now pushing 70, but still a successful age-group bodysurfer on the California circuit. "I'd go through the last couple of pilings on an angle, a really nice left, and take it all the way to the beach. To this day, I prefer going left."

In his way, Porter was the Mark Cunningham of the 1930s: innova-tive, low-key, decidedly skinny, and a capable swimmer in any surf. "The biggest I can remember was October of '42, and I had fins," he recalled recently. "A huge swell came in, a solid 20 feet on the face, and destroyed the end of nearly all the piers—Sunset, Venice, Ocean Park, Santa Monica. They all came down. I ran into Perry Black that day; he was a swimmer from Venice High who became a pilot and died during the war. We saw that the waves were feathering, like big San Onofre. So we ran out to the end of the Venice Pier, jumped off during a lull, swam out there and bodysurfed a couple."

Getting this information out of Porter was not easy. "I've known this guy 40 years," marveled one of Cal's friends. "Only now do I find out he was the first bodysurfer to ride the shoulder."

Every beach has its local hero, some guy who crawls out of the woodwork during a huge swell and bodysurfs the set waves alone. These are just a few names who merit mention when the sport's his-tory is written:

George Kalama: For all we know, the first Hawaiian bodysurfers were performing centuries ago. With such beautiful waves, and no equip-ment required, it seems entirely likely. But Kalama was the first to catch the eye of visiting Californians in the late 1940s and early '50s. "We just called him the Old Man," says Noll. "He had an old, rusted-out '32 Coupe, and he'd sit in there for three or four hours at a time, waiting for the right winds, swell and tide. Then he'd hit it, and the way he'd come through waves was just amazing. He'd be right there, alongside your board, like he was locked in a draft or something. Spectacular guy."

Buffalo Keaulana: Clips from Noll's old films show the great Buffalo in vintage form at Makaha, cruising majestically with his right arm tucked in and his trail arm extended parallel to the water. He would become the best in Hawaii, no questions asked, with a smooth and easy style befitting the island's tradition. "When the haoles first came down to surf with their balsa boards, they were outnumbered by body-surfers," Buffalo recalls. "We kind of had a rule out there: If you ride a surfboard, you have to surf outside of us. Everybody had respect for each other."

According to Noll, "Buffalo was the first to do a barrel roll, like so many bodyboarders do today. You know that backwash at Makaha; somewhere along the line, Buffalo got thrown up into the air, did a little flip, and came back down. That's how the whole thing got started. He turned it into a functional move, where he'd pull off the maneuver and keep on riding."

Buffalo responded with typical Hawaiian modesty and grace. "Naw, I didn't start that," he said. "Guy named Joe Kaeo, from Nanakuli, did it way before me."

Peter Cole: Here's a man with his own way of doing things. To this day, Cole surfs big Sunset on a single-fin long-board without a leash. His swimming ability is legendary on the North Shore, and in all his years of recreational bodysurfing—get this—he's never used fins. "Just my purist's approach, I guess," he says. "Same with my brothers, Lucky and Corny. We just took the approach we didn't need fins, and in six-foot surf at places like Pipeline, Makapuu or Rocky Point, we really didn't. I know I'm stubborn. And when people say 'Do this, do that,' I get even more stubborn."

During the past winter, someone ran this story past Cunningham. "He doesn't bodysurf with fins," said Mark. "That is so Peter Cole."

Larry Lumbeck: According to Gerry Lopez, Lumbeck was the bodysurfing king of Pipeline before Cunningham arrived. Best described as a classic '60s character, Lumbeck was also a fine guitarist, fairly well known in rock circles. As the story goes, Stephen Stills was in Hawaii one winter and looked up Lumbeck for a jam session. Somebody found Lumbeck in the water at Sunset and told him the news. "Sorry," said Larry. "Surf's perfect."

Mickey Muñoz: Of the many fine California bodysurfers of the '50s, Munoz stood out with his mind-blowing series of maneuvers. A great stand-up surfer in any size, Munoz carried that passion into his bodysurfing and dominated the Laguna Beach contest scene with his innovative style. A typical first wave would find him launching an underwater takeoff, pulling off spinners and layouts, riding all the way to the beach, running up onto the sand, then heading out for his next wave. There would be more to come, but the contest was already over. The only question was who would finish second.

Mike Cunningham: Widely recognized as the standout bodysurfer in California today, and no relation to Mark. "We played water polo against each other when I was at UCLA," he says. "When the coaches yelled out, 'Cunningham!' it was like, which one?"

Now 37, Cunningham grew up in Manhattan Beach under the tutelage of Bruce Macklin, Bob Holmes and other standouts of the Gillis Beach Bodysurfing Association. But he has surpassed everyone on the West Coast with a heavy arsenal, notably the underwater takeoff. "I've been watching this guy for years," says Porter, who is not easily impressed, "and I've never seen anybody like him. Nobody even comes close. He'll start off way outside, when the wave isn't even cresting, then you'll see him just shoot out onto the face, like a dolphin. Then he'll go back under, and as the wave starts to pitch, he'll come back out again. He'll do that several times, plus all the other moves you can think of. It's incredible to watch."

Mike is the man to beat on the current California circuit: Manhattan, Carlsbad, Oceanside, Santa Cruz, Ventura. And how did he perfect that underwater takeoff? "It just came from sitting in the tower every day, all these years, watching dolphins ride waves," he says. "I've worked on it constantly, trying to perfect it. This is a totally different sensation from surfing, because you're truly harnessing the wave's energy. It's a real distinct power you feel under the wave, and it's pretty exciting."

The two Cunnighams have competed once against each other in Hawaii, finishing 1–2 (Mark winning) during a nationally-televised contest in 1980. "It was real serious Pipeline—big, with shifty winds, and I was lucky enough to get second," says Mike. "I have a great relationship with Mark. There's no jealousy trip or anything like that. I've seen him pull off those rides at Pipeline where he went all the way across. The Ehukai Express, they called it. He's a tremendous individual and a great waterman."

Fred Simpson: The Wedge is a story in itself—probably a full-fledged book. So many great ones have passed through the epic Newport spot, from pioneers Jim Scanlon, John Forbes and Don Reddington to the crazed warriors of the present, including the renown Terry Wade, Mel Thoman, Mark McDonald, and the man simply known as Cashbox.

It was Simpson, however, who showed the Wedge could be ridden, not merely challenged. Performing on terrifying faces up to 20 feet, Simpson pioneered the so-called "outrigger" stance: leaning back into the wave, using his arm, shoulder and back for ultimate speed and planing position. Thanks greatly to Simpson, Wedge riding was transformed from kamikaze-style freefalls to slashing power drives through the tube. "He's done more for the sport than anyone I've ever known," says Thoman.

With his years of Hawaiian experience, Cunningham doesn't have much use for the Wedge. "Like Sandy Beach or the Waimea shore break, it fits the old bodysurfing stereotype," he says. "Just crash and burn, and who can take the worst wipeout. It's like all those old surf movies: 'And now, here's our bodysurfing sequence.' You'd see a few one-second rides, guys flying over the falls, then cut to the guy with his head buried in the sand and his fins sticking in the air (laughs). 'Hey, that's bodysurfing.' The sport is still trying to overcome that stereotype, and for a lot of people, that's the experience they'll have. Here in Hawaii, if you're patient and pursue the right lineups, you can get nice, long rides. I have a feeling if I pulled up on a 20-foot, California-style day at the Wedge, I'd say no fucking way, thanks. That looks like a good way to maim yourself permanently. I mean, I can see why the local city government doesn't allow any contests there."

Mark McDonald: A 6'5", 225-pound Wedge rider they call "Big Daddy," McDonald is a regular visitor to Hawaii. Although he fiercely defends his home break and calls Terry Wade, "The best big-wave bodysurfer I've ever seen," he admits, "we're so spoiled at the Wedge. Jump right into the pit, and you're there—it's just cake compared to the Islands. Pipeline guys have to deal with currents, a huge playing field, competition with red-hot surfers, and if you hit the reef—that's a whole new deal. If you don't know what you're doing out there, you'll end up like me."

Two winters ago, during a break in the local Pipeline contest, McDonald swam out to join some North Shore locals in a bodysurfing exhibition. "It was a solid, 8-foot day, and I was just off the plane," he says. "I saw a set outside and hesitated just enough, not sure if I wanted to hang tight or try to swim under it. This wave hit me right in the middle of the back. Blew off my fins, just like that. Knocked the wind out of me and shoved me straight to the bottom. I was unconscious underwater, I was gone, couldn't hang on any more. If it hadn't been for Terry Ahue and Brian Keaulana, who were out with their jet skis on water patrol, I'd be a dead man."

After watching Cunningham shred Pipeline, time and time again, McDonald concludes, "He's the best all-around bodysurfer in the water. I've never seen anybody take off on big surf as gracefully and fluid as Cunningham. He's like Wayne Gretzky or Nolan Ryan out there. In his own league."

Mike Stewart: Very quietly, with his trusty bodyboards set aside, Stewart has joined the Hawaiian bodysurfing circuit. At last check, he hadn't lost a single heat in four years—including two victories over Cunningham (1991 and 1993) in the annual Pipeline Bodysurfing Classic. It seems impossible that Stewart could outdo himself, having body-boarded second-reef Pipeline, 20-foot Waimea, 15-foot Sunset and many international spots, and winning every contest in sight. But his bodysurfing ability is nothing short of astonishing.

Cunningham may still have the edge in style and tube riding, but Stewart has perfected a maneuver that has everyone else baffled: The full barrel-roll at Pipeline. "I've done it so many times on my board, it's just an extension of that," he says. "It's fun, another challenge, another way to enjoy it."

The clincher is that Stewart doesn't merely fling himself into the lip, bound for a rude demise. He disappears into the white water and invariably claws his way back out, still in the wave. "I mean, at that point, you're just dog meat, eaten up, history, start over," says Cunningham. "But this guy, five seconds later, he pops out of the water and he's heading to the beach. And it's like, where the hell has he been? What's he doing in there? I have no idea. I can't do that, and I've never seen anybody else do it. It's something he's done 10 zillion times on his bodyboard, and somehow he's transferred it into bodysurfing."

The circumstances of Stewart's '93 victory were less than dignified. He had apparently missed the contest altogether, having flown from Los Angeles to Honolulu that morning and arrived on the beach at Pipeline during the quarter final heats. But the contest organizers were waiting for Stewart, the man who would truly round out a world-class field. They sent him straight into the water, where he was quickly sent back to the beach by a very angry local, who finished the heat and then stormed off the premises in disgust.

That appeared to be the end of Stewart, but wait a minute—now the officials were offering him a chance to create his own heat. In the already-completed first round, no less. "Just find four other guys, come up with the $30 entry fee per man, and you're in," they told him. Within minutes, Stewart produced the $120 himself and headed out with four of his bodyboarding partners. Many felt the contest had become a farce, but Stewart continued on in the glorious, 6-foot conditions, all the way to the finals, where he scored a very narrow victory over Cunningham.

"I want to be the nice guy and say we got empty Pipeline on one of the best days of the year," Cunningham said later. "But the mechanics of the meet left a bad taste in my mouth. It was wrong what they did, letting Mike pull that off. In hindsight, I'm really sorry I didn't kick his ass in that final. I wish I'd been a little more pissed-off mentally."

If there was a bright spot, it set up considerable anticipation for the next Stewart-Cunningham meeting (the two are close friends). After all these years, Mark's longstanding dominance has finally been challenged.

> "Mark's got a real edgy side to him, sort of a naughty side, and that's his saving grace. Otherwise, he'd be all goody-goody, too good to be true. He'd be almost nauseating."
> —Linny Morris Cunningham

"All I know is, I busted my ass to get there," said Stewart, "and my intention wasn't to bum out anyone. I was the only guy that was smiling the whole day. A lot of other guys were crying about this, bummed out about that, and you know, I really didn't give a shit. But tell you what, I'd have been equally stoked if Cunningham won. He's still the top guy. He's acquired an intangible sense about the ocean that you can't really describe—something that goes way past rollos and spinners and other maneuvers. He's one of the few people really tuned-in at that level, and I'm honored just to be out there with him."

It is a sparkling February afternoon on the North Shore, a mostly ragged winter suddenly reminiscent of past perfection. A couple of expert bodysurfers have arrived from California, anxious to spend a little water time with Cunningham. One of them sports a gaudy yellow handboard on each hand. The other is a bit animated, shall we say, launching into takeoffs with the blind ferocity of a man fleeing a swarm of hornets.

"Ladies and gentlemen," Cunningham announces, "meet my friends: Omega Man and Captain Seizure."

Here we find a key ingredient of Cunningham's persona: a biting sense of humor from which no one escapes. As Linny describes it, "He has this power of observation where he can go right to the essence of someone, find the obvious quirk, maybe something they're trying to hide, and call 'em on it. For people he thinks are getting too inflated, he is the pin that punctures them. Like Mike Stewart. Mark's completely mean to the guy. Nobody else can talk to him like that, and Mike respects it."

Cunningham was once approached by a dinosaur bodyboarder, a mid-40s type preaching the benefits of fiberglass and a single fin. "Tell you three reasons why I don't like sponges," he began. "First, that spinner stuff is just ridiculous."

"Okay, you get dizzy," said Cunningham. "Go on."

"Well, I don't understand this 'air' stuff. That's not true surfing."

"Okay, you're afraid of heights," said Cunningham. "What else?"

His argument shot down in flames, the poor guy never got around to the third reason.

These are the essential moments for Cunningham, ones that bring his personality to life. While the lifeguard's existence might seem like a happy-go-lucky path to nirvana, it really isn't. Whether it's outright acts of heroism or some tourist asking, 'Y'all got a Band Aid?' The job is hardly a barrel of laughs. Cunningham's standard look is one of deep concern, reflecting years of stress, strain and squinting into the late-afternoon sun. Quite often, he seems thoroughly unapproachable.

"Sometimes it's like, wow, Mark, you gotta chill out," says Asmus, like Cunningham a lifeguard since 1976. "Some of us wonder if he gets a little too involved, to the point where he almost makes the beachgoer uncomfortable, and we'll be thinking, damn, Mark's gonna have a heart attack if he doesn't relax a little bit."

Nobody realizes this more than Cunningham, but few understand the depth of his relationship with the North Shore. In his youth, only the bodysurfers rode Pipeline on those jagged, windy days. They rode it with joy and abandon, savoring their secret little place among surfing's elite. It was also an era when drugs ran rampant, as commonplace as toothpaste or toilet paper. "Everybody was either growing, selling or using out here," he says. "We went from acid to weed and into the little white powder, about everything there is. There's a common feeling among most of us who are still around, that we went through that period, heavily, and now we're sort of past it, and it's okay to talk about it."

Some may find it surprising that Cunningham is a charter member of the Hui O He'e Nalu, the group formed in the mid-70s to counter arrogant visiting surfers with intimidation. He was, and is, one of the few haoles in the organization. "I was at one of the first meetings, and it took all the balls I had to say, 'I want to be a part of this, but I'm not beating anybody up.' All the guys are like, 'What the hell are you talking about? We're gonna kick some ass here.' "

"I just felt the emphasis on violence was uncalled for," he says. "I wasn't raised that way. I mean, you got the feeling every Friday night, we were gonna go tar-and-feather somebody. But as far as establishing some type of presence, I was all for that. A lot of guys got out of line back then, particularly the Australians. People have to know they'll have to answer to somebody."

Things have changed over the years. "The whole emphasis of the Hui has changed," he says, "it's mostly paddleboard races, Water Patrol, contest security, Easter egg hunts . . . and of course, the occasional butt still gets kicked." But that hardly tempers Cunningham's frustration over the bodyboarding craze at Pipeline. Years ago, he was almost guaranteed a rip-roaring bodysurfing session on his lunch break, even if it meant sitting way out on the shoulder at Pipeline. There just wasn't anyone else around. Today, the good days find Cunningham seething about crowds and an increasing tone of hostility.

"I don't think of myself as the salty dog of the sea, you know, let's throw a charity bone to the old lifeguard, but sometimes it seems that way," he says. "We used to have time to talk story, bullshit as we swam out, and just relax. Now, English is like a fourth language out there. Japanese, Portugese, Australian—kind of its own brand—that's what you're finding. And there's a nasty, uptight vibe now, even among the top guns. Before, there was a lot of sharing and communication; you knew whose number was up. Now they're yelling and getting pissed off, calling one another out, and this is among the top Hawaiian guys. The wave hasn't changed, but the atmosphere definitely has.

"I can't really hold a grudge against the bodyboarders, because they rip out there. If I was a 20-year-old bodyboarder on the North Shore in 1993, I'd think I was the luckiest guy in the world. I just wish less importance was paid to Pipeline. It's always (bitterly) 'The Morey Boggie World Championships,' you know, at 'The Banzai Pipeline,' and everybody's got to come here to get their photo incentive shots. I wish the world sponging championships were at Bumfuck Appaloosa, or wherever (laughs). Please, let's take the spotlight off Pipeline. It's withering under the heat."

It's little wonder Cunningham cherishes his new home, amid the soft air, lush vegetation and waterfalls of the Nuuanu Valley, a truly gorgeous slice of old Hawaii. Out there it's just Mark and Linny, a successful and widely traveled photographer who grew up in Kailua and attended Parsons School of Design in New York. There are few hints of Mark's body-surfing; most of his trophies are stashed away in boxes somewhere. The house interior is bright and cheery, great splashes of color on a white background, featuring handmade tiles, an eclectic glass and art collection, and the worldly tone of the couple's conversation.

"We really don't have much in common as far as interests go," says Linny, "but we are both non-conformists, and that's the glue. We both question tradition. We just don't see the point in doing things the way everyone else does them, just to be accepted. We don't have children, because mankind is just way out of whack right now. We don't eat meat, because it's not good for the body, or the planet, or certainly not for the poor animal. And we believe in complete harmony with the environment, and Mark is very special in that regard. He's a gentle soul—much gentler than I am."

Indeed, this cynical, wise-cracking surf dog takes on an entirely new personality around home. He creates tiny little art exhibits, always in keeping with some theme from their daily life. He gathers spectacular flower arrangements and delivers them regularly to friends on the North Shore. And he tends affectionately to a massive family of cats, some 20 in all: regulars, strays, curiosity seekers, nearly all of them healthy and robust. "People can take care of themselves," Mark says. "The animals need help."

Once or twice a week, in the waking hour of a weekday morning, Cunningham can be found at Haleiwa Harbor, feeding the wildcat population. "It's a pretty sad situation out there. You'll see cats with BBs and pellets in them, cats with fish hooks sticking out of their mouth. If I can get near enough to touch them, I'll take them down to the Humane Society to get them fixed and adopted. We may adopt a couple ourselves." Always prepared, Cunningham amazed one of his North Shore friends last winter, spotting a stray kitten and producing an instant, pop-top can to feed it.

Simply put, Mark tries to live his life the way he approaches his bodysurfing. He once found a passage in a magazine article that seemed to sum things up perfectly: "Holding form eventually simplifies the task," it read. "Fortunately for us spectators, and our aesthetic sensibilities, the most efficient way also turns out to be the most beautiful. The eye always delights in the simplest and the most direct physical solution. That's what makes all of sport so beautiful."

Cunningham was so taken by the passage, he clipped it out and taped it to a photograph of Lopez surfing Pipeline. "I'd like to think it holds true for the way I ride waves," he says. "Bodysurfing is absolutely in keeping with that. It's grab the fins and away you go, as opposed to rig up the sail, tie down the lines, or any kind of new technology. I love the zen and simplicity of bodysurfing."

And when the crowds make it impossible, well, it's the unapproachable Cunningham once more. Things seemed to hit rockbottom last February when a roaring, pure-west swell hit Pipeline for three solid days and Mark got only a few fleeting moments in the water. As luck would have it, he was researching his magazine piece on Rell Sunn at the time.

"I was really bitter about what was going on. I can still hear myself (whiney voice), 'Oh, I can't get any waves, it's too big, it's too crowded, my lunch break was at the wrong time, or the winds went onshore,' I mean, I think I came off as a real jerk. I'll be the first to admit it. Then I spent some time with Rell, a person who has literally been at death's door several times, and she's pulled through. I was asking people for impressions of Rell, and it was always vital, sharing, loving. Tommy Holmes said she was 'self-effacing to a fault.' Like, any time she got a compliment, she'd be like a fighter ducking a punch, trying to escape it.

"She apparently has gone through every treatment possible, and it's just the strength of her spirit, divine intervention, that she's with us. I can only imagine what it's like, trying to live with that. But I'm finding I'm a much better person, after learning so much from her. I think back on the past with gratitude, the sense that I was so lucky to have had that. And I don't think it's Greg Noll or Gerry Lopez or Jock Sutherland who's my hero or role model anymore. I think Rell just skyrocketed to the top, and I don't know how anybody's gonna knock her off."

Cunningham has never attached much importance to his place in the surfing world, but his contributions were richly rewarded last December when he won the Aikau Waterman's Award which is given annually by a committee spearheaded by George Downing and the Aikau family.

"I have a tough time seeing myself in that 'waterman' category," Cunningham said in response. "I think the term is bandied about too easily. To me, a waterman is somebody who surfs everything from 2 feet to 25 feet. Somebody who goes diving for his dinner, windsurfs outside Phantoms, knows his way around a jet ski, canoe or a boat. Hell, I just look at a boat and I get seasick (laughter). But I was so touched to receive this. I'm up there at the podium, and people like the Keaulanas, the Aikaus, Barry Kanaiaupuni, Jeff Hakman and Titus Kinimaka are giving me a standing ovation. Good lord, I nearly peed in my pants. But it blew me away. It's the honor of my life."

In a fine and essential development, neither Mark nor Linny is terribly worried about his longevity, either as a bodysurfer or lifeguard. "He gets such unanimous respect," says Linny, "and that makes it easy for me. He's doing what he should be doing in life. Sometimes I wish we made more money, or that Mark would develop other skills so he could make a seamless passage into some other life. Then again, I'm not sure what that is. Sitting behind a desk would kill him. It would kill his spirit."

Without hesitation, Cunningham seconds the notion. "What am I gonna do when I grow up? People have been asking me that question for years. Here I am, pushing 40, the happy idiot, falling from one good situation to another, and I don't really know the answer. When I get my ass kicked real good, or someone doesn't make it because I wasn't paying attention or couldn't get through the shore break, then we'll give it some heavy thought. But I'm still getting the job done now. We have Jimmy Blears and Butch Ukauka lifeguarding up at Sunset, who have to be pushin' 50, if they haven't tagged home plate already (laughs), so I'm not real worried. I'll tell you this: It could all end tomorrow night, and I'll have come out a winner. I scored."

Not long after one of our interviews alongside Tower 26, Cunningham spotted one of those magic windows at Pipe, a precious little slot in time. He hit the water quickly with a couple of lifeguards, and to their delight, the only surfers in the water were James Jones, Bill Sickler and Perry Dane.

"Kaku [barracuda]!" yelled Dane, seeing Cunningham.

"So I'm stroking down the face of this wave," cracked Sickler, making sure Mark was within earshot, "and I see this enormous Stick Fish, like six feet long. I took a little closer, and it's Cunningham."

It was a session from some other time, and all of these time-honored characters knew it. They just ripped the place apart, in mellow 4–6-foot conditions, under the bright Hawaiian sun. Everyone was in rhythm, just like the old, no-leash days when lost boards bounced crazily through the soup. "I've been waiting for this all winter," Cunningham said later. Right then, he just might have realized a basic and glorious truth: In surfing, there are no laws of retirement. The call is strictly your own. With a little luck, it may never come at all.

The Last Wave
from Da Bull: Life Over the Edge

by Greg Noll
and Andrea Gabbard

Greg Noll (born 1937), aka "Da Bull," was an early big-wave surfer on the North Shore of Hawaii. Some of his peers claim that the wave he rode at Oahu in December 1969 was the biggest wave ever surfed.

n many ways the winter of '69 was the peak of my life. I was thirty-two. I had built a successful career of surfing and making surfboards. Although I had a wife and two sons, a ladyfriend named Laura had entered my life. That winter in the Islands happened to be the one trip that Laura made with me during that period. I'm glad she was there to share it with me. As it turned out, she became my lifelong companion and the mother of two of my children.

As usual, we stayed with Henry Preece in Haleiwa. I had stayed at Henry's house nearly every year, since I first met him and Buffalo Keaulana in the fifties, when I had first started coming to the Islands. Here I was, fifteen years later, still coming to the Islands each season for the big winter swell.

Henry's little wood-frame house is about four blocks from the water, where you can hear the surf and feel it when it gets big. About two o'clock one morning, I woke up to the sound of a far-off rumble, rumble, rumble and the rattle of dishes in the kitchen. Half asleep, I thought, "Hell of a time to run the tanks through." Every once in a while, the Army would drive its tanks down from Wahiawa, through Haleiwa and out to Kaena Point. I got up to take a whiz, and suddenly realized there were no tanks. It was the rumble of huge surf, breaking from the horizon.

I started pacing, tried to sleep, paced again. By sunrise my stomach was full of butterflies: My adrenaline was pumping. I was ready to go take a look at Waimea Bay. As soon as Laura and I got there, I could see that the whole North Shore was closed out. Solid whitewater as far as you could see. You can't go out when it gets that big. For the most part, on the very rare occasion when it gets that big, it's done all over the island.

Laura and I decided to go take a look at Makaha just for the hell of it. Every once in a while, when the North Shore closes out, Makaha Point still has ridable surf. Less often, when the North Shore closes out, Makaha does this wonderful, magical thing that I had heard about over the years from older surfers like George Downing and Buzzy Trent. If God sees fit to have that north swell come in at an absolute, perfect direction, Makaha gets unbelievably monstrous swells, as big or bigger than the ones that attack the North Shore, except they're not peak breaks. These Makaha giants peel off from the Point in precise, seemingly endless walls.

In the fifteen years that I had been coming to the Islands to surf, I had never seen Makaha do its magic. Sure, I had ridden a number of big Makaha Point days when the waves were breaking twenty feet, but compared to Waimea's hang-on-to-your-balls super-drop, Makaha Point surf just didn't have it for me. I had heard the stories. Supposedly the really huge surf at Makaha only happens about once every eleven or twelve years. I had missed the day in '58 when Buzzy Trent and George Downing rode some monster surf at Makaha. I was convinced that Waimea is where it's at. The ultimate go-for-broke spot. There's not a bigger place on the face of God's earth to ride than Waimea. That's the way it is and always will be, world without end.

Was I wrong!

Still, there was nothing to do on the North Shore, so we headed to Makaha, taking the road that led around Kaena Point. We figured the worst thing that could happen is that it would become a good excuse to see my old pal Buffalo, do a little beer drinking and talk stories Hawaiian-style.

Talking stories is part of surfing. Every surfer has stories to tell. I had started surfing when I was eleven years old and had heard a lot of stories from some of the great old board shapers, guys like Dale Veizy and Bob Simmons.

Simmons was one of the first to experiment with lightweight surfboards. He was a Cal Tech engineer who was into competitive cycling before he ever heard of surfing. One day he got into a terrible accident on his bike—got hit by a car and went right through the windshield. Wrecked up his arm. As it turns out, in the hospital he was put in a room next to a guy who surfed. This guy starts telling Simmons about surfing and Simmons gets real interested. This is how Simmons told the story:

"This guy tells me you take off on these waves and you start down the side and you angle off one way or the other and these waves throw out over the top of you. Suddenly you're inside this enclosure, a green room, and the wave has broken completely over you. If you want, you can yodel or yell and the noise bounces off the side of the walls. You go on like this for a while, then you go flying out of the other end of this tube into daylight."

Simmons' first indirect exposure to surfing really captivated him. He was determined to go out and get into that green room. He believed that every wave was like this, not realizing that it's every surfer's dream to spend even a second or two in that "green room."

I felt the intensity of twenty years of surfing bigger and bigger waves pent up inside me that day. As we approached Kaena Point we noticed several places where gigantic storm surf had already washed across the road. I told Laura to walk across the bad spots while I drove the car across. I held my door open, ready to bail out if a wave hit the car.

As soon as we reached Kaena Point, I knew this day was going to be different. Terrifying waves of fifty feet or bigger were pounding the end of the island. We stopped at a couple of places to take pictures. One memorable photo from that day shows a giant wave dwarfing a couple of beach shacks in the foreground. *Surfer* magazine printed it in its March 1970 issue with the description, "Kaena Point at forty, fifty, sixty or seventy feet." That day, the waves demolished several shacks on Kaena Point and nearby areas as well as a great portion of the road.

As we got nearer to Makaha Point, I said, "Holy shit. It's happening." Makaha was doing its magic.

Usually, no matter how big the north swell is, by the time it gets around to the Makaha side of the island, it dissipates or you're looking at full-on stormy, windy, nasty weather. The horizon off Maili Beach, south of Makaha, becomes what the old-timers call Maili cloudbreak. The rate of speed of big swells creates wind and spray that rains down on the ocean. On this day, the water was nearly as smooth as glass, beautiful, and the waves were so big that they literally put the fear of God in me.

The radio began to broadcast evacuation orders for people in homes on Makaha Point. The police had just started to put up barricades on the road, but we made it through and out to the Point. And there it was, not just ridable Makaha—great, big, horrifying Makaha.

You couldn't even see the break from the normal place on the beach. You had to get back up on the hill above the beach. On a normal, smaller day, the break comes off an inside reef. On a big, twenty-foot Point day, the break comes around the Point in a long wall and forms into a huge section referred to as the Bowl. The unique thing about Makaha is that under perfect conditions, waves will hold their shape at twenty-five feet or—so the stories go—bigger. Today, that's what it looked like, bigger.

The waves were breaking on a set of reefs I didn't even know existed, just inside where the blue water began. They looked like they were breaking out twice as far as usual. I started going into a mental freeze-up at this point. A haze settled over my brain, like I was in a dream.

There was just a handful of guys out in the water. Along the shore and on the hill above the beach, people were already lining up to watch. With the break so far out, it was almost impossible to see the surfers in any detail, let alone take clear pictures.

I got my board waxed up, started looking things over, setting up a plan. I saw that the cross-current was raging, so I knew that, to survive, I would have to swim like a sonofabitch for the Point or I would end up way down the beach, past Clausmyer's house. This house marks the place that is your last hope of getting in in one piece before the shore turns to solid rock. On a big day like this, if you don't eat it in the surf, the rocks can easily get you.

I got waxed up and headed into the water. It was surprisingly easy to get out. People have asked me, "How in the hell did you even get out?" Most of the breaks that would have been normal Makaha waves were just backed-off soupy slop and not that difficult to paddle through. It was like that almost out to the Point. Beyond the Point is where the waves were actually breaking.

I paddled way over to the left of the bowl, then headed straight out for a long ways past the break before I could paddle over to where a group of guys were sitting. They all were well-known big-wave riders, including Fred Hemmings, Bobby Cloutier, Wally Froiseth, Jimmy Blears. I had surfed different places with these guys for years. You could tell that this was no normal day. Usually, we're out there laughing, joking, giving each other a hard time. When the surf gets really big, all that bullshit goes out the window. At Waimea, for instance, when the surf starts coming up, guys' attitudes would change. Peter Cole would get a little more hyper, Buzzy Trent would start talking faster, Pat Curren would get quieter. Peter likes to joke about how I'd start hyperventilating extra loud to try to psych guys out.

Today it was serious business. No laughing, no joking. Some of the guys were glassy-eyed and there was talk of calling in the helicopters. Since that morning, when many of the guys had first paddled out, the surf had been steadily building. Now, it was at a size where all but the most experienced big-wave riders call it quits.

I sat there with the guys for at least forty-five minutes, watching these big, thunderous giants coming down out of the north, from Yokohama Bay, towards us. At times they looked so perfect you'd swear you were looking at waves at Rincon or Malibu, only these waves were thirty feet high with a lip that threw out thirty yards or more. At other times the waves broke in sections of two or three hundred yards across. They were horrible, absolutely horrible. As they peeled off towards us, a giant section would dump, and we'd count, "One thousand one, one thousand two, one thousand three . . ." then, *boom!* The wave would bottom out and, even though they were a quarter to a half-mile away, the impact of the breaking waves was so tremendous that it made beads of water dance on the deck of our boards. I'd never seen that happen before. The whole situation gave me a sick feeling in the pit of my stomach.

And the surf was still coming up! A few guys caught waves off the backside of smaller sets, hit the channel and paddled in. Nobody was going for the big ones.

The bottom line was obvious to every one of us out there: if you took off on one of the big waves and missed it, and there was a bigger wave behind it, you'd get caught in the impact zone where your chances of drowning were probably about eighty percent or better. If you paddled for one of these monstrous bastards and you didn't get to the bottom, but instead got caught high by catching an edge or hesitating for even a second, you'd tumble down the face of the wave and the whitewater would just eat you alive. It would be like going off Niagara Falls without the barrel. It looked to me like my only chance was to paddle as though the devil himself was on my ass, then get to my feet and drive as hard as possible straight down the face of the wave. If I could at least get to the bottom before the lip folded over, then maybe I'd have a chance of drilling myself a hole at the bottom of the wave, and the mass of the wave would pass over me instead of pummeling me along until I just ran out of air.

I analyzed the situation a little longer and gave myself better than a fifty-percent chance of surviving one of these monsters. I just figured I had an edge, since all my surfing had been devoted to big waves. My motivation was also competitive. Deep down inside I had always wanted to catch a bigger wave than anyone else had ever ridden. Now, here was my chance. After a lifetime of working up to it, the time had finally come to either shit or get off the pot. The chances of this type of surf occurring again might be another eleven or twelve years away, and out of my grasp.

Even though I had put a lot of time into riding big waves, I knew there was no chance of actually riding one of those waves all the way through. Not the way they were folding over in such huge sections. The best I could expect would be to get down the face to the bottom of the wave, make my turn, then put it in high gear and get as far as I could before the whole thing folded over on me. Then I'd have to take my chances on the swim in. Getting in would be half the danger—if I survived the impact zone, I'd have to fight my way through that strong side current and into the beach before I reached the rocky shoreline.

By this time the crowd in the water had thinned way down. I paddled about fifty yards away from the other guys to sit and do some more thinking. That's my whole deal. I can wait. Like Peter Cole and Pat Curren, I've always been willing to wait for the bigger sets. I always preferred to wait it out, catch fewer waves but, I hoped, bigger ones.

Everyone else had paddled in. It felt very lonely out there, but I was working on an adrenaline high. A lot of conflicts were racing around in my head. My chance of a lifetime—am I going to blow it or do something about it? I've got a family, kids and people I care about a great deal—is this goddamn wave really worth risking my life? I felt kind of crazy even considering it.

What it came down to was that I realized that I'd come all this way, all these years, for this moment. This "Makaha magic" was only going to happen once in my lifetime and that time was *now*. The next time it happened I'd either be hobbling around on a cane or dead of old age. In either case, I'd forever miss my one chance to catch a wave this large.

I've always had one kind of approach to surfing big waves. That is "Don't hesitate. Once you decide to go, go. Don't screw around." You get into more trouble trying to change your mind midstream—or midwave—than you do if you just make a commitment and go for it.

I spent about half an hour going through this mental battle before I came to my decision: "I want to do this. It's worth it to me." Above all, if I let this moment slip by, I knew I would never forgive myself. As cornball as it sounds, this probably was as close to the moment of truth that I would ever get.

I paddled back to my lineup. I was oblivious to the fact that I was now the only guy left out there. All my thoughts were focused on catching *the wave*. The wave that might be my biggest and my last. Finally a set came thundering down that I thought looked pretty god-damn good. "OK," I said to myself, "let's give this thing a shot."

Every board I built for big waves was designed to catch waves. That meant that each board had to include three main things: length, flotation and ample scoop in the nose. The scoop enabled me to point the nose down the face of a wave and paddle hard without worrying about the nose catching a little water and causing me to hesitate. You can lose a good wave by having to pull back at the instant of takeoff, just to prevent the nose from going underwater. I wanted enough scoop in front so that when I laid that sonofabitch down and started grinding, I'd never have to hesitate.

Boards can do funny things at high speeds. If the board isn't shaped right, or the fin is set even slightly wrong, the board can track or catch an edge, sending you ass over teakettle. I was very familiar with my board. I had made it for big waves and used it for three seasons. For me it was the perfect big-wave board. At eleven feet, four inches long with a one-and-a-half-inch scoop in the nose, it was a big gun for big waves.

The first wave in the set looked huge. Something inside me said, "Let it go." As I paddled over the top of it, I caught a glimpse of my wave. It was even bigger. I turned and began paddling, hard. I felt a rush of adrenaline as the wave approached, lifted me and my board began to accelerate. Then I was on my feet, committed.

You could have stacked two eighteen-wheel semis on top of each other against the face of that wave and still have had room left over to ride it. I started down the front of the wave and my board began to howl like a goddamn jet. I had never heard it make that noise. I was going down the face of the wave so fast that air was getting trapped somewhere and the vibration was causing an ear-shattering *WHOOOOOOOOOOOO!*

I flew down the face, past the lip of the wave, and when I got to the bottom, which is where I wanted to be, I looked ahead and saw the sonofabitch starting to break in a section that stretched a block and a half in front of me. I started to lay back, thinking I could dig a hole and escape through the backside of the wave. The wave threw out a sheet of water over my head and engulfed me. Then for a split second the whole scene froze forever in my mind. There I was, in that liquid green room that Simmons had talked about so long ago. I had been in and out of this room many times. Only this time the room was bigger, more frightening, with the thunderous roar of the ocean bouncing off its walls. I realized I wasn't going to go flying out the other end into daylight. This time I was afraid there might be no way out.

My board flew out from under me. I hit the water going so fast that it felt like hitting concrete. I skidded on my back and looked up just as tons of whitewater exploded over me. It pounded me under. It thrashed and rolled me beneath the surface until my lungs burned and there was so much pressure that I felt my eardrums were going to burst. Just as I thought I would pass out, the whitewater finally began to dissipate and the turbulence released me. I made it to the surface, gulped for air and quickly looked outside. There was another monster, heading my way.

There have been many times at Waimea when I've lost my board while trying to catch a wave and had to dive deep to avoid getting caught by the whitewater, or soup, of the next wave. As a big wave passes overhead, it causes tremendous pressure to build in your ears and you have to pop them to clear it.

Here at Makaha I waited for each wave to get within fifty to seventy-five yards outside me, then I dove down about twenty feet and waited for it to pass. When the first wave broke overhead, I popped my ears and waited a couple of seconds before I heard the muffled sound of rumbling whitewater. The underwater turbulence of the giant wall of whitewater overhead caught me and thrashed me around. These waves were so big and there was so much soup in them that, each time I went under, the pain from the pressure in my ears was almost unbearable. In waves like these, if you can't equalize the pressure by popping your ears, you can lose an eardrum.

I figured the best I could do was try to remain oriented towards the surface and let the turbulence carry me away from the main break. By the time I had cleared the impact zone, the waves had carried me inward about three hundred yards. I started swimming hard for the Point.

I knew the current was bad and that my survival now depended on reaching the shore quickly. I reached for every ounce of strength I had left. I was still a hundred yards or so off the beach. I could see Claus-myer's. I could see the rocky beach coming up. I was never a great swimmer, but on that day I had a real incentive to make it. I swam my ass off.

Even the shorebreak was breaking big. I kept thinking, "If I don't make it to the beach before the rocks, I'll have no place to come in. Did I go through all this hell just to lose it in the rocks?"

By now I was swimming almost parallel to the beach. I could see my good friend Buffalo in his lifeguard jeep, following me on shore. The current was so strong that the beach looked like it was smoking by me. I finally hit shore about fifty feet before the rocks began. I crawled up on the sand and flopped there on my stomach, just glad to be alive. Buff was there with the jeep and a cold beer. He got out, stood over me and shoved the beer in my face.

"Good ting you wen make 'em, Brudda," he said. " 'Cause no way I was comin' in afta you. I was jus goin' wave goodbye and say 'Alooo-ha.' "

My board survived that day. I still have it hanging in my garage. The image of getting buried in Simmons' green room remains very clear in my mind. I know that any surfer who has been in that green room never forgets it. I also know that if you screw around with it long enough, you'll get to know it intimately. It might be the last room you're ever in.

I don't know how big the wave was. I will say that it was at least ten feet bigger than anything I had surfed at Waimea Bay and far more dangerous. There were people there who saw it. Everyone has an opinion of how big it was. I'd like to leave it at that.

After I had analyzed what I'd done, I asked myself, "You're not going to top that, so where do you go from here? What do you do now?"

I didn't want to be like a punch-drunk fighter, going around and reliving that big moment. At first I felt a letdown. I thought everything would be downhill from there. In time I felt sort of relieved. That feeling gradually turned into a great sense of satisfaction. Now, I could go enjoy myself, my family. For a period of two or three years I just left off. No competition, no pressure. I just enjoyed the ocean. Eventually I stopped going to the Islands. It was years before I returned.

Surfing: The Royal Sport
from The Cruise of the Snark
by Jack London

Jack London (1876–1916) in 1907 set out to circle the globe in his 45-foot yacht, the Snark. He planned a seven-year voyage. The cruise lasted only 18 months, but London did manage to try surfing in Hawaii.

That is what it is, a royal sport for the natural kings of earth. The grass grows right down to the water at Waikiki Beach, and within fifty feet of the everlasting sea. The trees also grow down to the salty edge of things, and one sits in their shade and looks seaward at a majestic surf thundering in on the beach to one's very feet. Half a mile out, where the reef is, the white-headed combers thrust suddenly skyward out of the placid turquoise-blue and come rolling in to shore. One after another they come, a mile long, with smoking crests, the white battalions of the infinite army of the sea. And one sits and listens to the perpetual roar, and watches the unending procession, and feels tiny and fragile before this tremendous force expressing itself in fury and foam and sound. Indeed, one feels microscopically small, and the thought that one may wrestle with this sea raises in one's imagination a thrill of apprehension, almost of fear. Why, they are a mile long, these bull-mouthed monsters, and they weigh a thousand tons, and they charge in to shore faster than anyone can run. What chance? No chance at all, is the verdict of the shrinking ego; and one sits, and looks, and listens, and thinks the grass and the shade are a pretty good place in which to be.

And suddenly, out there where a big smoker lifts skyward, rising like a sea-god from out of the welter of spume and churning white, on the giddy, toppling, overhanging and downfalling, precarious crest appears the dark head of a man. Swiftly he rises through the rushing white. His black shoulders, his chest, his loins, his limbs—all is abruptly projected on one's vision. Where but the moment before was only the wide desolation and invincible roar, is now a man, erect, full-statured, not struggling frantically in that wild movement, not buried and crushed and buffeted by those mighty monsters, but standing above them all, calm and superb, poised on the giddy summit, his feet buried in the churning foam, the salt smoke rising to his knees, and all the rest of him in the free air and flashing sunlight, and he is flying through the air, flying forward, flying fast as the surge on which he stands. He is a Mercury—a brown Mercury. His heels are winged, and in them is the swiftness of the sea. In truth, from out of the sea he has leaped upon the back of the sea, and he is riding the sea that roars and bellows and cannot shake him from its back. But no frantic outreaching and balancing is his. He is impassive, motionless as a statue carved suddenly by some miracle out of the sea's depth from which he rose. And straight on toward shore he flies on his winged heels and the white crest of the breaker. There is a wild burst of foam, a long tumultuous rushing sound as the breaker falls futile and spent on the beach at your feet; and there, at your feet steps calmly ashore a Kanaka, burnt golden and brown by the tropic sun. Several minutes ago he was a speck a quarter of a mile away. He has "bitted the bull-mouthed breaker" and ridden it in, and the pride in the feat shows in the carriage of his magnificent body as he glances for a moment carelessly at you who sit in the shade of the shore. He is a Kanaka—and more, he is a human being, a member of the kingly species that has mastered matter and the brutes and lorded it over creation.

And one sits and thinks of Tristram's last wrestle with the sea on that fatal morning; and one thinks further, to the fact that Kanaka has done what Tristram never did, and that he knows a joy of the sea that Tristram never knew. And still further one thinks. It is all very well, sitting here in the cool shade of the beach, but you are a human being, one of the kingly species, and what that Kanaka can do, you can do yourself. Go to. Strip off your clothes that are a nuisance in this mellow clime. Get in and wrestle with the sea; wing your heels with the skill and power that reside in you; bit the sea's breakers, master them, and ride upon their backs as a king should.

And that is how it came about that I tackled surf-riding. And now that I have tackled it, more than ever do I hold it to be a royal sport. But first let me explain the physics of it. A wave is a communicated agitation. The water that composes the body of the wave does not move. If it did, when a stone is thrown into a pond and the ripples spread away in an ever widening circle, there would appear at the center an ever increasing hole. No, the water that composes the body of a wave is stationary. Thus, you may watch a particular portion of the ocean's surface and you will see the same water rise and fall a thousand times to the agitation communicated by a thousand successive waves. Now imagine this communicated agitation moving shoreward. As the bottom shoals, the lower portion of the wave strikes land first and is stopped. But water is fluid, and the upper portion has not struck anything, wherefore it keeps on communicating its agitation, keeps on going. And when the top of the wave keeps on going, while the bottom of it lags behind, something is bound to happen. The bottom of the wave drops out from under and the top of the wave falls over, forward, and down, curling and cresting and roaring as it does so. It is the bottom of a wave striking against the top of the land that is the cause of all surfs.

But the transformation from a smooth undulation to a breaker is not abrupt except where the bottom shoals abruptly. Say the bottom shoals gradually for from a quarter of a mile to a mile, then an equal distance will be occupied by the transformation. Such a bottom is that off the beach of Waikiki, and it produces a splendid surf-riding surf. One leaps upon the back of a breaker just as it begins to break, and stays on it as it continues to break all the way in to shore.

And now to the particular physics of surf-riding. Get out on a flat board, six feet long, two feet wide, and roughly oval in shape. Lie down upon it like a child on a coaster and paddle with your hands out to deep water, where the waves begin to crest. Lie out there quietly on the board. Sea after sea breaks before, behind, and under and over you, and rushes in to shore, leaving you behind. When a wave crests, it gets steeper. Imagine yourself, on your board, on the face of that steep slope. If it stood still, you would slide down just as a child slides down a hill on his or her coaster. "But," you object, "the wave doesn't stand still." Very true, but the water composing the wave stands still, and there you have the secret. If ever you start sliding down the face of that wave, you'll keep on sliding and you'll never reach the bottom. Please don't laugh. The face of that wave may be only six feet, yet you can slide down it a quarter of a mile, or half a mile, and not reach the bottom. For, see, since a wave is only a communicated agitation or impetus, and since the water that composes a wave is changing every instant, new water is rising into the wave as fast as the wave travels. You slide down this new water, and yet remain in your old position on the wave, sliding down the still newer water that is rising and forming the wave. You slide precisely as fast as the wave travels. If it travels fifteen miles an hour, you slide fifteen miles an hour. Between you and the shore stretches a quarter of mile of water. As the wave travels, this water obligingly heaps itself into the wave, gravity does the rest, and down you go, sliding the whole length of it. If you still cherish the notion, while sliding, that the water is moving with you, thrust your arms into it and attempt to paddle; you will find that you have to be remarkably quick to get a stroke, for that water is dropping astern just as fast as you are rushing ahead.

And now for another phase of the physics of surf-riding. All rules have their exceptions. It is true that the water in a wave does not travel forward. But there is what may be called the send of the sea. The water in the overtoppling crest does move forward, as you will speedily realize if you are slapped in the face by it, or if you are caught under it and are pounded by one mighty blow down under the surface panting and gasping for half a minute. The water in the top of a wave rests upon the water in the bottom of the wave. But when the bottom of the wave strikes the land, it stops, while the top goes on. It no longer has the bottom of the wave to hold it up. Where was solid water beneath it, is now air, and for the first time it feels the grip of gravity, and down it falls, at the same time being torn asunder from the lagging bottom of the wave and flung forward. And it is because of this that riding a surfboard is something more than a mere placid sliding down a hill. In truth, one is caught up and hurled shoreward as by some Titan's hand.

I deserted the cool shade, put on a swimming suit, and got hold of a surfboard. It was too small a board. But I didn't know, and nobody told me. I joined some little Kanaka boys in shallow water, where the breakers were well spent and small—a regular kindergarten school. I watched the little Kanaka boys. When a likely-looking breaker came along, they flopped upon their stomachs on their boards, kicked like mad with their feet, and rode the breaker in to the beach. I tried to emulate them. I watched them, tried to do everything that they did, and failed utterly. The breaker swept past, and I was not on it. I tried again and again. I kicked twice as madly as they did, and failed. Half a dozen would be around. We would all leap on our boards in front of a good breaker. Away our feet would churn like the sternwheels of river steamboats, and away the little rascals would scoot while I remained in disgrace behind.

I tried for a solid hour, and not one wave could I persuade to boost me shoreward. And then arrived a friend, Alexander Hume Ford, a globe trotter by profession, bent ever on the pursuit of sensation. And he had found it at Waikiki. Heading for Australia, he had stopped off for a week to find out if there were any thrills in surf-riding, and he had become wedded to it. He had been at it every day for a month and could not yet see any symptoms of the fascination lessening on him. He spoke with authority.

"Get off that board," he said. "Chuck it away at once. Look at the way you're trying to ride it. If ever the nose of that board hits bottom, you'll be disembowelled. Here, take my board. It's a man's size."

I am always humble when confronted by knowledge. Ford knew. He showed me how properly to mount his board. Then he waited for a good breaker, gave me a shove at the right moment, and started me in. Ah, delicious moment when I felt that breaker grip and fling me. On I dashed, a hundred and fifty feet, and subsided with the breaker on the sand. From that moment I was lost. I waded back to Ford with his board. It was a large one, several inches thick, and weighed all of seventy-five pounds. He gave me advice, much of it. He had had no one to teach him, and all that he had laboriously learned in several weeks he communicated to me in half an hour. I really learned by proxy. And inside of half an hour I was able to start myself and ride in. I did it time after time, and Ford applauded and advised. For instance, he told me to get just so far forward on the board and no farther. But I must have got some farther, for as I came charging in to land, that miserable board poked its nose down to bottom, stopped abruptly, and turned a somersault, at the same time violently severing our relations. I was tossed through the air like a chip and buried ignominiously under the downfalling breaker. And I realized that if it hadn't been for Ford, I'd have been disembowelled. That particular risk is part of the sport, Ford says. Maybe he'll have it happen to him before he leaves Waikiki, and then, I feel confident, his yearning for sensation will be satisfied for a time.

When all is said and done, it is my steadfast belief that homicide is worse than suicide. Ford saved me from being a homicide. "Imagine your legs are a rudder," he said. "Hold them close together, and steer with them." A few minutes later I came charging in on a comber. As I neared the beach, there, in the water, up to her waist, dead in front of me, appeared a woman. How was I to stop that comber on whose back I was? It looked like a dead woman. The board weighed seventy-five pounds, I weighed a hundred and sixty-five. The added weight had a velocity of fifteen miles per hour. The board and I constituted a projectile. I leave it to the physicists to figure out the force of the impact upon that poor woman. And then I remembered my guardian angel, Ford. "Steer with your legs!" rang through my brain. I steered with my legs, I steered sharply, abruptly, with all my legs and with all my might. The board sheered around broadside on the crest. Many things happened simultaneously. The wave gave me a passing buffet, a light tap as the taps of waves go, but a tap sufficient to knock me off the board and smash me down through the rushing water to bottom, with which I came in violent collision and upon which I was rolled over and over. I got my head out for a breath of air and then gained my feet. There stood the woman before me. I felt like a hero. I had saved her life. And she laughed at me. It was not hysteria. She had never dreamed of her danger. Anyway, I solaced myself, it was not I but Ford that saved her, and I didn't have to feel like a hero. And besides, that leg-steering was great. In a few minutes more of practice I was able to thread my way in and out past several bathers and to remain on top my breaker instead of going under it.

"Tomorrow," Ford said, "I am going to take you out into the blue water."

I looked seaward where he pointed, and saw the great smoking combers that made the breakers I had been riding look like ripples. I don't know what I might have said had I not recollected just then that I was one of a kingly species. So all that I did say was, "All right, I'll tackle them tomorrow."

The water that rolls in on Waikiki Beach is just the same as the water that laves the shores of all the Hawaiian Islands; and in ways, especially from the swimmer's standpoint, it is wonderful water. It is cool enough to be comfortable, while it is warm enough to permit a swimmer to stay in all day without experiencing a chill. Under the sun or the stars, at high noon or at midnight, in midwinter or in midsummer, it does not matter when, it is always the same temperature—not too warm, not too cold, just right. It is wonderful water, salt as old ocean itself, pure and crystal clear. When the nature of the water is considered, it is not so remarkable after all that the Kanakas are one of the most expert of swimming races.

So it was, next morning, when Ford came along, that I plunged into the wonderful water for a swim of indeterminate length. Astride of our surfboards, or, rather, flat down upon them on our stomachs, we paddled out through the kindergarten where the little Kanaka boys were at play. Soon we were out in deep water where the big smokers came roaring in. The mere struggle with them, facing them and paddling seaward over them and through them, was sport enough in itself. You had to have your wits about you, for it was a battle in which mighty blows were struck, on one side, and in which cunning was used on the other side—a struggle between insensate force and intelligence. I soon learned a bit. When a breaker curled over my head, for a swift instant I could see the light of day through its emerald body; then down would go my head, and I would clutch the board with all my strength. Then would come the blow, and to the onlooker on shore I would be blotted out. In reality the board and I had passed through the crest and emerged in the respite of the other side. I should not recommend those smashing blows to an invalid or delicate person. There is weight behind them, and the impact of the driven water is like a sandblast. Sometimes one passes through half a dozen combers in quick succession, and it is just about that time that one is liable to discover new merits in the stable land and new reasons for being on shore.

Out there in the midst of such a succession of big smoky ones, a third man was added to our party, one Freeth. Shaking the water from my eyes as I emerged from one wave and peered ahead to see what the next one looked like, I saw him tearing in on the back of it, standing upright on his board, carelessly poised, a young god bronzed with sunburn. We went through the wave on the back of which he rode. Ford called to him. He turned an airspring from his wave, rescued his board from its maw, paddled over to us and joined Ford in showing me things. One thing I learned in particular from Freeth, namely, how to encounter the occasional breaker of exceptional size that rolled in. Such breakers were really ferocious, and it was unsafe to meet them on top of the board. But Freeth showed me, so that whenever I saw one of that caliber rolling down on me, I slid off the rear end of the board and dropped down beneath the surface, my arms over my head and holding the board. Thus, if the wave ripped the board out of my hands and tried to strike me with it (a common trick of such waves), there would be a cushion of water a foot or more in depth between my head and the blow. When the wave passed, I climbed upon the board and paddled on. Many have been terribly injured, I learn, by being struck by their boards.

The whole method of surf-riding and surf-fighting, I learned, is one of non-resistance. Dodge the blow that is struck at you. Dive through the wave that is trying to slap you in the face. Sink down, feet first, deep under the surface, and let the big smoker that is trying to smash you go by far overhead. Never be rigid. Relax. Yield yourself to the waters that are ripping and tearing at you. When the undertow catches you and drags you seaward along the bottom, don't struggle against it. If you do, you are liable to be drowned, for it is stronger than you. Yield yourself to that undertow. Swim with it, not against it, and you will find the pressure removed. And, swimming with it, fooling it so that it does not hold you, swim upward at the same time. It will be no trouble at all to reach the surface.

The person who wants to learn surf-riding must be a strong swimmer, and must be used to going under the water. After that, fair strength and common sense are all that is required. The force of the big comber is rather unexpected. There are mix-ups in which board and rider are torn apart and separated by several hundred feet. The surf-rider must take care of him or herself. No matter how many riders swim out with you, you cannot depend upon any of them for aid. The fancied security I had in the presence of Ford and Freeth made me forget that it was my first swim out in deep water among the big ones. I recollected, however, and rather suddenly, for a big wave came in, and away went the two men on its back all the way to shore. I could have been drowned a dozen different ways before they got back to me.

One slides down the face of a breaker on the surf-board, but has to get started to sliding. Board and rider must be moving shoreward at a good rate before the wave overtakes them. When you see the wave coming that you want to ride in, you turn tail to it and paddle shoreward with all your strength, using what is called the windmill stroke. This is a sort of spurt performed immediately in front of the wave. If the board is going fast enough, the wave accelerates it, and the board begins its quarter-of-a-mile slide.

I shall never forget the first big wave I caught out there in the deep water. I saw it coming, turned my back on it and paddled for dear life. Faster and faster my board went, till it seemed my arms would drop off. What was happening behind me I could not tell. One cannot look behind and paddle the windmill stroke. I heard the crest of the wave hissing and churning, and then my board was lifted and flung forward. I scarcely knew what happened the first half-minute. Though I kept my eyes open, I could not see anything, for I was buried in the rushing white of the crest. But I did not mind. I was chiefly conscious of ecstatic bliss at having caught the wave. At the end of the half-minute, however, I began to see things, and to breathe. I saw that three feet of the nose of my board was clear out of water and riding on the air. I shifted my weight forward, and made the nose come down. Then I lay, quite at rest in the midst of the wild movement, and watched the shore and the bathers on the beach grow distinct. I didn't cover quite a quarter of a mile on that wave, because, to prevent the board from diving, I shifted my weight back, but shifted it too far and fell down the rear slope of the wave.

It was my second day at surf-riding, and I was quite proud of myself. I stayed out there four hours, and when it was over, I was resolved that on the morrow I'd come in standing up. But that resolution paved a distant place. On the morrow I was in bed. I was not sick, but I was very unhappy, and I was in bed. When describing the wonderful water of Hawaii I forgot to describe the wonderful sun of Hawaii. It is a tropic sun, and, furthermore, in the first part of June, it is an overhead sun. It is also an insidious, deceitful sun. For the first time in my life I was sunburned unawares. My arms, shoulders, and back had been burned many times in the past and were tough; but not so my legs. And for four hours I had exposed the tender backs of my legs, at right angles, to that perpendicular Hawaiian sun. It was not until after I got ashore that I discovered the sun had touched me. Sunburn at first is merely warm; after that it grows intense and the blisters come out. Also, the joints, where the skin wrinkles, refuse to bend. That is why I spent the next day in bed. I couldn't walk. And that is why, today, I am writing this in bed. It is easier to than not to. But tomorrow, ah, tomorrow, I shall be out in that wonderful water, and I shall come in standing up, even as Ford and Freeth. And if I fail tomorrow, I shall do it the next day, or the next. Upon one thing I am resolved: the Snark shall not sail from Honolulu until I, too, wing my heels with the swiftness of the sea, and become a sunburned, skin-peeling Mercury.

The Animal
from Pure Stoke
by John Grissim

John Grissim's (born 1941) profile of Australian Nat Young captures a difficult man who played a crucial role in the development of surfing technique.

A mong the milestones that mark the sometimes erratic course of modern surfing are several occurrences which did not seem significant at the time, yet whose impact was destined to be immense. For example, the sensational 1963 footage of Butch Van Arsdalen at the Banzai Pipeline was for more than a million kids the world over the very first look at what surfing, and getting tubed, was all about. Not only did Van Arsdalen have the Pipe wired on a longboard but whenever and wherever he surfed in Hawaii the cameras followed—and with good reason. The original Mr. Pipeline once backdoored the peak at ten feet, trimmed high in the tube, then sat down cross-legged on his board and clapped his hands. On another occasion he took off on a Waimea monster and deftly pulled off a quick 360° spinner a mere instant before he set up for the drop. It matters not that Van Arsdalen's personal life was plagued by alcoholism (he died a few years ago of cirrhosis of the liver). His contribution was there on celluloid—incredible stuff that more than anything turned a world-wide generation of coastal gremmies into surfers.

Less splashy but no less momentous was George Greenough's 1965 encounter with Bob McTavish which led to the shortboard revolution, an event equal in importance to an earlier milestone: the introduction of polyurethane foam in 1956.

There are, however, those rare moments in which an event of such incandescence occurs that it not only changes forever the direction of surfing but leaves no doubt of that fact in the minds of those present that they are witnessing history in the making. Such a moment occurred in San Diego during the 1966 World Championships, the event marking the American contest debut of nineteen-year-old Australian phenom Robert "Nat" Young. Not only did he win the world title hands down but his surfing on a board of unique design was so sensational, so utterly different that it rewrote the book of performance standards and practically overnight triggered a complete rethinking on the subject of surfing's ultimate possibilities. Ah, the stuff of legends.

By way of background, surfing ability in the mid-60s was almost universally judged on the basis of how closely one came to the California style: smooth take-offs, graceful turns, and, above all, long nose-rides, the longer the better. In big Hawaiian surf the California style still dominated, emphasizing poise under pressure. The rider took off on a wave and established an optimum track, usually quite straight, and then positioned himself on the board in response to the wave's speed and breaking pattern. The best surfers would look for the optimum point at which to hang five or ten over, and do so as long as possible, often sacrificing most of the wave for this single maneuver. Equipment was well suited to this purpose. Board lengths ranged from 9'6" to 11' with fins roughly the size and shape of garden spades.

The California style had been successfully exported world wide in the form of early surf movies, most notably Bruce Brown's classic *Endless Summer*. Though Americans Robert August and Mike Hynson were the featured surfers, there is a brief Down Under sequence in the film showing a hot thirteen-year-old Australian at Bells Beach, in Victoria, shredding waves with a quickly executed series of nose-rides, turns, and cutbacks. His style was unique, radical, and a near-complete departure from the norm. His name was Nat Young.

Young's cameo appearance started no trends but it did presage his quick rise in the Aussie competition world. Tall, lanky, and muscular with huge hands and feet, Nat the teenager won several junior surfing contests on the waves around his hometown of Sydney. In 1963, at the urging of friends, he entered the senior (or open) event of the Australian Championships held at Bondi Beach—and won it. It was a remarkable win for a sixteen year old who as a gremmie years earlier had been considered rather too tall and gangling to ever become a first-rate surfer. Yet Nat's incredible determination, animal strength, and visionary sense of the possibilities that lay ahead in wave riding were only beginning to make their mark. When George Greenough brought to Australia his kneeboard spoons with their flexible, foiled fins and design concepts for surfboards that were much shorter, thinner, and lighter, it was Bob McTavish who incorporated those ideas into radically new configurations—and Nat Young who helped test those boards in the demanding Australian surf. McTavish replaced the usual spade-shaped fin with a hydrodynamic hooked fin, trimmed down most of his board dimensions, and used lighter fiberglass. The result was a quantum improvement in maneuverability and responsiveness that was truly a major breakthrough. Nat Young took that prototype board into the water and started a revolution.

When he arrived in California for the 1966 World Championship at San Diego, Nat Young was nineteen, had already been surfing for a decade, had developed an astonishing repertoire of maneuvers, and had brought with him a board of radically new design (which he had dubbed "Sam") and an approach to surfing that was absolutely unique. At that time the leading California stylist was Hawaiian-born David Nuuhiwa. In fact, with Nuuhiwa's nose-riding setting the standard, everyone expected Nuuhiwa to win. Everyone, that is, except Nat.

A lot of people had predicted that this young Australian would be a standout in the contest but no one anticipated the explosive display of surfing that Nat put on for the next few days. From his very first heat Nat showed that he was not only totally ignoring the California style but was going to surf the waves *his* way. Using a 9'4" board that was pounds lighter, thinner, tapered and fitted with a Greenough-inspired fin, Nat would take off on five-foot peaks, pull off a slamming bottom turn, set up on the wall, walk to the nose and hang five, shoot ahead of the surf, then quickly rip a cutback, sometimes burying his inside rail so deeply that the board deck was vertical to the water. Huge rooster tails of water rose into the air with every turn and cutback as Nat slashed and ripped, now tucking into the power pocket, now skating out onto the shoulder to dig in for a turn. His maneuvers were quick, powerful, and seemingly executed at will as this tall Aussie animal with oversized feet seemed utterly to dominate each wave. In contrast to fellow competitors whose strategy was to set up on a wave and wait to react to its movement, Nat seemed to throw himself into a maneuver before the wave had barely developed a shape. He would then extract from the face an amazing amount of speed and energy. That was it really. Nat Young owned his waves so totally that he could pull from them what *he* wanted, not what they offered. Compounding his performance, Nat was a terror in the line-up, easily paddling circles around the competition, consistently beating others to the take-off, and stealing waves right and left with a steely eyed aggressiveness that was totally intimidating. And when things didn't go his way he would often pound his board with his fist, an unheard-of gesture. In the words of one observer, Nat Young was Australia's answer to Bismarck.

"What stood out the most was his aggressive style," recalls Corky Carroll, a fellow contestant and at the time one of surfing's premier talents. "Nat's performance was a statement that there was a lot more to do on a wave besides nose-riding. And he not only had the ability to do a lot more but his board was an all-around vehicle designed to provide the flexibility he demanded."

Nat won the contest going away, besting a field of tough competitors who, in retrospect, were marching to a different drummer, both in style and equipment. Hawaii's Jock Sutherland finished second, Corky Carroll third, while Midget Farrelly, Rodney Sumpter, and Steve Bigler took fourth, fifth, and sixth, respectively. The following day, when filmed footage of the final heats was aired on California television stations, the shock waves began to spread. Northern California surfer Kirby Ferris, upon seeing the 30-second segment of Nat's rip-and-tear style, later remarked, "I knew right then that any board I was riding was a piece of crap. Nat Young had suddenly changed everything and, in a way, I resented it. I wonder how many dozens of guys went out the next day and torched their boards."

Actually, while Nat's win did represent a quantum jump in performance standards, ushering in an era of slashing, aggressive, freestyle competition, the change percolated rather slowly through the ranks of the mellow California stylists. One notable exception was Corky: "I picked up on Nat's design right away and incorporated the elements in the line of boards I put out through Hobie Boards, but sales were very slow. I myself switched to an 8'2", which was pretty radical at the time, and won a lot of contests but still the new designs didn't catch on. Over a twelve-month period I sold only thirteen boards in that configuration. It wasn't until Dick Brewer in 1968 came out with the first of his mini-guns that the changeover to shortboards began in earnest."

With his 1966 World Championship win Nat Young now shared the celebrity spotlight with his fellow countryman Midget Farrelly. Their names were—and still are—household words in Oz. But there the similarity ended. Whereas Midget was gracious, self-effacing, and respectable, a model Australian Mr. Goody Two-shoes who was the darling of the tabloids, Nat was, and still largely is, a different breed of cat. True, he could be all those things when he wanted (a consummate charmer at times) but he also had an equal capacity to be bullheaded, egotistical, immature, dissembling, and belligerent—sometimes all at once. His peers quickly nicknamed him "the animal," this at a time in Australia when being an animal was hip. What was refreshing, however, was that, although his stance was arrogant, it embodied an implicit rejection of the petty hypocrisies practiced by so many professional athletes—the false humility, the facade of clean living, and the kow-towing to the press. Nat was a product of an elite renegade class of hip surfers, who became the world's best surfer, whose conduct was in ways a vindication of the Australian surfer with his hard-charging, mocking blend of blarney, good times, "aggro," and superb go-for-it surfing. More-over, there were times when he could play the role beautifully.

Surfer Kirby Ferris, who is also a gifted teller of tales, remembers one eventful incident in 1969 when Nat pulled off a bit of flawless theater:

"I had moved to Maui from San Diego where I had more or less gotten out of surfing because I couldn't take the crowds and being has-sled by the Huntington Beach variety of punk surfer who made life miserable in the line-up and/or ripped off your car while you were out in the water. The Maui scene appeared much better until I realized that the tanned, long-haired soul brothers, with their beads and flowers, and who were always ready to get stoned on grass and acid, were the phoniest assholes imaginable. All was peace and love on the beach but once in the water they would snake around you, steal waves, drop in on you, and yell obscenities. I was truly disgusted. These people had no sense of humility whatsoever. The worst qualities of California were being exported to Hawaii to infect and suppress a culture of probably the most innately happy people on earth. Then one day at the Lahaina breakwater I was sitting on the beach watching the mob in the line-up when this rental car drives up. Out step surf filmmakers Greg McGillivray and Jim Freeman, and Nat Young. For a radius of about three hundred yards around the car everything came to a standstill as all eyes turned to Nat.

"Without saying a word, Nat pulls a board off the surf rack, strides to the water's edge, and slides onto the board like a big, mean crocodile silently snaking into the water from the river bank. Now the breakwater had a three- to five-foot right working that afternoon and Nat paddled right into the pack. By paddling I mean every time his hands clawed the water his board literally planed—he moved unbelievably fast and quick. The pack parted before him as though hypnotized and Nat continued on to pick up an outside peak that was just feathering. He took off, snapped a top turn, drove to the bottom, and skated a bit in front of the wave as it started to tube. Then he quickly carved a turn into the wall, piercing the curtain of the tube, literally raping it, screamed along in the tube, came out on the shoulder and kicked out so that his board came down on the backside with an incredibly loud SLAP! I swear the sound was so loud it could be heard for hundreds of yards.

"Not a surfer anywhere—on the beach or in the water—made a move or a sound. Utter silence. And as Nat knee-paddled back to the take-off point he glared at everyone he passed, making absolute eye contact. He had paralyzed the entire pack. Everyone seemed to cower in his presence. He seemed a kind of avenging angel, something powerful and sinister and certainly very dangerous. At that moment Nat Young vindicated every surfer who had ever been rat-fucked by some L.A. punk juvenile lightweight. I was totally stoked."

Years later, in the mid-70s, while living in Oz, I visited Nat to interview him for *Tracks* magazine and came away understanding just how much impact the man can make in the water. During an early morning go-out near his farm I watched this lanky, bearded, wet-suited animal paddling out to a pristine sunrise wave with rare grace and power, hooting and grinning happily as he plunged his size-twelve hands into Pacific glass, pushing great sections of water effortlessly behind him. He sat up for a few seconds, waiting for that timid virginal wall to offer itself—and when he wheeled about and stroked into the wave, I felt as though I shouldn't be watching.

It was, of course, a form of communion between Mr. Super Surfer and his mistress. Or was it mistress and slave? Any distinction would have been academic; for Nat, then twenty-seven, was still the outspoken radical Eminence of surfing, even though four years earlier he had quietly dropped out of competitive professional surfing. His reason for doing so is characteristic of the man: "I'd decided I'd really won them all for too long and really didn't feel like doing it any more. I don't know, it's hard to put it down to a loss of competitive drive due to drugs, or growing old or what. My drive is still there and I can develop it as much as I want but I don't particularly like it that much."

Nat really *had* won them all for a long time—literally dozens of contests during the years 1966 through 1970. Along with his success came a small fortune from product endorsements, much of which was carefully invested for him by his business manager and agent. Nat has since lived comfortably off those investments. Among his holdings is a 2,000-acre ranch and a hundred head of cattle some thirty miles from the town of Grafton in upper New South Wales. Nat moved there in 1973 with his wife Marilyn and their two toddlers (a daughter Nyaomie and son Beau) and built almost single-handedly a home which featured an oval-shaped central atrium nearly sixty feet across. Whether or not marriage, family, and the responsibilities of a farm played a role, Nat's once-legendary aggressiveness has since mellowed, particularly regarding his reputation for not liking anyone else on a wave he chooses to ride:

"I still consider that some waves are made for me, or come for me. And if I feel that strongly about a wave I . . . call it dash, arrogance, or whatever, but it happens a lot less now because I have a lot more respect for others. But when I was younger it was a very tenacious feeling—I felt like, This is my wave and therefore I'm going to have it. . . . I knew that my ability was probably better than anyone else's and that would justify it. It's understandable now but I don't think it's very admirable."

A certain distance from those tumultuous years of early fame and money has brought with it a comprehension of brash behavior in and out of the water that was both his hallmark and one of young Nat's least attractive attributes: "I'm glad I'm not completely into that end of it any more. It was that whole aggressive youthful thing that sort of led from one thing, and then the ego came into it because I was getting away with it and started believing it. . . . I wanted everything, so I'd fight to get it. And if it meant knocking off milk money to get it, or fuckin' grabbing that babe down there, then that was the way it was gonna be."

Nat's approach to riding waves, however, has remained unchanged: "I can't carve in two-foot junk. Don't know anybody that can, really, although a lot of people can gimmick it out. There's not many who carve on surfboards anyway, because a lot of people aren't into pressure and a lot aren't into carving. I want to feel that kind of energy and to leave my mark on a wave when I do it. I'm glad the track is wiped out as soon as I finish it. To me that's the essence of good art. It's instantaneous. I don't want to remember it forever. All I want to do is *feel* it."

As my visit to his ranch was drawing to a close, Nat mentioned that prior to his building his home on an expansive hilltop, a designer friend had thrown the *I Ching* to check out the energy level. That savvy oracle spoke pointedly of Fire on the Mountain, most apt for a sometimes headstrong Scorpio with a lot of water in his natal chart. Aside from these metaphysical signposts, I sensed that beneath his confident, easy-going, hospitable exterior, Nat Young, the former-world-champion-turned-rancher-and-family-man, was smoldering. He seemed at bottom an adventurer anxious to hit the road once more and again live on impulse.

The impression stemmed from the interviews. His earnest talk of having settled down and of getting into stay-at-home farming was not so much a statement of a conviction as it was a projection of hope—something he wanted to want, if only to silence the restless animal within. Deep down, it seemed, he was still quite ill-at-ease with his new role. Of his wife Marilyn and of his then-pending departure for a four-month round-the-world trip (via the pro contests in Hawaii) he said, "She understands I love her. I've always gone away and I've always come back." What many of Nat's friends could not understand was his leaving just a few weeks after his son Beau was born prematurely. But he admitted he was struggling to reconcile his commitment to a family with an older and perhaps more familiar commitment to surfing.

Then, too, there is more than just surfing. Nat has always loved traveling and meeting new people and partying and mixing with elegant types like Marisa Berenson and Baron Whoever and generally being, well, the legendary Australian surfer Nat Young, particularly in Europe where his reputation in many ways has yet to be superseded. Nat is also fascinated by hip people with style and flash and power, particularly those who love to work in quick and shrewd ways (his friend Mickey Dora comes to mind). Nat himself possesses some of those same qualities, something which sharply delineates the quality of his personality. He is on the one hand a hard-working family provider and on the other a flash star with a quick smile and a ready wink—as long as you don't stand between him and what he wants. The former role is admirable, albeit mundane; the latter is simply jive.

Admittedly, neither of the above considerations has a direct bearing on Nat's phenomenal physical courage and ability as a surfer. In fact, that ability largely (but not completely) excuses him from so much that may have been inexcusable in the water in the years past. To put this into perspective bear in mind that his idea of an easy stretch is surfing Angourie at twelve feet by moonlight. The man is definitely a connoisseur of edgework.

But waves come in differing sizes and manifestations, both physical and emotional, and it may be that the years following his move to the country brought with them tough challenges. Nat's decision to return to the contest circuit in the late 70s, for example, was not accompanied by his return to the top of the ratings. Ironically his earlier success had spawned a new generation of hotties, many of whom were armed with financial backing from surfing-related industries and a white-hot commitment to win big. Under those circumstances, Nat may have opted out of the pro circuit rather than accept a middling performance rating. The late 70s also saw the breakup of his marriage, an event which should not necessarily be construed as a failure in the conventional sense because Nat Young is not a conventional person. By 1980 he once again was living north of Sydney not far from his boyhood haunts of Collaroy, working on a documentary called *Fall Line* (about surfing, hang gliding, and skiing), and regularly traveling to Europe, California, and assorted exotic islands.

"I'm a lot closer now to the things I stand for," he replied during a recent visit to California. He added that for any future on-the-record conversations he would like time to think things out: "Like right now I'm shaping several blanks before I leave for Sydney. That's a physical activity but it gets me clear. Then I can sit down and talk." But he readily admitted during a swell the previous week he had spent five days surfing the best waves to hit California in months, leaving more mundane matters to be wrapped up prior to jumping on the plane.

Clearly the fire and enthusiasm that have always characterized Nat Young are still there, guaranteeing that one of the finest athletes Australia has ever produced will be around to make waves, and surf them, both in and out of the water. And that's as it should be, for, at bottom, the significance of Nat Young in the world of surfing is not so much what the man has to say, but what he does, and doubtless will continue to do with consummate style and skill in the water.

"Surfing is a very nice thing to do," he once remarked during an afterdinner conversation that had turned pleasantly philosophical. "And to go surfing and get tubed, too . . . well, there it is. That's really where it is. There's been an awful lot written and said about that beautiful little place inside waves. And I certainly like to get there as often as possible. I'm primarily someone who would like to hang around inside that tube as much as I can. Everybody knows it's there, but very few get there themselves, and fewer still get there all the time."

Alaska: The Land Duke Forgot
by Dave Parmenter

Surfer *magazine sent Dave Parmenter (born 1961) to a*
place where you need a rifle, wool socks, rain pants and a
sleeping bag to go surfing. His story ran in January, 1993.

O n the left side of the aircraft there's a great view of the
Malaspina Glacier, which is bigger than the state of Rhode
Island," came the even, Chuck Yeager–modulated voice of
the pilot.

Halfway through our Naugahyde omelets, Brock Little and I looked
at each other and chortled. We'd been in Alaska only a short while, and
yet we'd run into this Rhode Island comparison a number of times. It
had already become a private joke.

Thirty-eight thousand feet below, an impossible landscape scrolled
past the portholes; brutal snow-caked mountain ranges hooked across
the eastern Gulf of Alaska like a giant mandible of ogre-ish chipped
teeth. Massive panes of crevassed rhino-hide ice creaked in glacial
strain toward the ocean, some as big as . . . well, Rhode Island.

Alaska is so huge, its features so outsized, that the place borders on science fiction. The currency of measurement is as elephantine as the state itself. Features are constantly scaled to this Rhode Island standard: the glaciers, the mammoth forest tracts, the medicine-ball cabbages from the fertile Matanuska Valley, the manta ray–sized halibut. Rain is measured in feet, wholesale—rather than sissy California inches. Even the name itself is derived from the Aleut native word "Alashka," or "great land." If there is any "greater" or more bizarrely gorgeous land on the globe, George Lucas will have to build it at Industrial Light and Magic.

Surfing Alaska? Surely an oxymoron if ever there was one. A lot of things have drawn people to Alaska in the past: fur, fish, gold, oil, even elbow room. But never surfing. It's not exactly what Duke Kahanamoku had in mind.

People thought we were pulling their leg. Were we for real or just eccentrics on a cavalier whim, like mad flagpole-sitters intent on defining some new parameter in discomfort? We weren't sure ourselves, stepping off the plane into the mid-summer drizzle of Sitka, Alaska. Wrangling bulging Pro-Lites around like hog-tied steer, we drew quite a few quizzical stares.

"Whatcha' got there son, a canoe?" someone wearing a CPO jacket and hip-waders would invariably ask. Maybe we were potential canoe-borne invaders of his favorite trout lake.

"Naw, it's a surfboard."

Now in Alaska, it's a safe bet that if their rejoinder isn't a hearty, "Them's good eatin'!" you'll be of no further interest and can pass on your way without further scrutiny.

Brock Little, Josh Mulcoy, Bob Barbour and myself heaved and dragged our burdens into the terminal, and we felt a hell of a lot better when the entire surfing population of Sitka was there to greet us. Both of them.

Charlie Skultka and his brother-in-law Todd. We all shook hands, piled our gear into Charlie's truck, and within an hour or so were blasting out of Sitka Harbor in a 14-foot aluminum skiff. This was the

Alaskan equivalent of driving down to T Street to check the surf: an hour-long Mr. Toad's Wild Ride to one of the innumerable swell-exposed islands that make up the Alexander Archipelago of South-eastern Alaska.

The no-wake rule in the harbor gave us plenty of time to take in the city's layout. It's a quaint yet utilitarian harbor town, set on the low terraces beneath snow-capped coastal mountains snaking around Sitka Sound. Spruce trees carpet every square foot in verdant deep-pile, even on nearly vertical angles. Grimy, diesel-sooted fishing trawlers grappled with incoming cruise liners as immaculate and white as a first communion dress. Sea planes were hauled up on slanted docks, guzzling fuel with happy-hour zest.

Once clear of the fish and diesel smell of the inner harbor, we got our first lungfuls of pure Alaskan air. Glacier-chilled and imbued with the Christmas-tree scent of a billion spruce, the air was so rich and pure that it verged on being an intoxicant.

The outer harbor was dappled with dozens of small, craggy islands. Some were sizable enough to have cozy New England–style homes built on them. Others were mere tree-stubbled sea stacks.

Charlie had a dozen marine charts detailing more than 1,000 islands with something like 10,000 to 15,000 miles of potentially surfable coastline. We'd point to a likely looking setup on a chart and yell over the drone of the outboard motor, "What about this point?" Every inquiry was answered with a shrug and, "No one's ever been down there."

Charlie and Todd had worked over a handful of spots that they knew well, bashing out into wild seas in small skiffs, sometimes camping on a deserted beach, trading rainy gray waves in the loneliest surfing real estate on Earth.

Charlie was a Haida, a native Indian in the region. Solidly built and ruggedly handsome, he had a certain Hawaiian bearing, which showed up even more when he surfed. A surfer of modest ability, he rode with a definite Hawaiian regalness—upright and proud—with none of the exaggerated Wilbur Kookmeyer flailings that plague most intermediates.

"A lot of people say our people migrated here from Hawaii," Charlie told us. As if to support this claim, Charlie gave us the story on his first board. A fellow fisherman had found it drifting far out to sea. It was a mossy, water-logged longboard called a "Tiki," a '60s pop-out from Southern California. Most likely it drifted up from Hawaii in the northwesterly-flowing Japanese current. Charlie scraped the moss from it, dried it out, and repaired the dings with bluish-marine resin. He learned to surf at Sandy Beach in Sitka, the one sliver of swell window actually in town and accessible by car. If there's a 12-foot swell on the outer waters, Sandy Beach might be 3 feet and like a good day on Lake Superior.

I told Charlie about the hairball landing we had sweated out at Juneau. Fog kept us circling over aluminum-cleaving peaks for almost an hour until the pilot found a vein of clearness.

"Oh, yeah. Happens all the time. Those glaciers above the city make their own weather," Charlie said. "That ice field is bigger than Rhode Island."

We anchored off a low, spruce-shaggy point on the southern tip of a volcanic island. A black slab of pitted lava tilted into the ocean with that perfect inclination and sweep that sets surfers a'blubbering from Rincon to Raglan. There wasn't much swell, but a few glassy, head-high peelers wrapped around the point, rehearsing their lines for better days.

It resembled a small day at Third Point, Malibu, may it rest in peace. Except Gidget would have some pretty stiff nipples here, and the bears have even less patience with the Vals than Dora did. This was as far away from the teeming mouse hole of surf culture as you could get in America. Well, almost. . . .

Let he who hath understanding reckon the number of the Beast, for he is a California refugee. We hadn't been in the water 10 minutes when a guy in an aluminum skiff like ours sidled up to the line-up during a lull. I instantly recognized the phylum and class. The beard, the dog as Man Friday, the vibe.

"I know what this guy ate for breakfast," I thought. "If we were on Highway One, that skiff would be an El Camino."

"You the *Surfer* Magazine guys?" asked the guy, whom we'll call "Dick," for a number of reasons mutually agreed upon later.

"Yep," Charlie answered. He seemed to know Dick.

"Which one of you is the writer?" He had those oversize polarized glasses you see on fuddy-duddies timidly pulling out of Leisure World in Buick Le Sabres.

"That'd be me," I said, thinking, Laguna Beach? Santa Cruz? Palos Verdes? He's behind the times; nowadays, you're supposed to hassle the photographer.

"You're not going to tell everyone about this place are you?" Dick asked. "I've been surfing here for 10 years." I looked for the bandanna on the dog. Nope, must have been in the wash.

"Uh . . . that's not the idea. We don't intend to . . ." I trailed off thinking, "This is unfuggingbelievable."

"Thank you," he said with finality and motored off into the channel, leaving us on a shriveling, ever-smaller planet. Even here, on a remote and uninhabited island, one of thousands in the Gulf of Alaska, where one wrong move or fey lash of weather means a mossy skeleton in six months, there is still the stereotypical Californian paranoiac looking over his shoulder to make sure Salt Creek isn't gaining on him, sweating out the fever of Invasion Fear, as if tomorrow we'd have introduced a leprosy of condos and 7-Elevens and parking meters at his personal retreat.

Charlie was pissed. He explained that Dick hadn't wanted us to come here. Dick was a bodyboarder, and, if that wasn't bad enough, he had also written a book about the self-same island, using personal or native endearments for place-names. Bob and I later read it, a deeply felt and poetic but overwrought Boy and His Dog love letter to the island. Reading between the lines, one could find that smug sanctimony so many refugee Californians assume, as if having the wisdom to turn their backs on Californication grants them the moral highground and the deed to their personal Walden Pond.

"Sorry, you guys," Charlie said, his eyes clouding over. "Not many people around here like that guy. No offense, but . . . they think he's a typical Californian."

The waves were fun, head-high on the sets, and for a half an hour the sun popped out and baked the shoulders of our wetsuits. I asked Charlie what this wave was like at 6 feet.

"Actually, this is the first time I've ever surfed this place," he replied.

"What?"

"I don't go backside very good," Charlie offered. "But this place is 'kill.' I'll have to come out here more."

The next day we decided to start fresh and begin exploring the outer coast of this Catalina-size island. There were a lot of places on the charts that looked suspiciously like a Klondike of Rincons, Burleighs and Mundacas. Venturing on such a quest into the open ocean here is not something to be taken lightly. If by definition "adventure" is adversity rightly viewed, then by all rights anytime you take a boat into Alaskan waters, it qualifies as adventure. Or certainly adversity.

Preparing for extended camping in this wilderness is a serious undertaking. Most camping in the lower 48 isn't real camping. There you phone up Ticketron months in advance, and your credit card reserves you a sandbox-size cubical of "wilderness" that is really more Festival Seating Motel 6 than Communion with Nature.

But this was the real thing. Alaska has a total tidal shoreline of 47,300 miles. Virtually none of it can be reached by car. So it's boats or sea planes. The tidal range can be 12 to 18 feet. When the tide goes minus, it leaves a pre-tsunami scree of exposed sand and rock, often stranding your boat 100 yards from where you want it to be. When you're lost here, man, not even God can find you.

The region of Alaska we were in can get more than 200 inches of rain in a year—Cornwall on steroids. In medieval Cornwall, when the foul weather drove people batty, they invented witchcraft to cope. Here, they just drink. After a week of constant dreary rain, you can imagine the faintly audible gritty sound of whiskey bottles being unscrewed under rain-slashed roofs across town. After September, the tourist trade fizzles, leaving the locals alone with four-hour days and 100 inches of rain.

"How do people cope?" I asked Charlie. Just one week of fog in Morro Bay and I look like Jack Nicholson just before he lost it in *The Shining*.

"Ninety-nine percent of the people drink," he said evenly. "The other 1 percent are court-ordered not to."

Charlie didn't drink, at least not anymore. Once, flush with $5,000 in cash after a long fishing job, he got so bombed that he woke up in . . . Mazatlan. He couldn't remember how he got there; just woke up in a hotel in tropical Mexico with a hangover that would have toppled a Cape buffalo. He had $2,000 left.

As our strategy gelled, there remained one final obstacle, Mr. Bear. First and foremost, Alaska is bear country. Bears, bear tracks, bear shit and bear lore absolutely pepper the countryside. Every point in Alaska is Charlie Bear's Point. Charlie Bear don't surf, but he can run 35 mph, swim like Mark Spitz, and climb a tree faster than a scalded cat.

Even in the urban areas, according to a newspaper account, bears "ruined by their taste in garbage" hang out at dumps like Insta-Teller muggers.

In the coupon section of the local newspaper, sandwiched between the Renuzit Fragrance Jars and the Hostess Ho-Hos, is a device known as a Bear Bell. For 59 cents (with coupon) you get a cube-shaped bell that affixes to your clothing, the idea being that, when tromping over hill and dale, or taking an old mattress to the dump, you'll clang and peal like a Salvation Army Santa, thus signaling to any marauding bear, "Hey, comin' through."

Surprising a bear in repose (or any pose for that matter) is a pretty one-sided affair, if you're a stickler for all that statistical stuff. Of course, the Bear Bell is the rock-bottom, low-end ticket in bear repellent. It's sensible and field-tested effective; and for about five bucks you can bell yourself, the fam, the mailman, baby Herman, even Rover. But dammit, it's also un-American. It's what Gandhi would have done to ward off bears.

Which is why you should do what 99.999 percent of Alaskans do:

purchase a big ol' mofo firearm and cart it everywhere like a fifth limb. This is the preferred linchpin in the Guerrilla War with bears in Alaska.

Not that you'll ever really need your "smokewagon." Chances are you'll never encounter a bear that will interrupt his berry-slurping or wood-shitting to charge you. But at least you can lend a hand in what seems to be a statewide industry of reducing wind resistance on road signs and mailboxes.

Being lower-48 greenhorns in Alaska, we were constantly teased. "Look out for them bears, boys," they'd warn us with a twinkle in their eyes. We'd explain that Bob, Josh and I were from the notorious Red Triangle in Central California, and that once a person reconciled the fear of a sudden, fatal attack by a white shark, well, "bearanoia" seemed almost laughable. One wildlife expert, stretching hard for a great sound-byte on a local news show, called the grizzly bear a "terrestrial version of the great white shark." We howled at that. Bears declare their major well in advance, unlike the stealth-torpedo tactics of a white. It's not like a grizzly suddenly rockets upward from some ursine gopher hole and takes your leg in a splintered second.

Although we had ultra-trick Patagonia rain gear, some Rubik's Cube North Face tents, and 14 cartons of Pop Tarts, we realized it was time to step up and arm ourselves. Brock was elected sergeant-at-arms. He was the most macho and was used to dealing with big, grumpy locals. He was also the only one of us who had any money.

We went shopping for our peace-makin', lead-spittin' bear control at a little shanty perched over the harbor on stilts. It was called Ye Old Rod and Reel (no lie), and the scene inside was familiar to any veteran surf shop patron. Racks of guns, new and used, stood erect in an intentionally phallic way across the showroom. Two grizzled good ol' boys—one easily measuring on the Rhode Island Standard—sporting NRA sideburns and CPO jackets, tried to sell Brock the firearm equivalent of a 12-foot Brewer gun, when all he really needed was a Becker.

Brock was keen on a 30.30 Winchester. He cocked the lever and checked the "action," the gun version of kicking the tires on a used car. The elder gun nut scoffed.

"That won't stop no bear," he said, sucking on a cigarette like a snorkel, partially obscured in that pall of acrid smoke that most Alaskans live and work in. "What you need is sumthin' like this here 7mm." He brandished a huge rifle, a dreadnought with a bore like a garden hose. "This'll stop 'im right in his tracks." Yeah, and uproot the tree behind him. It would also some in handy if you wanted to bore a new cylinder into an engine block.

But Brock was set on the 30.30. Ten minutes later, he left the shop cradling his rifle, beaming proudly. The day's provisioning was over.

"I've got a rifle, some wool socks, rain pants, and a sleeping bag. I'm ready," Brock exclaimed with satisfaction, "to go surfing."

No sooner had we packed the boats when the unthinkable happened . . . the weather cleared up. A rogue slab of glacial high pressure nosed into the soupy overcast, and soon we were smack dab in the middle of the best weather of the year.

Alaska has a feminine, brooding beauty. She is a gorgeous and enchanting woman, even cloaked in her chador of rain and gloom. But when the sun comes out and the mountains glow green, you feel singled out and special. Your heart lifts. It's as if you've just passed a beautiful and classy Garbo in a crowd, and she smiles directly at you.

Of course, as soon as the weather turned glorious, the swell hissed flat like a punctured tire. We motored around the far side of the island for half a day, finally making camp near a rivermouth deep in a wide bay, with a melding of forest and foreshore that made Big Sur look like a wilted Disneyland diorama. Three conical Puerto Escondido–style sandbars were scattered about near the rivermouth, teasing us with 1-foot replicas of perfect surfing waves.

"You guys should have come in November," Charlie mused.

"Yeah, or we should have brought Rob Machado," I countered, watching a perfect 13-inch set peel down a black sand G-land.

The weather stayed great, and the surf flat, so we put on our camping heads. Our setup was idyllic. Salmon were lobbing out of the river as if each gurgling bend were an inexhaustible silo of fresh silver protein. Bob would stand in the icy river for hours, jacking huge dog salmon onto the bank, his voice fairly cracking with emotion: "This is the J-Bay of fishing. . . . It's like some beautiful dream."

The beautiful fish caught was one Bob spotted trapped in a large longshore pool, cut off from the river and sea by the extreme low tide. Josh, Brock and I chased it through the pool like a greased pig in a rodeo event. Brock finally cornered it, quickly rolled it up the bank, and drilled its head with three lightning-quick North Shore hay-makers. Within two hours eight pounds of salmon steaks were grilling over our campfire.

Walking through the forest you could snack on raspberries and blueberries, which grew on everything, and wash them all down with ice-cold, snow-fed river water. On sand banks deeper in the interior, we found the recent tracks of bears and the leftover viscera of salmon lunch. One set had paw prints as big as dinner plates. Charlie extended his rifle overhead to show us the approximate size of that bear. Great. No surf, but at least the bears were double overhead.

A couple more days of no swell followed, and we started to wonder if perhaps we weren't camped out at Rincon waiting for a big north swell in July.

The weather began to sour one afternoon, with all the evil portent of an approaching winter in a Stephen King story. By nightfall, a gale was upon us. We moved camp into the protection of the forest, and huddled around the fire, grilling the last of the salmon as all hell broke loose out at sea. In Alaska, they don't call the wind Mariah. They call it Cujo.

Brook and I lay in our tent listening to the creaks and groans of the gale-torn forest, waiting for a bear in the Double-Overhead Club to take us like a nylon Bon-Bon. There'd be a horrid ripping of fabric and he'd come and he'd . . .

The tent flap flew open and a dark head poked through. It was Charlie. "I need some help with the skiff." Charlie had that understated, taciturn manner most Alaskans have, as if constant exposure to the grandeur of their surrounding had stripped them of all futile adjectives.

We geared up, abandoning our warm cocoon with longing, and followed Charlie's swinging, fluttering lantern out onto the beach.

The skiff was sunk. Luckily it was sunk right near shore, but regardless, it was well on the way to a more traditional burial. The millpond anchorage of the previous day was now a heaving, wind-nagged 4-foot shoredump. The skiff was broadside to the waves, which were breaking directly into the sorry craft. Half a ton of sand had gathered along the floor, pinning the skiff in the ceaseless shorebreak. And the incoming tide was still two hours from peaking.

The three of us wrestled the motor off the mount and set about reclaiming our vessel, scooping water and sand in gut-busting desperation, trying to stay a beat ahead of the incoming flushes of water and sand. Rain slashed through the lantern's wavering sphere of light at a 45-degree angle. The wind was the bastard offspring of a banshee and a chain saw. Waves broke completely over us as we grappled with the boat. A few times the lantern blew out, and one of us had to relight it as the other two bailed furiously.

By 2 a.m., we were able to monkey the skiff up out of reach of the tide. The last of the dry driftwood was thrown onto the fire back at camp. I put a pot of coffee on, and we squatted near the flames, steam beginning to waft from our sodden clothes. For some perverse reason, this moment was the highlight of the trip, and we all sensed it. "Welcome," Charlie deadpanned, "to the real Alaska."

One of us said in the morning, and I don't recall who, "Enough of this boat shit!" We broke camp and limped back to Sitka in the remnants of the storm. Confused spikes of windswell hammered our 14-foot skiff, and it took most of the day to gain the calmer waters of Sitka Sound.

The next morning we were on the dawn flight to a place I'll call Cape Tanis, leaving Charlie and Todd to their lonely sentinel in Sitka. We'd heard tell of a better swell window a few hundred miles up the coast. Best of all, the area had dirt roads leading out to most of the surrounding coastline. The prospect of not having an outboard hangover every day pleased us, as did eliminating the expense of hiring two boats.

Cape Tanis was a small, remote fishing and hunting Mecca, sort of a salmon Tavarua. In August and September the silver salmon head upstream and the few local lodges fill up. The population swells to 900, three times the winter desolation of 300. People in Sitka warned us that people in Cape Tanis weren't too friendly, that they didn't like outsiders, but we found it to be one of the friendliest places any of us had ever been. Every single person waved when passed on the road. It was a habit that came remarkably easy to we veterans of the 405 Freeway. All you had to do was extend the remaining four fingers normally crumpled in the customary L.A. freeway greeting.

We stayed at the Happy Bear Lodge, strangers in a strange land. The bar and restaurant were wallpapered with the skins of bear and lynx. Stuffed salmon gaped vacantly from mahogany plaques, and over the kitchen door was what I swear had to be the world's largest taxidermied king crab. Over by the jukebox stood a posthumous member of the Double-Overhead Club, stuffed and mounted in a snarling rictus. A placard at the base read: "Old Rover, shot by Bad Bob Fraker in May 1979. R.I.P."

The hunters and fishermen regarded us with curiosity, but most were so ensnared in the fishing *plak tow* that they didn't even notice us. We were as out of place as a luge team on Nias. But we all had the same spirit, more or less. At the bar I read a magazine called *Alaskan Hunter*, and a passage in the "Taxidermy Tips" column caught my eye:

"Each year as we get out the hunting gear for the first time, there's a feeling of excitement and anticipation as we think of the hunt. Maybe this will be the year we finally get that big one we've been looking for all these years. As we gaze at our living room wall, or think of how we'd feel if our bear or sheep was standing proudly in a public place for all to see, we dream of that moment, when we finally realize our big dream!"

It's obvious we were of a breed. We were brothers.

Force 7 winds had whipped up a solid 8-foot swell. We'd heard quite a few fish stories about a left point at Cape Tanis; on the charts it looked too good to be true. We set out in our rented van and drove as far as we could in the general direction of the point. When we could go no farther we got out and hiked through the foliage, Brock on point with the 30.30.

We found ourselves at the terminus of a large bay. A mile seaward was the graceful sweep of a sand-shoal left point, so we hiked along the beach to get a better look. The wind was offshore here, and at the top of the point, thick, lumpy swells staggered around the cape, punch-drunk and slobbering from a beating out to sea. They refracted into the stiff offshore wind, sifting and smoothing into progressively cleaner lines. Halfway down the quarter-mile point certain waves would bend so severely that they actually became thick Trestles-like rights that wound to the beach like spokes around a hub. It was possible to ride a hundred yards or so from the top of the point on a left, and then bank off a swelling hump on the shoulder that in turn swung its energy right for another 50 yards, ultimately depositing you on the sand with burning quads. From there, it was a short jog back to the top of the cape for another circuit.

To the north was a staggering backdrop, as alien and transfixing as a Martian landscape. The Saint Elias Mountains, at 18,000 feet the highest coastal range in the world, soared into the chilled Alaskan sky, crusted with snow and flanked by the ivory shards of some of those "Rhode Island" glaciers.

Having access to roads set us free. After a day or so of scouting, we were able to make surgical strikes at the point and various beach-breaks. On smaller days we hit the beachbreaks at high tide for some thick, wedgy bowls that strongly resembled Hossegor. In one week we got two 8-foot swells. We spent these at the point, surfing five or six hours a day, stopping only for peanut butter sandwiches shared around a roaring bonfire, which we kept stoked between quarter-mile rides down the sand point.

So what was it like to surf Alaska? How different was it than, say,

Oregon or Northern California? All I can say is that it wasn't a matter of how the water felt or what wax to bring, or even how your lungs burned running up the point, sucking in volcanic ash from a nearby eruption. I felt something so much bigger than mere . . . surfing.

They call Alaska the "Last Frontier," but it's more than that. It's the last place where America, its true atavistic spirit, exists. It's the America of John Ford, where accountability and self-reliance still mean something. It's not the litigation-snarled America we have today, full of blame-shirkers and moral cowards. If you break down, you don't call the Auto Club. If a bear looms up on the trail ahead, you don't slap an injunction on him or sue the state because you weren't mollycoddled with warning signs every 10 yards. And if you get into trouble surfing, you don't flag down the rescue copter or whistle for Darrick Doerner to swim out and save your lily-white helpless ass.

Elephants, rhinos, even spotted owls all have their sanctuaries now. But what of that breed of Americans also so endangered? The wild-eyed misfits who webbed prairie and desert with the ruts of countless wagon wheels, beating the wildest continent on Earth into docility, staying always one step ahead of the preachers and lawyers and bureaucrats. What of them? Maybe they just took a dogleg turn north when they ran out of "West" generations ago. Alaska is their reserve.

Studying my creased and fish-stained chart one night, I happened upon a discovery that made my heart swell with the rhapsody of my forefathers. A 50-mile chunk of coast, some accident of desolation, was inscribed with that rarest and loveliest of all words: "Unsurveyed."

Alone

by Dave Parmenter

Dave Parmenter's (born 1961) trip to Africa suggests how far some contemporary surfers will go to get away from the crowds at their local beaches—and conveys a sense of the rewards reaped by those willing to go the distance.

Manuel spent his last dawn digging his own grave. The sandstorm had ended with an eerie suddenness late in the night, almost arbitrarily, as if a vengeful god had grown tired of that particular torture and was casting about for a new method. The jackals seemed closer then, their wails amplified by the empty ringing stillness. Finally, toward sunrise, the fog coasted in from the southwest and muffled their mournful retreat back into the hinterland behind the towering sand dunes.

Manuel drank of the fog by wringing the dampened square of canvas into his mouth. A pitiful few drops of brackish water, soaked up instantly by a bloodstream thick and sluggish after five days of unbearable thirst. But it was enough to keep his throat from fusing shut and a little strength seeped into his limbs. Strength to dig.

A lone castaway after his ship had torn its bottom to shreds on some fog-shrouded offshore reef, Manuel was just another of the growing ranks of doomed sailors cast up on the alien shores of southwestern Africa. As the Portuguese began pushing their barques south of the Horn of Africa in the mid-15th century, they ran into a welter of fog, wind and currents that seemed to work in malevolent collusion to strip timber from keels and flesh from bone.

Manuel dug and thought how it was odd what finally made a man give up hope. Vanity. His arm had been lacerated on barnacles during the struggle ashore and now, days later, was streaked with angry, sup-purating sores. Gangrene. The realization struck him that even if by some miracle he was saved immediately, he would lose his arm, and the thought of being less than a whole man withered his resolve.

Not that there was any hope of being saved. The coast unspooled for hundreds of miles either way; a brutal empire of sand dunes and drifting fog, unrelieved by even the slightest trace of vegetation. The only water came from the morning fog each night once the daily sand-storms died. The beach was littered with seal skulls and mangled bits of pelt. At dusk the jackals and hyenas would begin skulking out to the seal colony on the headland, and he would hear the horrifying cries of the seal pups being dragged away from their mothers, followed by the grunts and snuffling of the dogs as they set upon their prey. Manuel could hear the bones crunching in the oversize jaws, and he spent the nights shivering in a hollow at the base of a small dune, trying to drown out the slaughter by repeating prayers and psalms over and over, aloud, until his voice cracked or he shivered himself asleep.

Manuel had always been a devoutly religious man. For the first day or so as a castaway, he had brandished his childlike faith as one would hold a cross to a vampire. But now, with his gangrenous, evil-smelling arm drawing the jackals nearer and nearer in their death-vigil, he had a sudden and terrifying glimpse of the true workings of life, a lightning-flash illumination of a nightmarish charnel house that had lain hidden beneath the facade of incense and salvation and braying church organs.

He finished digging into the side of the dune. It was big enough to crouch in, and he had piled up the sand in a loose crest overhead so the wind would blow it over him. Not much time left. His throat had begun to glue shut, and he had heard that when a man's eyes glimmered with bright light it was over soon after. As long as the jackals didn't get to him, Manuel thought, anything but that. He crouched in the hole and hugged his knees, drained of his last energy, and waited for the lights to sear his vision.

After a while the wind came up strong from the southwest, scraping away the fog and blasting curling wraiths of sand along the beach. The fine, powdery crest over Manuel showered down around his feet in little sprinkles at first, then mounds. By mid-afternoon the little grotto was half-filled. The sand weighed against Manuel's chest, but he was far, far away in an impossibly green garden where water poured from fountains with the sweet tones of music. The sand blew all that night, and all through the next day.

> "What better place to end one's life than Primordial Africa?"
>
> —Miki Dora

I was sitting out in the lineup alone at a perfect left point on Namibia's Skeleton Coast, popping kelp bulbs and daydreaming between sets. The sun was going down and I was trying, with as much empathy as I could muster, to imagine what it must have been like to be suddenly flung onto these shores after some disaster at sea, and to realize the utter hopelessness of it. I pondered the riddle of the crouching skeleton, a man found buried alive very close to where I was surfing, hunched in a little womb-like grave. Most of the books dealing with the shipwreck lore of the Skeleton Coast found it to be a mystery. They concluded he must have been buried in a sandstorm while taking shelter in a hole. Just another riddle among hundreds on this coast.

Then I saw the jackal. He was on a little rise at the top of the point 30 yards away, just sitting on his haunches staring at me. At first I thought he was curious, with his pricked-up ears and comically serious stare. In our culture, generations removed from real wilderness, we anthropomorphize animals. Dogs "smile," lions wear crowns, and bears are cute, cuddly things that bounce on our laundry.

It didn't take me long to understand that the jackal was sizing me up as potential prey, scanning through the predator checklist for some sign that I might fit the profile: old, young, weak, sick . . . alone? Even though there was absolutely no danger, it gave me a shiver to be considered as food, as well as a little insight as to why a man might prefer premature burial to being jackal fodder like the countless torn seals that carpeted every square foot of shoreline for miles around the rookery at the cape.

Carnage is what the Skeleton Coast is all about. The name is derived from the profusion of bones strewn along a 400-mile swath on the northern coast of Namibia. From literally any random vantage point, some sort of pitiful remains can be seen: bleached whale ribs, broken-backed ships, piles of seal bones, and perhaps the tangled skeleton of some hapless castaway who made it ashore and died wishing he hadn't.

I was pretty keen on making it to shore myself. The last set of the day hit the outer indicator at Robbenspunt and filed down the half-mile point toward my lineup, the second perfect left point in a two-mile stretch. With a rookery of 100,000 Cape Fur seals just up the point, there's a pretty good chance of some sort of encounter with a white shark. Also, lions have been known, in years of drought, to sneak up on the seals as they sleep and have a little high-cholesterol snack. Most surfers live in a smug cocoon of invulnerability, and why not. With a good car in view, a jerrycan of water, a wetsuit, Swiss Army knife, duct tape, and a little common sense, surfers are practically immortal. But with the sun all but gone, surfing alone without a leash, the nearest town 100 miles away, I began to feel the hair stand up on the back of my neck, and shivered to some involuntary primordial warning surging down my spine. A quarter-mile down the point, Lance had lit up the car as he packed away the gear—a cozy sphere of warmth and safety. I was tired of loitering in the food chain. The first wave of the set approached, a perfect 5-foot wall that roped down the point for

200 yards. I caught it, pulled my feet out of Triassic Park as I stood, and glided toward the 20th century.

> "No country abounds in a greater degree with dangerous beasts than Southern Africa."
>
> —Charles Darwin

"PUFF ADDER BITES JOGGER THREE TIMES!" screeched the bold headline. A "colored" newsboy stood in the median, one foot on his bundle of papers to keep them from blowing away in the Capetown gale. I'm in South Africa all right, I thought. Fresh off the plane from a mild-mannered summer in California, I couldn't reckon with this bizarre world where raging winter storms spun out of the Southern Ocean still tasting of Antarctica, and poisonous snakes vented their reptilian angst on innocent joggers.

It had been five years since I had been to Capetown. Much had changed, and local surfer/photographer Lance Slabbert gave me the rundown as we tore through the gloom that creamed into the sloping sandstone cake layers of world-famous Table Mountain. South Africa could well be the most beautiful country in the world, especially for a surfer. I fell in love with the place long before I'd even been there, enchanted by Bruce Brown's voice-over in *The Endless Summer*: "If you want to be alone in South Africa, you're welcome to do so." That and his vistas of empty highways, buzzing veldt and huge sand dunes hiding perfect pointbreaks in sphinx-like secrecy. When California was all about black beaver-tail wetsuits, circling the wagons against outsiders, buying the "right" to surf the Ranch, lifeguards and blackball, South Africa promised a new, adventurous melding of archetypes: Allan Quatermain crossed with Kevin Naughton, a fresh romantic offshoot from the tired old roots of Waikiki beach boys and Santa Monica misanthropes.

But now, South Africa seems to be in sad decline. And it's nothing like what you think, not nearly as simple as your "Free Mandela" bumper sticker on the ol' Volvo. Say what you will about apartheid, injustice and civil rights from your lofty American pulpit, but unless you've been there, you have no opinion. South Africa is an antipodean America, with common bloodlines. In both cases, whites migrated away from bureaucracy into native tribes with Bible-thumping arrogance. The difference, and the real reason South Africa is in the international doghouse, is that our grim deeds were done long before CNN and bumper stickers.

Arm the Apaches with dirt-cheap AK-47s, waggle some Fervent Insurgency Dogma in front of them, and basically you've got South Africa in 1993. Driving around the outskirts of a city like Capetown, snipers take occasional potshots at passing motorists. Bridges and overpasses are approached with dread, as terrorists have taken to hurling bricks into oncoming windshields. The N-2 freeway out to the airport has been dubbed "Hell Run," as it passes near a huge squatter camp with an apparently limitless quarry of bricks. It's Super Mario Capetown, with everyone zooming through the narrow, hilly lanes, dodging Koopas and Goombas, seemingly always in a manic rush to reach home—in most cases pastoral white-washed Cape Dutch cottages that belie surveillance and alarm systems that would rival Fort Knox.

The second largest growth industry in South Africa is home protection: guns, alarms, video monitors, window bars. The largest is getting the hell out. The business sections of the newspapers are flooded with immigration ads entreating South Africa's best and brightest (and richest) to move overseas to more stable havens like Toronto, Sydney or Laguna Beach, where if a snake bit you it would probably be only once, and at least you could sue somebody or sell the screen rights.

Of course, there's always Namibia. Lots of people were moving up into that newly independent country, which was formerly a sort of territory of South Africa. I had stopped at Windhoek, Namibia's capital, on a flight years ago, leaving me with the impression that Namibia was 300,000 square miles of Bakersfield. But Lance had been up there on a surf trip recently, and his description of quaint colonial seaside towns, stately dunes, and lonely left pointbreaks sounded much more sporting than the usual surfari to J-Bay, which has become more and more a Surf City. I could picture Derek Hynd patrolling that fabled lava point, notebook in hand, wallowing in self-imposed exile, seeking his canine brethren. Also, Pro World was due to arrive soon, and that alone was a good reason to head off in the opposite direction.

"Our nature lies in movement; complete calm is death."

—Pascal

Leaving Capetown and driving to the Skeleton Coast is the spiritual equivalent of going on surfari from Dana Point to Vancouver . . . in 1936. The Namibian Coastline is roughly the same length as that of California, but with twice the total area. Namibia means "land of no people," and even then most of the million or so inhabitants live in landlocked Windhoek or a narrow swale of arable land along the northern border near Angola. The coast is basically empty.

Just a few hours out of Capetown the highway is deserted. Small towns are spaced farther and farther apart, finally giving way to forlorn, ramshackle settlements that seem to be nothing more than concessions to the shortcomings of the average gas tank. There are few towns on the coast from the cape all the way to Angola, as there are only a handful of decent harbors. Most can only be reached via a 50- or 100-mile sidetrack on a graded dirt road. Heading to the coast off of the N-7, the main north-to-south highway, these secondary roads can be traveled for hours without seeing another vehicle.

It seemed completely normal, then, when we pulled up at the legendary Elands Bay on a gorgeous, offshore, 6-foot morning and there was . . . no one out. There were a few guys camped next to their car, trying to work up a mojo next to a crude fire pit. They were in no rush. I got to fulfill a boyhood dream by surfing Elands as good as it gets for almost an hour, completely alone. It's a world-class left point often described as a flopped-negative cousin to Jeffreys Bay. But surfing in Atlantic waters on the west coast is a far cry from the comparative warmth of Jeffreys Bay 400 miles away in the more temperate Indian Ocean. At Elands the water was like cold Santa Cruz, about 53 degrees.

The icy Benguela current socks a stiff uppercut punch into the guts of southwest Africa, sweeping in chilled water from the Antarctic nether world. The water temperature is rarely over 55 degrees. Thick and pulpy with upwelled plankton, the increased water density feels "faster," and the illusion of speed is increased as you fly through the tangle of bull kelp, the muscular bulbs flashing by like the blurred white lines on a highway.

There were 300 miles more of promising coastline before the Namibian border. On the map, the coast was kinked with the telltale squiggles of one left point after another. But three quarters of this coastline is the domain of the infamous De Beers Diamond Company, which invented localism 60 years before Dora first kicked his board at a kook wearing cutoffs. Security measures and treatment of trespassers is rumored to be harsh, sometimes beyond the law. All things being equal, I'd rather face some grumpy, walrusine "owner" at the Ranch than an X-ray and sigmoidoscope at gunpoint.

Here is the world's Last Great Reserve of temperate climate surf, virtually untapped from Lambert's Bay to Walvis Bay. Seven hundred miles of points, reefs and beaches that have been a *sperrgebiet* or "forbidden region," since Duke Kahanamoku was about 6 years old. The same antediluvian alchemy that made this the richest diamond field in the world also gave it limitless surfing potential, with alluvial headlands and ancient, upthrust marine terraces forming a serrated coastline the length of Baja.

Lance had arranged for us to visit a 50-mile chunk of one of the mines. After filling out security-clearance forms and waiting around a few days, we were allowed to enter as "official visitors."

In one short afternoon, even with our limited access to the beaches, we catalogued a half-dozen world-class waves easily comparable to the Margaret River region of Western Australia. Headland points were spaced at regular intervals, often flanked by grinding reef peaks or wedging beachbreak—the Ranch if Wayne Lynch designed it. Toward evening we surfed a right point that was like a high-voltage Supertubes. Eight to 10 feet and no way of knowing if it had been surfed before. In the middle of the bay was a gaping left that poured over a shallow wedge of sandstone reef. From talking to people in the area, we're fairly certain some lucky guys surf on this coast occasionally. If you don't mind surfing alone in the kind of chilly waters that scream, "White shark!" like a berserk Ouija board, and if you don't object to the odd X-ray and personal body search, this place is for you.

The farther we got from Capetown, the deeper we plunged into Afrikaner territory. The accents grew thicker and thicker and the food more indigestible. Afrikaners are looked down upon as provincial rednecks by the English, but they really are the heart and soul of all that is good and bad in South Africa. The Afrikaans language sounds like variety show mimicry of Colonel Klink, a harsh-sounding derivative of Dutch and Flemish. "Thank you" sounds exactly like "buy a donkey," and "please," or "assebleif," sounds like some arcane gay password. And "drankwinkle," or "bottle shop," sounds like some monstrous derivative of the great Australian party trick "spitting the winkle," but let's not give them any ideas.

It was a Friday evening when we crossed the border into Namibia, and Afrikaner families were flooding over from their Spartan farm towns, heading into the parks and reserves of Namibia like beleaguered Norte Americanos stumbling into Baja for a little Margaritaville respite.

Afrikaners are great carnivores. Waiting in line at the border for our passports to get stamped, I exchanged pleasantries with a family who had seen our surfboards on the car. I told them we were going on up to the Skeleton Coast to do a little surfing, and they looked at me with that forced grin used the world over to tolerate eccentrics and crackpots. They were heading up to Windhoek on a pilgrimage to see the "1,000 Meters-O-Meat," an attempt to cook the world's biggest shish kebab at a rugby stadium. A black day indeed for the slower cattle in the herd, and a red-letter day for Clark W. Griswolds everywhere.

Some will contend that man's greatest achievement is language or flight or the printing press. But on a bone-rattling, kidney-torquing journey into the Namibian outback, you'd swear that the pinnacle of human left-brain accomplishment is . . . duct tape. After 750 miles of jouncing along at 85 mph, everything not welded in place was working loose. Mysterious little bolts and screws littered the floorboard, tapes warbled and choked, and the peanut butter never had to be stirred. This was the Skeleton Road, a bitumen artery through the middle of Namibia, ramrod straight at times for hundreds of miles. Twice a day a town would appear ahead, wavering in mirage, with osterizing dust-devils scraping across the flinty, rust-orange gravel plains. A gas station, some sad little plywood shanties and gaily painted donkey carts: a Baja fish camp plopped down in an artist's conception of Mars.

There are two strategies for occupants of the desert. Hole up and accept the worst, or migrate. The Namib Desert is the oldest desert in the world; its inhabitants have had some 80 million years to get their acts together. Ants lick the dew off one another's back, lions scavenge dead whales along the littoral, and the weltwitchia, the bizarre "living fossil plant," lives up to 2,000 years on the wafting fog.

The few surfers in Namibia have had to adapt to a brutal environment that is a long, long, way from Polynesia Idyll. The cold water creates a semi-permanent canopy of fog, up to 340 days a year. The water is made colder by the prevailing southwesterly trades, a chill rasp of a wind that churns up the cooler, nutrient-rich water from the deep, and gives the beaches a briny red-tide smell. The only surf not completely blown to rags by the southwesterlies are the twin left points of Robbenspunt, a hundred miles from the nearest population. Beach-break, beachbreak everywhere, and not a peak to surf. One day we scrutinized 50 miles of coast, and although it was a sunny, offshore, 4-foot day, and I applied the dogged search pattern used to survive 17 years of similar cruelty on California's Central Coast, we didn't find one decent peak.

By this time, Lance had imported his Performance Seals to add what magazine editors call "color contrast." I'm not a very colorful or even modern surfer. I have no tattoos, and if my fins slide out I feel a great shame. Our Performance Seals were very nice kids from Durban: Carl and Paul. Like almost all young South African surfers, they were polite, well-behaved gremmies who put their logos right where their sponsors told them and phoned home twice a week. They also had that unique adolescent ability to fold up and shut down like C3PO and sleep anywhere at the slightest hint of downtime.

And we had plenty of downtime on the hundred-mile drive up to Robbenspunt. Camping nearby was out of the question. Aside from the sandstorms and nightly jackal and hyena sorties, there was the biting, litter-box stench of 100,000 seals stewing in their own effluvia. Technically, it's illegal to surf the top point because the cape is a seal reserve, and the park wardens don't want the seals "startled." I don't see the sense in this, as seals are like cows: They're permanently startled. Anyway, the marine bovines have staked out the whole top of the point and swim through the lineup in such thick herds that the waves are literally warped into sagging ruin. A 6-foot wave will peel through this pinniped Ganges for hundreds of yards, finally elbowing its way into the uncontaminated final run down the point, which is still twice the length of a good Rincon wave.

Deeper into the bay is another point next to some settlement that appeared to have been built piece by piece from shipwreck detritus. Until recently, an old German caretaker would sit out on the porch with a shotgun to keep away pesky surfers. When we arrived, the place was deserted. We didn't see another surfer in two weeks of surfing here. Four- to 5-foot lines peeled over the delicately ribbed sand bottom, translucent green in the settled calm of the inner bay. Not a gnarly Indonesian racetrack, but not some snail's-pace California point, either. Surfers have been hounding Scorpion Bay for 15 years without getting surf as good as it gets here monthly.

In the winter months, high pressure areas fatten and bulge in the interior of southern Africa, occasionally steepening to form a hot, dry offshore wind not unlike the Santa Ana in California. This is the dreaded Namibian *ostwind*, an unnerving, grating rasp that scrapes up sand, melds into a gritty furnace blast, and brings life to a standstill for days at a time. Temperatures can exceed 100 degrees, and the sandstorms are so thick that you often can't see 20 yards ahead. During *ostwinds,* a rime of fine dust covers every surface in even the most tightly sealed home. Cars have their number plates scoured to illegibility. Teeth take on an unpleasant abrasive sensation. Tempers flare at stoplights, and after a week under the Vulcan canopy, the suicide rate always soars.

Driving around in a sandstorm, we watched huge rooster tails of sand curling off the crests of giant dunes being torn into tornadic rotors. Flung instantly into the sea, they flailed into the spume of oncoming waves, blotching the white spray into a brown haze. Sea birds fluttered in awkward side-slip with grimaces of strained concentration. In town, Lance had to jerk the car out of the path of one stout old Germanic matron who had wobbled into the road from either heat stroke or sand-blindness, walking with that erratic pattern that on the savanna says, "Fair game!"

In the desert, time is measured on a vaster scale than the clocks and calendars of man. Standing on the ridge of the highest dune for miles, my jacket and pants cracking in the wind like a luffing mainsheet, I watched a sandstorm swirl over thousands of acres of trackless dunes. Casting aside the measure of our pitiful 70 or so years on the planet, a deceitful benchmark, I could see this desert as a sort of anti-matter ocean. Even on our day-to-day clock, dunes will crest and "break" like an ocean wave when they get too steep, sending out a roar. How would the desert appear from the vantage point of thousands of years of time-lapse photography? Wouldn't it appear to swell and crest in the ceaseless wind side by side with the Atlantic?

People from rich, green lands have always had to reconcile their mortality when confronted by the desert. Here a plant may live 2,000 years, diamonds are forever, and a man's tracks may last a thousand years on the delicate gravel plains. In the rain forest, things topple hourly and decay under a riot of growth and change, but here in the desert, the ebb and flow of an entire race of people is a mere second hand on the geologic clock that marks the passage of waterless eons and patient, creeping dunes.

The Bushmen of the nearby Kalahari Desert have acquired from their desolate origins a pragmatic grasp of mortality not unlike that learned on the Skeleton Coast amid the poking ribs of men and ships long dead. To them, there is no afterlife, no trumpets blaring at Pearly Gates. "When we die, we die," they shrug. "The wind blows away our footprints and that is the end of us."

Surfacing
from Maverick's
by Matt Warshaw

Matt Warshaw (born 1960) is a former editor of Surfer
magazine. Here he describes a young surfer's experience
at Maverick's, the central California surf break known for
huge waves, 50-degree water, powerful currents and dangerous rock formations.

Sixteen-year-old Jay Moriarity from Santa Cruz was so intent on
paddling into his first wave of the day and pushing up into the
correct stance—and he nailed it, feet spread wide across the deck
of his board, head tucked, weight forward and low—that he
didn't at first realize he'd lifted off the water and was now surfing
through air, just ahead of the curl, thirty feet above sea level.

Moriarity, as the big-wave expression goes, didn't penetrate. The
wave had pulsed and expanded as it rolled over Maverick's reef,
passing quickly from canted to vertical to concave, at which point
Moriarity should have been two-thirds of the way down the face,
driving like a javelin for flat water. But a draft of wind had slipped
under the nose of Moriarity's surfboard—and instead here he was, still
in his best big-wave crouch, levitating near the wave's apex. Now the
nose of his board lifted up and backward onto a near-perfect vertical

axis, its brightly airbrushed underbelly exposed and sharply limned in the morning light. Beautiful and condemned. The crest hooked forward, and Moriarity's arms came up and spread out from either side of his board, creating a Maverick's tableau that couldn't be taken as anything other than a kind of crucifixion.

The religious metaphor is an easy one to make—since big-wave surfers themselves so often use spiritual terms to characterize and illustrate their sport—but it makes you wonder how God, or Lono, or any such divine presence, could have decided to flick Jay Moriarity, Maverick's youngest and sweetest surfer, into the abyss. He was *Jay,* no nickname, friendly, wholesome, and unjaded—as compared to Flea, Ratboy, Skindog, and a few of the other red-hot and moderately profane Santa Cruz surfers known collectively as the Vermin. Moriarity won sportsmanship awards at surf contests. Recalling his first day at Maverick's during a surf magazine interview, the Georgia-born teenager gushed with Mousketeer enthusiasm: "I felt like I had just conquered Mount Everest or won a Gold Medal in the Olympics! I really felt on top of the world!" For the past two years Moriarity had been openly thrilled with the practice and promise of riding huge surf. He fell asleep thinking about big waves, then dreamed big-wave dreams. When the surf was down, he drove to Maverick's to survey the angles and contours of the reef, like a Formula One driver walking the track before a race. He wrote essays about big-wave surfing. Over the summer he'd paddled thirty-five miles across Monterey Bay to help build stamina and strength. For a moment, in fact, while still airborne, unaware that he'd just launched into what would soon be described as the most spectacular big-wave wipeout on record, Moriarity had the confidence to tell himself, "No problem, this one's *made.*"

The previous evening, at about 9 p.m., halfway through his evening shift in the kitchen at Pleasure Point Pizza in Santa Cruz, Moriarity phoned the National Weather Service for the updated buoy and weather report. For the past few days, he'd been tracking a North Pacific storm, and his eyebrows went up in stages as he discovered that the surf was going to be bigger than he'd thought, and it was due to arrive in just a few hours. Moriarity had ridden Maverick's twice that season already, and twice the season before. Driven to distraction by the prospect of a fifth session tomorrow, he clocked out, drove to Pleasure Point, suited up, and hit the water for a soothing round of night surfing.

At 5 a.m. the next morning, Moriarity steered his mother's Datsun pickup north on Highway One out of Santa Cruz, a pair of ten-foot, eight-inch surfboards stacked diagonally in the truck bed, their back ends jutting out past the tailgate. An hour later he pulled off the highway near Pillar Point Harbor, just a few hundred yards north of the Half Moon Bay city limit. Maverick's wasn't visible, but out past the harbor jetty, Moriarity could see smooth, wide-spaced ribbons of swell moving toward shore. Big for sure. Maybe bigger than he'd ever seen it.

Another two dozen people—surfers from San Francisco, Santa Cruz, Half Moon Bay, and Pacifica, along with a few surf photographers and spectators—were also driving toward Maverick's in the predawn light. Most parked in the small dirt lot just east of the Pillar Point headland, but Moriarity parked near the harbor, where he was going to catch a ride on *Lizzie-Lynn*, a twenty-six-foot fishing boat hired by one of the photographers. Moriarity unloaded his car and jogged toward the dock, a surfboard under each arm and a nylon backpack hanging off one shoulder. The weather was dry and brittle, in the upper 40s, but a steady east wind made it seem colder. Moriarity wore a black sweat-shirt, jeans, and sneakers, with a black wool watch-cap pulled down low on his forehead. He stepped aboard *Lizzie-Lynn*, nodding and smiling to photographer Bob Barbour and the boat captain as he set his boards down, then he brought both hands up to his mouth and blew, to warm them. The boat began to pitch and roll as it cleared the harbor entrance, but it was a short ride, and ten minutes later *Lizzie-Lynn* pulled into a deepwater channel adjacent to Maverick's, about seventy-five yards south of the breaking surf.

It was just past 7 a.m. Ten riders were already in the water, loosely clustered and sitting on their boards, alert but casual as they watched the ocean and waited. The surf had been relatively calm during the boat's approach. Now, almost on cue, a set of waves shifted through the water about a half mile past the surfers—all of whom snapped to attention like pointers. One of them dropped and began sprint-paddling to the west, recognizing that the advancing waves were going to break ten or twenty yards beyond the group's current position. The other surfers, in a pack, followed.

Moriarity watched the first wave track across the distant part of the reef, which served as a kind of anteroom for Maverick's-bound swells. The wave, shaped like a broad-based pyramid, grew steadily, then fringed along the crest as it intersected with the group of surfers, their arms like pinwheels as they clambered up the face and dropped, safe, down the back slope. No takers. Not even an exploratory sidelong look. Everyone vanished from sight as the wind aerated the uppermost few inches of water and spun out an enormous sunlit corona of mist, which trailed behind the wave like a cape.

The crest arced down and exploded across the flat water with a low-pitched ripping noise, as if the air itself had split open, and the wave transformed into a cyclonic thirty-by-fifteen-foot tube, through which the rural tree-lined cliffs of Moss Beach, two miles away, were briefly visible. The canopy then imploded and a geyser of water shot out from the now-shrinking mouth of the tube, like a sharply exhaled cloud of smoke. A "spitter"—the salacious and climactic big-wave moment. The wave rumbled on, still big, powerful, and noisy, but dissipating, until it washed over a stand of rocks thirty seconds later and poured into the nearby lagoon.

Jay Moriarity stood like a tuning fork on the deck of *Lizzie-Lynn*, staring, almost vibrating with nervous anticipation, three words looping through his mind—*huge and perfect, huge and perfect.* Then a pragmatic thought: *too much wind.*

Surfers welcome a gentle land-to-sea breeze—an "offshore" wind—because it brushes out the nautical flaws, chops, and burrs and casts the sea's littoral, or near-shore, field in a dreamy sort of brine-sparkle. The wind on this particular morning, though, was of a different order. A 20-knot easterly was being amplified through the nearby coastal range mountain passes, then amplified again as it whipped up and around each breaking wave. An incoming surfer, Moriarity knew, would be temporarily deafened by the noise and partially blinded by the saltwater spray blowing off the front of his board. You'd have to do part of the takeoff by feel, he told himself. And once into the wave, you'd have to get low and *stay* low to fight down through the wind. Don't straighten up. Penetrate.

As he ran down his tactical checklist, Moriarity watched Evan Slater wheel his board around and paddle into the second wave of the set. Slater got to his feet smoothly, but the wind flicked him sideways—just like that. He landed midway down the face on the small of his back, skipped once, twice, then disappeared as the tube threw out around him like a giant blown-glass bubble and collapsed.

"Oh my *God!*" someone on the boat yelled. Two or three others added yowling surfer-shouts, thrilled and shocked, and everyone scanned the wave's white-foaming aftermath until Slater's head popped up about a hundred feet shoreward from where he'd gone down. More wild shrieks of amazement—"That was in*sane!*"—voices tinged with nervous relief. *Lizzie-Lynn* had been in the channel less than two minutes.

Moriarity squatted down, unzipped his nylon backpack, and pulled out a full-length hood-to-ankle neoprene wetsuit, black with blue accents, plus a long-sleeve polypropylene undershirt, a pair of wetsuit booties, and a pair of webbed gloves. The ocean temperature was a skin-tightening 52 degrees, but with this layered outfit he might stay in the water for hours. Moriarity could get fully rigged-out in less than two minutes, but he stopped halfway through and told himself to slow down. Stripped to the waist, now unaware of the cold, he breathed in, counting slowly to five. Then a five-count exhale as the wind gusted and the arm pieces of his wetsuit fluttered around his knees. Another breath to five, then he lost patience, rammed his arms into the rubber

sleeves, zipped up, grabbed his board, and slipped over the edge of
Lizzie-Lynn, gasping as he hit the water.

As Moriarity paddled toward the Maverick's lineup, Half Moon Bay's
twelve thousand residents were getting showered and dressed, pouring
coffee, reviewing the Monday morning headlines, and glancing outside to take note of the ongoing stretch of temperate weather. Com-
muters moved onto the highways, driving north to San Francisco,
south to San Jose, east to Silicon Valley. Most of Half Moon Bay High's
students were still sleeping through their first few hours of Christmas
vacation.

What Half Moon Bay locals were not doing was paying any attention to the fact that Moriarity, Slater, and the rest were at that moment
tilting against waves bigger than anything surfers had ever faced anywhere in the world outside of Hawaii. Maverick's would in the days
ahead produce international headlines. It would eventually produce
bigger surf. But that morning, December 19, 1994, the huge wind-
sculpted waves were changing the big-wave surfing landscape—and
doing so in showy, dramatic style.

That it was happening in near-seclusion was partly a matter of geog-
raphy, as Maverick's is hidden from view behind Pillar Point's silt-and-
sandstone headland and the adjacent boat harbor breakwater. But
Maverick's was also relatively unknown: it had publicly debuted to the
surf world just eighteen months earlier, in a six-page *Surfer* magazine
feature story. For two years before that, it had been something of a
shared secret among twenty-five or so northern California surfers.
Before that, no one outside of Half Moon Bay had even heard of Maverick's, and it was ridden by only one person, a local carpenter.

In addition, Half Moon Bay wasn't a hard-core surf town, and never
had been. San Francisco, twenty-five miles north, had long occupied a
special niche in the surf world—partly due to the incredibly photogenic
wave that breaks under the southern span of the Golden Gate Bridge,

but more so because of the curious and pleasing fact that surfing could take root and flourish on the perimeter of such a famous, sophisticated urban center. Santa Cruz, meanwhile, fifty-eight miles south of Half Moon Bay, had a strong claim as the world's greatest surf city. High-quality surf breaks are strung together like beads along the Santa Cruz coastline, and the near-Homeric scope of local surf history goes back to 1885, when Edward, David, and Cupid Kawananakoa, three blue-blooded Hawaiian teenagers attending a local military school, crafted boards for themselves from redwood planks and tested the shorebreak near the San Lorenzo rivermouth—becoming not just the first surfers in Santa Cruz but the first surfers in America. Wetsuit magnate Jack O'Neill opened his first shop here in 1959. Tom Curren, three-time world champion and American surfing icon, opened his 1990 world title run with a contest win at Steamer Lane, Santa Cruz's best-known break. A few years later, Darryl Virostko, Josh Loya, Chris Gallagher, Peter Mel, Kenny Collins, Jay Moriarity, and other young Santa Cruz locals had collectively become the hottest regionally connected troupe of surfers in California.

Half Moon Bay, meanwhile, wasn't off the surfing map entirely in 1994. Some of the reefs north of town occasionally produced good, powerful waves, and the long crescent-shaped beach south of the harbor was a fallback when the surf was small. Two Half Moon Bay surf shops were doing slow but steady business. Local surf history, though, was thin and mostly unrecorded. Just a few people, for instance, knew the story of Maverick, the white-haired German shep-herd who, one winter's day in 1961, tore into the water behind three Half Moon Bay surfers as they paddled out to try the distant waves off Pillar Point. One of the surfers, Alex Matienzo, who lived with Mav-erick's owner, thought the surf looked too rough for the dog. Matienzo paddled back to the beach, whistled Maverick in, and tied him to the car bumper. The waves ended up being too rough for the surfers as well; they soon returned to the beach without having done much riding, and left Pillar Point alone after that. Because Maverick the dog had obviously gotten the most out of the experience, Matienzo and his friends called the intriguing but vaguely sinister Pillar Point surf break "Maverick's Point"—or just Maverick's.

Surfing and surf culture hadn't yet made any real impression in Half Moon Bay, which by 1994 was known more for its weathered rows of cut-flower greenhouses and its neatly groomed acres of brussels sprouts, broccoli, and artichokes, for the horse stables, the stately Beaux-Arts city hall building, the sublime foothill views along Highway 92, and an elaborate and well-attended annual pumpkin festival appropriate for a city billing itself as "The Pumpkin Capital of the World." While strip malls had gone up near downtown and touristy seafood restaurants and nautical-themed gift shops were clustered by the harbor, local slow-growth advocates had been masterful at keeping large-scale commercialization at bay. They had shut down all attempts to widen Highway One and expand the Half Moon Bay airport. Residents, for the most part, were happy to be at a friendly but distinct remove from San Francisco.

Half Moon Bay, the oldest city in San Mateo County, nonetheless has a long and interesting mercantile connection to the sea. Portuguese whalers, in the late nineteenth century, dragged California grays and humpbacks onto the sandy hook of beach just inside Pillar Point, where they rendered slabs of blubber in enormous iron cook pots. Wooden ships were often gutted on the nearby reefs, some producing horrible scenes of splintered planks and floating corpses, others bringing sudden windfall. "Locals rushed to the scene," writes June Morrall in *Half Moon Bay Memories*, describing the gently beached and evacuated *Columbia* steamer, which ran aground in 1897, "and stripped luxurious staterooms of their white and gold molding. Others removed copper wire and within days every yard in the vicinity proudly displayed a new copper wire clothesline."

During Prohibition, Half Moon Bay bootleggers filled their customized shallow-hulled boats with cases of Canadian-made scotch, rum, gin, and champagne, darted through the surf at night, and made their prearranged drops in the shadowy coves south of Pillar Point. Most of the liquor was rushed up the coast to San Francisco speakeasies, though some went straight into the hollowed-out walls of nearby roadhouse/dance hall/bordellos like the Princeton Hotel and the Ocean Beach Tavern. Federal authorities were for the most part out-generalled by the bootleggers, but in 1932, a midnight skirmish between a Coast Guard patrol boat and a local rumrunner in high seas off Moss Beach resulted in rifle fire, machine gun fire, *cannon* fire, a kidnapped government agent, some hypothermic open-ocean swimming, two separate chases, and four hundred cases of high-quality booze being tossed overboard.

Big fines and the prospect of serious prison time may have forced bootleggers to run this kind of no-surrender gauntlet. But it must have been fantastic open-ocean sport, too. "You experience a thrill and fear at the same time," big-wave surfing pioneer Buzzy Trent wrote in 1965, in a passage that might apply equally to Prohibition bootleggers and Maverick's surfers. "You hear that crack and thunder, you feel the wet spray, [and] you just power through, hoping you won't get the ax. And then if you *do* make it, you get a wonderful feeling inside."

Jay Moriarity had a different feeling inside—not so wonderful—as he lifted off the face of his giant wave, spread his arms, and hung like a marionette just ahead of the crest.

Ten minutes earlier, Moriarity had paddled without hesitation from the starboard side of *Lizzie-Lynn* to the Maverick's lineup, smiling and calling out "Hey" to three or four surfers. He offered a curious, irony-free greeting to Evan Slater, who'd returned from his awful wipeout just a few minutes earlier: "Evan! Fun out here, huh?"

Then another set lifted into view, prompting a few moments of lineup shuffling and repositioning, and by luck or design Moriarity was on the spot for the first wave. Nothing but reflex now as he spun his board and began paddling, eyes nearly shut against the wind, barely conscious of the shouts of nearby surfers—one voice yelled, "Go, Jay, go!" or "No, Jay, no!"; he later couldn't remember which—all of whom were freaking at the growing size of Moriarity's wave as he got to his feet.

Moriarity, thirty feet above the trough, levitated for a little more than a second. The wind then flipped his board back over the top of the wave, and the curl, distended and grossly thick, pitched forward and blotted Moriarity from view. For a half-beat the wave poured forward, untouched and unmarked. Then Moriarity's surfboard reappeared from the wave's back slope and was swiftly pulled forward "over the falls" into the growing thundercloud of whitewater—a bad sign. Moriarity's board was tethered to his ankle by a fifteen-foot, nearly half-inch-thick urethane leash, and the only way it could have been brought back into play was if Moriarity himself, deep and unseen inside the wave, had been dragged down into Maverick's aptly named Pit.

The wave was now a thirty-foot levee of whitewater, crowned by fifty feet of swirling mist and vapor. Below the surface, energy and mass burst downward, creating a field of vertical-flushing gyratory columns, and Moriarity, trapped inside one of these columns, spun end over end until his back and shoulders were fixed against the ocean floor. He clenched, and a bubble of oxygen rushed past his teeth. Maverick's was a deepwater break, he'd been told; nobody ever hit bottom. The next wave would be overhead in another ten or twelve seconds, and Moriarity wondered if, from this depth, he could get to the surface—to air—before it arrived. A two-wave hold-down put a surfer one big step closer to drowning, and Moriarity had used this grim fact to inspire his training, but never had he imagined himself pinned to the rocks like an entomological display, trying to figure out if the overhead Neptunian rumble was from the diminishing first wave or the oncoming second.

He at least had his bearings. The trip down was disorienting, the water now dark, but Moriarity didn't have to pause to figure out which way to swim. Navigation is often a problem during a big-wave wipeout. Underwater flips and turns can disable a surfer's internal compass to the point where he might begin swimming for the surface only to bang head-first into the reef.

Moriarity pushed off and took a huge, sweeping breaststroke. He opened his eyes to near-opaque blackness. Four more strokes, five, legs in a flutter kick, exhaling slowly, eyes staring upward, stroke, the light becoming a diffuse gray-green, stroke, throat clamped shut, then one last thrust to break the surface—and he threw his head back, mouth stretched open. He'd been down for just over twenty seconds, but he'd beat the second wave—barely. Two quick breaths, and he hunched over defensively as the whitewater roared over, sending him on another underwater loop, shorter but just as violent. Pinpoints of light were zipping across his field of vision by the time he resurfaced.

Moriarity's breath was deep and ragged. There was no third wave. His respiratory rate eased, and as his eyes refocused, he saw that his surfboard was broken in half: the smaller piece—the tail section—was still attached to his leash; the rest floated nearby. Evan Slater suddenly appeared, looking concerned. Did he need any help? Moriarity shook his head. No, he'd be okay. He swam over to the front half of his surfboard, hoisted himself on deck, and began slowly paddling back to *Lizzie-Lynn*.

In the late eighties, a surf magazine writer theorized that the essential requirement for big-wave riding is not courage, or daring, or fitness, but a nonarousable imagination. Where an ordinary surfer taking full measure of a wave like Maverick's will lose himself in one of a near-endless number of death-by-misadventure scenarios, the big-wave surfer, fantasy-free, paddles out with some degree of aplomb. And as the untroubled imagination reduces fear and anxiety beforehand, it may also smooth things out afterward. Jay Moriarity, a week later, couldn't do much more than sketch out in the most obvious terms the big-wave vignette—generally described as the worst wipeout, or at least the worst *looking* wipeout, in surfing history—that soon appeared on the cover of *Surfer* and the front section of the *New York Times Magazine*. "I started to stand up," he told *Surfer*, "and thought, 'This will be a cool wave.' Then the whole thing ledged out and I had time to think, 'Oh shit. This is not good.'"

But maybe that's unfair. Moriarity's banal reaction may have had less to do with a deficient imagination than with the general inarticulateness of sixteen-year-olds. Or perhaps he was just following the form of big-wave protocol that says, play it down, play it *cool.*

Either way, there was nothing banal about what Moriarity did for an encore that morning. After tossing the pieces of his broken board onto the deck of *Lizzie-Lynn,* he took a short breather, grabbed his reserve board, ran a bar of sticky wax across the top for traction, and paddled back into the lineup.

Forty-five minutes later he caught another wave, nearly as big as the first one, and made it. In the next five hours he caught eight more waves—and made them all.

The Last Wave

by Peter Wilkinson

Hawaii-based surfer Mark Foo flew from Hawaii to California just before Christmas, 1994. Foo came to ride the big waves at Maverick's.

t made sense that he would go. Maverick's was finally breaking, waves 15 to 25 feet, perhaps the best swell in years. Reports also indicated sunny weather, unusual for what is normally a gray, forbidding strip of beach. In his oceanfront home on Oahu's North Shore, Mark Foo dug out his plane ticket, an open round trip on United he'd had for almost a year, stashed in a drawer. It was Dec. 22, 1994.

Foo and Ken Bradshaw, another professional big-wave surfer, drove down U.S. Highway 2 past the sugar-cane fields and pineapple plantations for the red-eye from Honolulu to San Francisco. Maverick's lies about 22 miles south of San Francisco, near Half Moon Bay. Full of anticipation, Foo had trouble sleeping on the plane. Waves on the North Shore had been disappointing all winter, the victim of fast-moving low-pressure systems and disruptive southwestern winds. When you devote your life to riding big waves, waiting months, sometimes years for consistent, organized sets, you have to be ready to rush after them on a moment's notice. Would Maverick's still be breaking big by the time they got there, Foo wondered. Or would he be disappointed again?

One of the world's top riders of big waves (more than 15 feet) for more than a decade, Foo had made his reputation surfing Waimea Bay on the North Shore, big-wave riding's Indianapolis Motor Speedway, a proving ground where reputations are made and lost. With its tropical sun, aquamarine water and gentle trade winds, Waimea is the sacred setting where big-wave surfing was born in the late 1950s.

Recently discovered by the California hard core, Maverick's offers a chilly vibe. Maverick's is perilously rocky. The water is often 50 degrees, and the waves seem thick and nasty. You don't see untied bikini tops there. What you do notice, up on a cliff, is an Air Force radar installation brooding like the break itself. Ambience was not Foo's first concern, however. To him, Maverick's was the only major big-wave spot he had yet to conquer, the only significant challenge still unmet.

As Foo and Bradshaw flew over the Pacific, a large press contingent was preparing to descend on Maverick's. The surf magazines would be out in force with photographers staked out on a cliff overlooking the break, bobbing alongside the waves in rented fishing boats and buzzing overhead in a helicopter. The Hawaiians were coming: Foo, 36, the small, frenetic first-generation Chinese-American who'd made surfing a career and done so loudly; Bradshaw, 42, the burly, square-jawed former high-school football player from Texas who earned a modest living shaping boards and who believed big waves and big money didn't mix; and Brock Little, a spidery, fearless North Shore regular who at 27 was perhaps the hottest of the young big-wave stars and who in temperament was part Bradshaw, part Foo.

Throughout his 11 years as a big-wave rider, Mark Foo always followed an agenda larger than that of the so-called soul surfers, purists like Bradshaw who surfed big waves for the sheer gut-spinning thrill of it. Nobody doubted Foo's commitment. He tracked storms and pored over weather-service faxes like other full-time riders. But Foo also invested endless hours in decidedly nonsoulful endeavors. He actively sought magazine covers and between Waimea sessions networked like an investment banker—in person, by fax and by phone, at times running up bills of $2,000 a month. Foo's stated mission: to raise the profile of big-wave surfing worldwide, to help members of the unwet world understand it. If Mark Foo's profile was raised in the process— and it was—so be it.

Foo's self-promotion had always bugged Bradshaw. "Mark, above all else," says Bradshaw, "was a businessman." Foo described himself in his résumé as "surfing's pre-eminent big-wave rider" and "surfing's consummate living legend." Bradshaw felt that was pushing it. He tolerated Foo because the guy could surf. At 36, Mark Foo was actually getting better. Even Bradshaw admits that, grudgingly, and has a theory about why: "Mark realized he had to live up to the image he'd created." With squadrons of guys out in the water these days crowding the lineup, taking off sometimes six at once, big-wave surfing was becoming even more dangerous. In the past few years, Bradshaw had come to regard Foo less as an annoyance and more as a trusted co-pilot, the sort of veteran who knew how to take care of himself in almost any situation.

United Flight 184 landed in San Francisco at 5:20 a.m., a few minutes ahead of schedule. It was still dark. Foo was exhausted. As the skies brightened over the airport, Bradshaw handled the Alamo car rental and drove the two of them into town to rendezvous with a couple of local surfers, the first stop before the 35-minute trip to Maverick's. The plan was to surf all day, then fly back the next night in time for Christmas Eve in Hawaii. With Bradshaw at the wheel and two big-wave "guns" strapped to the roof, Foo dozed in the back seat, resting up for the last ride of his life.

The moment in surfing history that crystallized Mark Foo's reputation as both a big-wave rider and a salesman had occurred a decade earlier on the stellar afternoon of Jan. 18, 1985, at Waimea Bay. That day, Foo, then 26 years old, paddled into a behemoth estimated at 30 to 35 feet, close to what is generally considered the outer limit of ridable size.

A west swell started pumping out 15- to 18-foot sets in the morning. Fire-station rescue helicopters swooped down to snare a few riders grabbed by the rip currents. After noon, Waimea got even bigger: classic Waimea, epic Waimea, real Waimea. Whatever you wanted to call it, using whatever mythic-heroic surf term that came to mind. Mark Foo arrived on the beach and did his ritual public stretching. Foo's body, as usual, looked ejected from the Perfect Surfer mold: He was only 5 feet 8 inches tall, which helped him keep a low center of gravity on the board, and he was lithe and muscular, which is ideal for quick maneuvering to the takeoff spot and inside the tube. Foo went out that day on a 9-foot-6-inch gun feeling kind of rusty; recovering from the flu, he'd surfed only once in the previous two weeks.

Then something amazing happened. A wave variously estimated at between 48 and 80 feet steamrollered through the bay. Foo and a couple of other riders dove for cover, Foo being the only one to come up with his board still leashed to his leg. More surfers grabbed helicopter rides out of the maelstrom, having tasted enough epic Waimea for one day.

"The helicopter guys come out to get me, but I wave them off 'cause I figure I can ride one in," Foo wrote later in a local newspaper. A 30-foot-plus wave roared in—as tall as a three-story building. (It was probably even larger; Hawaiian big-wave riders are famous for their conservative wave-size estimates. A wave that is 10 feet from trough to peak probably has a 20-foot face when cresting but will still be called a 10-foot wave.) Foo scurried up on his board, dropped into his trademark low crouch, got his front arm straight out and stationary. "But then it sucks out in the middle of the channel," wrote Foo, "and I'm in the lip, bunching myself over what looks like a moving cliff. There was really no chance, but I was already committed and charging. I free-fall vertically on my feet—a good 20 feet before impacting the bottom—then the lip of the wave unloads on top of me. The thing about wiping out at Waimea is that you are going so fast, and there is so much power that when you hit, it's not like hitting water, it feels more like concrete, and today the water was particularly hard. I have the worst wipeout of my life, break my 9-foot Lunder thruster, lose my watch, and the bay is white water all the way across."

So Foo hadn't technically ridden the wave. He'd ridden lots of big waves, make no mistake. He was extremely good at it—as brave as they come and an innovator, probably the first guy to ride a tri-fin board at Waimea. But the ballsy attempt on that 30 footer became legendary, especially when Foo's version of events moved over the news wires and later ended up in an expanded form in various surf magazines. A big-wave rider for about two years, Mark Foo was suddenly a recognized star. He commanded new respect at Waimea and at Sunset and Pipeline, the two other main big-wave breaks on the North Shore.

Some sages there, guys like Ken Bradshaw, who'd surfed the place almost daily since the early 1970s, began to wonder whether Foo, the upstart, deserved his new status and whether sufficient dues had been paid. Unlike Bradshaw, Foo had not sought to ride big waves almost from the moment he stuck his toe in the water as a boy. Foo bought his first board at the age of 11 with money he saved from a paper route. He concentrated almost exclusively on small waves, getting up at 3 a.m. to surf before school and then sessioning again after classes, perfecting his technique. "He never considered doing anything else," says SharLyn Foo-Wagner, his older sister. "He was completely focused and obsessed."

When the family moved back to Washington, D.C., in 1970 after two years in Hawaii—Mark's dad, Charles, worked in the U.S. Foreign Service—Mark was 12 and despondent. "He cried every day," recalls his mother, Lorna Foo. "He locked himself in his bedroom and kicked the door." Mark begged to go live near the water with the family of a friend in Pensacola, Fla. "You gotta talk them into it!" Mark implored SharLyn. Reluctantly, Lorna Foo assented, hoping for a quick end to her son's surfing mania. Mark kept buying boards and assuring his mother that nobody surfed past the age of 35. In 1974 the family moved back to Honolulu. A year later Mark blew off his commencement at Roosevelt High to go surfing.

Mark Foo lasted one semester at the University of Hawaii. He joined the competitive surfing circuit in 1977 and traveled the world. Over the next five years his ranking never broke 66th, and he struggled financially. To fulfill a strong sense of personal ambition—and a need to prove to his mother that surfers weren't losers—Foo began to reconsider his options. And so it was in 1983, only two years before that epic day at Waimea, when Foo made the switch from small waves to big, thus beginning a sort of second surfing career.

The sport is not a crowded one. Compared with the thousands of men and women who surf small waves (6 feet or less), only about 50 men around the world surf big waves with any consistency. It can take an already proficient surfer three to five years of regular practice to competently surf waves in the 10-foot range, then years more to gradually climb the ladder and adjust to waves that are 5, 10 and then—for the very few—15 feet bigger. "It comes down to desire," says Bobby Owens, a longtime friend of Foo's who has ridden big waves for two decades, mainly on the North Shore. "A lot of people don't want to get near big waves."

The sport's macho mystique draws the most dedicated individualists, and they are a patient breed. Because waves are so unpredictable—the sport's World Series, the Quiksilver/Eddie Aikau invitational, usually held at Waimea Bay, hasn't taken place since 1990 for lack of steady 20-foot surf—big-wave surfing has historically had trouble attracting major sponsors, the sort of companies accustomed to pumping their money into predictable events held in man-made stadiums and sheltered from nature's whims. Big-wave surfers get off on the exclusiveness of their club—that what they experience can never be understood by the great dry majority: nature's enormous power, increasing exponentially with every few feet of wave, felt through the soles of their feet. "The only people who understand big-wave riders are the people who race at 200 miles per hour or parachute out of planes," says big-wave expert Brock Little.

That thrill of hurtling down a wall of water produces a constant craving for waves. Foo's analysis of the sensation was oddly Zen-like. "For me, the more adverse the situation, the more peaceful I am," he once said. "That's when I become truly centered. It's really funny. Basically I'm kind of high-strung and nervous. I'm scared of speed, I'm scared of heights, I don't gamble. I'm not really into athletics. Surfing big waves is the combination of all these things that are against my nature."

Approaching the riding of big waves as something less than a calling—like Foo did—turned off pros like Bradshaw, who never invited Foo over to his house on Ke Nui Road. Foo asked Bradshaw over once. "Our relationship was in the water," Bradshaw says tersely. Foo openly dismissed soul-surfer thinking as rather precious: Why not earn money surfing? If you could make money doing what you loved like other pro athletes, then you had more time to do what you loved. You had more time to surf instead of working as a lifeguard or painting houses or shaping boards. What was impure about that?

These ideas became central to what Mark Foo referred to as his Foo-losophy, and they enabled him to become one of the first professional surfers to be sponsored by a major nonsurf company, Michelob, in the mid-1980s. Earning $800 a month, Foo took to wearing bright yellow and purple wet suits and riding logo-slathered boards. "That's how the wheels of industry turn!" Foo would exult, working the phones, monitoring the progress of his various surf-related ventures. He talked incessantly, even while eating, food spraying from his mouth. A friend says: "Mark was always trying to find the right angle, find the right sponsorship, meet the right people. You'd get a headache if you took all his marketing ideas seriously."

With a financial assist from his mother, Foo even delved into real estate—the surfing kind. He opened Surf 'n Bed, a hostel for traveling surfers, around the bend from Waimea Bay. Board-toting nomads came in droves. What could be cooler than chartering all the way to the vaunted North Shore from Sydney, Australia, or Sao Paulo, Brazil, or Santa Cruz, Calif., and actually hanging out with a surfer god in a place where you paid 10 bucks a night to bunk? As Surf 'n Bed expanded—called Backpackers Vacation Inn International today, capacity 100—Foo, a skilled delegator, turned day-to-day operations of the business over to his sister SharLyn, who had left her job as a flight attendant for Eastern Airlines.

Already a local celebrity for his biweekly surfing-news column for the *North Shore News*, a free paper in Haleiwa, Hawaii, Foo set about raising his national and international profile. He hosted surf shows on ESPN and Prime Network. Unlike a lot of surfers, Foo could clearly convey what he knew on television. Chasing swells, he surfed the world: Australia, Bali, Nicaragua, Tahiti, Peru, Mexico, Brazil, South Africa and Japan. Accounts of some of these trips led to features for *Surfer* and *Surfing* magazines, on the covers of which Foo appeared many times—and the photographers of which, through no coincidence, became regular guests, gratis, at the Backpackers Inn.

That largess, at least during Foo's early years on big waves, did not necessarily carry over to fellow surfers. Foo disliked sharing waves; he'd drop in and stay in, forcing another surfer attempting the same wave to veer off. So incensed was Bradshaw during one session that he swam up, tore a fin off Foo's board and shouted, "You don't have any respect for anybody out here but yourself!" At the 1986 Eddie Aikau invitational, when the waves at Waimea stayed at 20 feet for eight hours, Foo finished second. Several months later he announced in a magazine, "I don't think anyone surfs at 20-foot Waimea better than I do."

Foo partisans like the accomplished big-wave rider Dennis Pang saw Foo as a prototype, a man for our fame-addled age: big-wave surfer as marketer, a wiseman who could explode the surfer-as-gelhead stereotype. Sales of surf clothing were going through the roof in the mid-1980s, hawked mainly by high-performance small-wave riders, while big-wave surfing meandered along as lazily as it had since the late 1950s—the frontier days of the North Shore—its riders admired but comparatively undercompensated. "There's a saying that the Chinese can make a dollar out of 15 cents," says Pang, a friend of Foo's for 25 years. "Well, Mark could make $5 out of 15 cents." Foo pushed people's buttons even when money wasn't involved. "There was an ulterior motive in everything he did," Pang says. "He'd call me up and ask me to go out just because he didn't want to drive." Like Foo's other friends, Pang keeps pointing out that no matter what, the dude could *surf*. In the past few years, young big-wave surfers have been drawn to the Foo-losophy. "Mark worked hard at making money, and I loved it," says Brock Little. "The more money he brought in to the sport, I knew I'd be getting some of it." Promotional deals with Gotcha and other companies earn Little around $100,000 a year—top big-wave dollar.

Another subject Foo loved to discuss in connection with his career as a surfer, another Fooism that became a cliché, was his belief that he would die surfing big waves. "To experience the ultimate thrill," his refrain went, "you have to be prepared to pay the ultimate price." When the *Challenger* exploded, Foo wrote, "They died happy. That's the way I want to go." Ken Bradshaw detected further image burnishing as the motive behind talk like this. If Foo existed so close to death, then he must be riding the most dangerous waves, right? And, as a friend notes, "Mark talked about dying because it made good copy."

Nobody, of course, took Foo's preparing-for-my-own-martyrdom rap seriously. Why should they? No top-echelon big-wave rider had ever died on a wave, as remarkable as that sounded. Injuries? All the time. Foo's list: a large keloid on his left shoulder from an encounter with the bottom, a broken leg, a broken ankle, a jammed neck, tendon damage in one knee—the usual stuff. When he wasn't at the chiropractor, Foo was in physical therapy or eating Chinese herbs. (One current big-wave star, barely out of his teens, is starting to show signs of osteoporosis.) But a pro had yet to barrel into the morgue.

A primary reason for this is that most pros are not reckless. Riding big waves as well as he did, through years of sponsorships by a raft of corporations, Mark Foo carefully followed two basic principles: Publicity value aside, avoid massive wipeouts like the one he had at Waimea in 1985, and if one occurs, take levelheaded steps to survive such a wipeout. Usually the ocean is not vengeful and rewards rational behavior. This isn't to say, of course, that it is averse to teaching hard lessons of respect.

Foo could sense a wipeout coming: He'd taken off too late under the canopy of the wave and didn't have enough time to get down the face, and his board was losing contact with the water. Gulping a few short, deep breaths, then one big one, Foo would dive straight toward the bottom—this is called getting penetration—and wait out the "hold down." Wiping out in a big wave, pros say, is like being blown down the street with water from a high-pressure fire hose.

The longer the hold down, the tighter the ocean closes its grip on the human brain. Anxiety is superseded by a feeling of well-being, a fuzzy sensation, and the desire to struggle recedes. Foo called this the brown phase of consciousness. It is a prelude to drowning. Usually, though, the mind sends out a blast of adrenaline, enough to send the thankful surfer spluttering to the surface. Two-wave hold downs, in which a second wave whacks the surfer after the first without giving him a chance to surface for a gulp of air, are extremely rare. So it's essential to be able to ride out the hammering, hold your breath for 10 to 15 seconds and, above all, not panic.

Until 1989 the notion of big waves in California was scoffed at. Jeff Clark knew better. Growing up on the beach in Miramar, going to Half Moon Bay High, Clark was always studying the ocean from his dining-room window at home. Breaking over a reef a quarter to a half mile off nearby Pillar Point in front of a jagged outcropping of Dumpster-size rocks frequented by sea lions, the waves were truly huge—and unsurfed. Clark started surfing them virtually alone in 1975 at 17.

It didn't take Jeff Clark long to realize why he had this place, named for a German shepherd that tested the surf, all to himself. Deep trenches in the reef allow the waves to maintain their energy longer. Average rides at Maverick's last 30 to 40 seconds—vs. 12 seconds or less at Waimea. And Maverick's waves break right in front of jagged rocks. Richard Schmidt, a big-wave veteran from Santa Cruz, came around to take a look "Waimea has a little bit of forgiveness," he says. "The wave hits the reef a lot faster here. At Maverick's, it was scary to think how big it can actually get." The rocks were hairy for a reason besides simple proximity: Covered with sea urchins, they've grown extra sharp from years of being perforated by the spiny creatures. Maverick's extends its unique hospitality in other ways. Sharks have been sighted in the vicinity. Around the impact area, the bottom—15 to 20 feet down—is rutted with crevices in which an ankle or a board leash can become stuck. And the water is so turbulent that hold downs sometimes run 19 seconds or longer.

Over the years, a trickle of doubting Hawaiians came across the ocean to test Jeff Clark's home field. How good could it be, they wondered. It was California. A wave outside Hawaii with half the volume of a wave at Waimea was hard to find. Word went back that Maverick's was indeed big. "The place actually had some juice," says Ken Bradshaw, who first surfed it in 1992 wearing a thick wet suit and rubber booties, which changes a surfer's feel for the board. Mark Foo was intrigued enough to fly over in the summer of 1992 and have a look. Maverick's didn't go off that day.

Though worn out after the flight from Honolulu, Foo came ready to surf Maverick's last Dec. 23. He worked out daily with a set of weights kept on the back porch of his place on Iliohu Highway. He avoided drugs and drank only a little. Foo did chase women, though: He juggled multiple girlfriends, was intermittently faithful and was the sort of fellow who is able to remain friends with the previous girlfriend after securing the next. Lately, Foo had been dating Lisa Nakano, a Japanese woman who works in the marketing department of Levi Strauss in Honolulu. A model who won Hawaii's Cherry Blossom Queen pageant in 1988, Nakano loved Foo and seemed to understand his priorities. "I accepted that surfing came first," she says, "as long as there was no other girl."

Foo had paid $500,000 for the Iliohu house in 1993 and in addition to Lisa Nakano had another female roommate, who instead of paying rent, cleaned and cooked Foo's meals for him—further testament to the efficacy of the Foo-losophy, although there were those on the North Shore who remained convinced, incorrectly, that Mark Foo made his money by dealing drugs. The truth was that though Foo was rich by surfer standards, the Iliohu house was heavily mortgaged. In a year he probably earned less than $100,000: $30,000 to $40,000 in endorsements for Free Style watches, Body Glove wet suits, Blue

Hawaii surfboards and Power Bar energy snacks, plus commissions as the Hawaii-Guam sales representative for Body Glove.

H3O, a cable-television surf show that Foo produced and co-hosted in Hawaii, was picked up by Prime Network. But the company that produced the program was running in the red. Foo took out a $120,000 personal loan to keep it operating. "Mark was the kind of guy who went for opportunities whether the money was in place or not," says Mike Latronic, Foo's television partner, who split with him last November after an argument over Foo's $8,000 travel expenses for a four-month surfing and business trip to Australia, Tahiti and Indonesia. "He was abroad expanding when he needed to be home consolidating."

Mark Foo looked forward to spending Christmas with Lisa Nakano, but Dec. 23 turned out to be a day for serious surfing, an unprecedented afternoon. At this point, Maverick's had been breaking for 10 days with consistent sets of 15- to 25-foot waves. In a weird reverse migration, the major big-wave pros from the North Shore and from Todos Santos, in Mexico—the No. 2 winter break—went to Northern California: Mark Foo and Ken Bradshaw represented the Old Guard. The new crew included Brock Little and two Todos stars, Mike Parsons, 30, of San Clemente, Calif., and Evan Slater, 23, from San Francisco, as well as a 16-year-old sensation from Santa Cruz named Jay Moriarity. Unprecedented day? Call it historic. Like Foo, many of the outsiders were virgins surfing Maverick's for the first time.

Foo walked three-quarters of a mile from the parking lot and arrived at the beach around 9:30 a.m. He scanned the water, which he knew was a bone-stiffening 52 degrees. Arranged behind sets of binoculars, a crowd of 100 spectators stood on the cliff. Jeff Clark looked at all this and felt a jolt of pride. Solitary old Maverick's, his haunted old break—she wasn't used to such attention. How would she react? What sort of mood would she be in? It would be interesting to see how these Hawaiians dealt with the muscular Maverick's waves.

Even though the water was cold, the air temperature was in the mid-60s—balmy for Maverick's—and early-morning offshore winds, which had cleaned up the waves, were calm. Everybody shouldered on their wet suits. Foo had brought two. "You think the 3mm will be enough?" he asked Mark Renneker, a San Francisco physician who rides big waves and goes by the name of Doc. Renneker said, "If you've got it, go thicker. It does get cold out there, especially when the wind blows."

"Yeah, but it has a hood," Foo said.

"All the better," Renneker said, "it keeps your head warmer, and it's safer, too." Foo changed into his 4mm.

"The waves were perfectly spaced and organized," Renneker says, "as if they'd been delivered from the spirit world." Friday, unfortunately, was shaping up as a smaller day: nothing much over 20 feet, most waves 12 to 15 feet, with a few 18 footers rolling in. "The day seemed run-of-the-mill," says Zachary Wormhoudt, a Californian who'd been out all week with his brother Jake. "Other days that week were more treacherous." As a result, Foo began to question the board he'd selected, a yellow and purple custom 10-foot-6-inch Blue Hawaii designed for 20-feet-plus conditions.

"I think I'll run hack and get my smaller board," Foo said. Reminded of the distance to the parking lot, he reconsidered. There was also a feeling that the swells would kick up, so he stuck with the gun he had.

Inevitably, grumbles of disappointment were heard from some of the Hawaiians, stuff along the lines that this would be a good warm-up day. Then they paddled out into something more than they bargained for. The Hawaiians were wiping out; in fact, almost everyone was. "People were going down, way down, people were hitting the bottom," says Jeff Clark. "But it wasn't so big that you thought anybody would get hurt."

Out in the lineup, Foo wanted to talk about women. He mentioned that he was thinking about getting an engagement ring for Lisa Nakano. They had been together about a year. Brock Little laughed and said, "Yeah, man, but when the waves are good, it's still gonna be like 'Sorry, gotta go!' " Foo agreed, looked around and turned to Doc Renneker. "You guys are lucky to have this spot," Foo said, paying Doc the highest compliment you can pay a local at his home break. "It's a great wave."

With all the photographers present and the surfers' every movement being cataloged, it didn't take long for a competitive atmosphere to form out in the water. As every surfer knows—pro and prospective pro —all it takes is one cool shot to make a magazine cover and multiply your name recognition overnight. Next step: sponsorship, stipends, free boards, free gear; goodbye, real job. Surfer nirvana. And the Mark Foo lesson still applies. Making the wave isn't absolutely necessary. Sometimes if you paddle into a monster and are annihilated spectacularly, a picture of that is just as good.

By 11 a.m., Foo and Bradshaw had caught about 10 decent waves apiece and were getting Maverick's dialed in. A bank of clouds appeared to the east, darkened to bronze by reflected sunlight, indicating a storm gathering just as one of the biggest sets of the day came through. Bradshaw paddled for the second wave, about a 12 footer, but found himself slightly out of position and pulled off. Foo, in better position, jumped up on his board, charging. His technique as always looked good: low crouch, front arm straight. Nothing seemed abnormal about the takeoff. In three seconds, though, Foo pitched forward awkwardly and fell away from his board: a belly-flop-style wipeout. Hitting the water with his stomach and rib cage, Foo went down, only to eerily rise up a moment later behind a curtain of water 8 to 10 feet to the right of his board.

Nobody saw Mark Foo surface after that, but because the wipeout didn't look out of the ordinary and because there were so many surfers in the water, Foo's absence did not raise an immediate alarm. Up on the cliff, spectators turned their binoculars to Brock Little and Mike Parsons on the next wave. They, too, wiped out. Now Little and Parsons were in trouble, being pushed onto the barbed rocks. "My leash was hooked onto the bottom," Parsons says. "I was 100 percent convinced I was gonna die."

Ken Bradshaw, meanwhile, successfully rode the fourth wave of the set all the way in and began paddling back out. As Bradshaw slid past one of the photo boats, Bob Barbour, a photographer, said, "Mark really ate it bad. You should be glad you didn't go. I think he broke his board."

"Well, where is he?" Bradshaw asked.

Barbour pointed toward the rocks where Little and Parsons were hung up and to another rock outcropping to the south. "I think he's one of the heads over there," he said. Bradshaw detected nothing strange. He figured Foo would head in for a new gun, a process—with the swim in and swim out, plus the hike up and back from the parking lot—that could take an hour.

Mark Foo, though, was not on land. A part of his board—the large center piece—was now visible in the north channel. Attached by his leash to the rear third of his board, Foo lay beneath the surface, drowning. "The piece was so small, maybe 2 feet by 10 inches, it offered no flotation," Bradshaw says. "It just went under the water with him and stayed under the water with him." The irony was inescapable: One of the most lionized surfers in history, surfing a crowded break while motor drives whirred, couldn't get anybody to pay attention to him when he needed it most.

Around 90 minutes later, the crew of *Deeper Blue*, a photo boat that was picking up stranded surfers, spied the small chunk of Foo's board floating in the mouth of Pillar Point Harbor. As *Deeper Blue* pulled up to examine the debris, Evan Slater saw Foo's leash and Foo still attached to it. "Turn the boat around!" Slater yelled. He dove in and hauled Foo into the boat. "But it was way, way too late," says Mike Parsons, who was also on board by this point. On the dock, paramedics tried for a half hour to revive Mark Foo, to no avail. Oddly, the weather, so perfect for 10 days, suddenly changed. Low storm clouds ambled in, the wind turned south, and that was the end of the swell.

What happened to Mark Foo that day at Maverick's? Videotapes of his wipeout were examined, again and again, frame by frame. The tape became the Zapruder film of the big-wave surfing community. Steve Hawk, editor of *Surfer* magazine, called Foo's death "the biggest single news story to hit the sport in the past 20 years. It may be the biggest ever." Cynics said it was just like Foo to have died on videotape.

Inevitably, the death of Mark Foo, master of surf-scene politics, became politicized. There was no question that he had drowned. The question was what had kept him down. Had Foo been hit on the head and knocked unconscious by his board, which would render the incident a freak accident, a piece of unpreventable bad luck?

Or had Foo or his leash become entangled on a rock or in a trench on the bottom? After all, the tail section of his brand-new board was chewed up, the fiberglass broken and scratched. There were only scrapes and cuts on his forehead, which didn't appear to be evidence of a knockout blow. This scenario, of course, implicated Maverick's. Dark whispers went around that some Maverick's regulars didn't mind this interpretation. Behind their talk about the need for increased safety, they were secretly getting off on the fact that Maverick's was *their* killer break; they surfed it, then the famous guys from Hawaii marched in and didn't take the place seriously, and that was why Mark Foo died.

"What happened to the buddy system?" asked Lisa Nakano tearfully a few weeks after her boyfriend's death. It is a question many big-wave surfers are now asking themselves. "What happened to water safety?" Nakano said. "How come nobody realized Mark was gone?"

"Mark just slipped through the cracks," derided Maverick's veteran Jeff Clark.

Looking back on what happened, if one were to follow the teachings of Foo-losophy, the whole event might have been seen as the greatest publicity stunt of all. A big-wave Top 5 surfer before, Mark Foo was now a certifiable big-wave legend.

On a Tuesday shortly after Mark Foo's death, a low-pressure system with 50-knot winds finally settles 800 to 1,200 miles west-northwest of Oahu. Big-wave surfers on the North Shore awake at 6 o'clock in the morning to find Waimea breaking. Sets will be 10 to 15 feet all day, some as big as 22 feet. Ken Bradshaw grabs a board and rushes out. Bobby Owens, the big-wave surfer who had been Mark Foo's best friend, decides to just watch. He jumps a fence on Kamehameha Highway, near the Backpackers Inn, and makes his way across a pile of black lava boulders to Waimea Point. Here you get the best sense of the size and power of the waves crashing a few hundred yards away—short of actually being in the water. The vantage point is made more dramatic by a small prospect of danger. A big set can come in and drench you. On a 25-foot day, you might be pulled out to sea.

Known as Mr. Sunset for his skill at the break just down the road, Owens is a kindly son with sun-bleached red hair and soft blue eyes. In the weeks before Mark Foo died, Owens says, Foo was still surfing two, three, sometimes four times a day, talking about starting a water-safety school and about a new promotional idea called Destination Extreme, in which Foo, camera crew in tow, would follow a storm around the world, on sea and land, surfing the waves it created and commenting on how snow boarders handled the powder. "Today is really a classic situation, dramatic big waves, though not the most epic day you'll see in five years," Owens says sadly, watching the bay in action. "Mark would be just spilling over with excitement. He'd have been out there first thing this morning."

Out in the bay, Shawn Briley, the new Waimea hellman, goes left on a 16-foot wave, an insane maneuver, which sends him sluicing toward the lava boulders. A human fireplug, 5 feet 7 inches tall, 195 pounds, Briley is only 21 years old. And he believes. He has taken up the Foo-losophy. He talks about getting "a continuous amount of coverage." His business card describes him as a "promotional subcontractor" first and a "professional surfer" second. Briley has yet to surf Maverick's.

"People say if Shawn keeps up that way, he's not going to be around very long," Owens says. "The new breed of younger guys are more brazen, go one step further for their reputation, their notoriety. Most people would say going left at Waimea is a hideous thing to do."

After an open-casket service in Honolulu, two memorials were held simultaneously for Mark Foo at Waimea and Maverick's. Hundreds came. At Waimea, 200 of Foo's friends paddled out into the water. Two circles were formed: one big outside ring and a group of about 10 of his closest friends holding hands to make an inside ring—Ken Bradshaw, Brock Little, Dennis Pang, Bobby Owens, SharLyn Foo, Lisa Nakano and Richard Schmidt, among others. Earlier, speeches had been given on the beach about Foo's dedication to big waves, his skills as a businessman, his loyalty as a friend, how he'd met his goals, had loved the life he lived. Now out in the bay, the mourners tossed leis and flowers into the water. Dennis Pang took a box from his backpack and spread Foo's ashes, which were taken up by the currents and carried out to sea.

As depressed as they felt about their loss, the mourners sustained themselves with the thought that Foo, wherever he was, had to be enjoying all the attention. "He knows," says Pang. "He's stoked. He's loving every minute of it."

Surf Dudes of Beach 89
by Charlie Rubin

Some of the world's most dedicated surfers don't have access to great surf. Charlie Rubin in 1997 profiled a gang of surfers who take the subway to the beach.

The Dodge van is making good time along the Belt Parkway. It should, because it's 8 a.m. on a Labor Day Sunday. Three Brooklyn Surfers are in the van. They all live in Manhattan, every one of them. Adam Mergan is driving. By day he delivers for a New Jersey pharmaceuticals company. He's 27. Beside him is his girlfriend, Casey M., 24, who's in real estate, and in back is Eric Watson, 41, a hairdresser from the salon at Bergdorf's, sharing the hard van floor with a bag of soda and six or seven surfboards.

They are heading out to Rockaway Beach for the waves. It is in the Rockaways that these three and scores like them got their nickname, Brooklyn Surfers, even though they are obviously Manhattan Surfers, because that is what kids from Rockaway, in Queens, call anybody who isn't a Rockaway Surfer.

There are people who surf Montauk and Jones Beach. Good for

them. This is a story about people who swear by beaches they can subway to, where the waves maybe don't "break steady" but satisfy an exploding population of mostly teen-agers and 20-ish surfers who design their lives around wave sizes, who track "ocean temp" on the Internet's "World Buoy Map of the East Coast" and storms via Doppler radar on TV weather and who take guff from weirded-out straphangers for lugging their boards onto the A train and give it right back, sprinkling Hawaiian words into their obscenities. It's these folks who have been raising eyebrows along Rockaway's 7.5 miles of beaches, because the "Rockapulco" Surfers know that the Brooklyn Surfers are as dedicated to wave-riding as they are. Maybe more. Because where you can't see surf, you must think it. All the time. N.B.W. Nothing But Waves.

Adam and Casey are discussing a jellyfish. "The lifeguard went right into it, face first," says Casey. "She's OK."

Adam says: "You get bit by a man-of-war like they have in Florida, it causes total paralysis. That I know for a fact."

Eric says, "I'm just going to keep my eye out for it." Adam parks a block from Beach 89, and everybody carries a couple of boards across Rockaway Beach Boulevard.

"I got a new stick," says Adam. "It's a fast little gun."

"I can't wait to ride my Mako," Eric says. This is a tomato-red, Beach Boys–era classic longboard that Eric bought, used, last week for $175.

"It's sweet," says Adam.

"It's a log," Eric says. He repaired it, adding a "Jesus Saves" sticker. "Was Pretty Boy out Friday?"

"Yeah," says Casey. "With that Brooklyn kid who dropped out of school to surf."

Adam suddenly says, "I gotta catch some swell!"

Eric says, "This homeless guy wanted to go surfing, but I couldn't find him."

Beach 89 is the hot beach. Beach 88 is the legal one, according to the Parks Department, but the lifeguards allow the surfers to migrate west to 92d with the waves. The guards are flexible in part because the other official surfers' beach, Beach 38, was quickly overrun by hookers and dealers. There were muggings, and one Brooklyn boy is famous for surfing with a knife taped under his board. These days, surfers who brave 38th drive their cars right up onto the boardwalk so they can surf while guarding their car stereos.

The Brooklyn Surfers are studying the ocean. Two months into hurricane season (which can run through November) and so far it's a serious dud; which, after a fierce '95 and a solid '96, is just killing everybody. "The tropicals are out there, enticing us," one says, but they aren't coming near enough. Still, Adam and Casey intend to start living in a tent on the beach next week.

Now they wrap towels around their waists and change from shorts into wet suits, pulling and fastening, done. Adam nudges Eric: "Look, that's a ridable wave. That's a nice righthanded wave." He unzips his silver board bags. Some surfers are moving into the water, to the right of the rock jetty. Adam paddles out. After 20 minutes he's back, and all the other surfers follow him to the left of the jetty. Adam has a quiet prominence here.

A kid goes by, announcing: "There's gonna be something Wednesday! Guy saw it on the Doppler!"

Eric gave away his boards when he moved to Manhattan from California 10 months ago, figuring that part of his life was over. Now he shouts, "Maiden voyage!" and rides his Mako all the way in on a nothing wave, beaming.

By noon, the sand is packed with "whoo girls"—local slang for women who get suntans until a surfer makes a good ride, then jump up and go: "Whoo! Whoo! Whoo!" Casey's different. She's usually the only female surfer on 89. "It's not really encouraged," she shrugs. "I just went in the water and did it."

Two examples of harmless surfer macho, from another day, on Beach 118: 1) Several surfers two-fingering raw soup from cans—a 15-year-old surfer called it a "pointless local energy fad." 2) Surfing with a Jets helmet on.

And then there's "localism."

Tommy Sena, 43, owns the Rockaway Beach Surf Shop. He learned surfing in the early 60's by watching John and Tom McGonigal, who had watched Pat Reen and the Schreifels, Wally and Kenny, who may have watched a lifeguard named Mickey McManamon in the 50's. Back then, nobody resented new surfers. The more the merrier. "Today," Tommy admits, "there's a little bit of pressure down the beach."

Turfy beach fighting among surfers is way up, according to a cop familiar with the scene. He broke it down this way: Rockaway's predominantly Irish surfers don't like being crowded off their home waves by Brooklyn's Italian and Jewish surfers. Nobody's delighted by the Hispanics who come over the Cross Bay Bridge from the Bronx or the Haitian and Jamaican "wave snakers" or the random gay surfqueen.

The surfer party line is that these clashes are about waves, not race, and only occur when the waves are way up, making the competitive stakes higher. (Rockaway veterans estimate great wave days at about one in six during the summer, much higher in winter, when the hardcore surf through blistering cold and nasty ice-cream headaches.) On exceptional days, surfers say, you can see the snarls on people's faces, and hear the "power surfing"—grunting and sneering while riding— out in the street.

Adam is talking about whether he's had problems on the beach with Rockaway Surfers: "No." Shrugs. "One guy, but we didn't go to fists. He backed off. Sometimes two or three people catch a good wave and no one seems to mind. He didn't want anyone on his wave. He said, 'Peek!' I said, 'You peek!' He left his board in the sand, he wouldn't come back for it. He had to be escorted off the beach by three guys." Adam adds: "I was a pretty wild guy. I'm sure you can tell by my tattoos. I tried to change my ways and be a human being now because I met a woman I love."

An 11-year-old surfer from Brooklyn, Michael Vagle, has been run down on the water by locals. Xavier Ceniceros, 26, snorts: "All the Irish geeks out there. They're shanty Irish. Young punks who think they have something to prove. But once you show that you're as determined as they are, you kind of earn your localism."

A surfer from Beach 135 says: "You know what the Brooklyn Surfers really hate? When we call 'em Brooklyn Surfers."

Oddly, for a while in the early 1980's, there was a shabby storefront near the Brooklyn courthouses that wore its name proudly: brooklyn surfers. It was a teen-age boys' clubhouse, and inside, in the dead of winter, you could see them marching around barefoot with surfboards while their girlfriends assembled a "Have a Surf Xmas!" window display. Several of them lived upstairs in a kind of surfer flop, having quit school to be boxboys or Xerox room guys or to take night jobs to surf all day. That profile still fits a lot of (real) Brooklyn Surfers.

In contrast to Rockaway kids from strong working-class backgrounds, who tend to live at home with parents who are policemen, firemen or schoolteachers, true Brooklyn Surfers are a muttier bunch. Is it any wonder why Brooklyn Surfer is a term of derision, and probably fear?

It's 4 p.m. and the Brooklyn Surfers from Manhattan are in the emergency room of Lenox Hill Hospital in the East 70's. Adam is pressing a cold soda can to his lower lip, which split open when he was bushwhacked by his own board in the water. He wanted to let the wound—which is ugly—heal on its own, but was finally convinced to let a doctor look at it.

An hour passes in the waiting room. Occasionally, Adam studies his lip in the men's room. He says: "That's the only reason I'm here. 'Cause I seen the meat hanging out." He wonders, could he just shove it back in with a Q-Tip? Eric says: "I tried to save a baby bird like that last summer. It fell out of a nest and hit its head on the pavement, and it had a piece like that sticking out, so I stuffed it back in. But it died."

Adam says, "Thanks for the story."

Famous surfers have surfed Rockaway, but no famous surfer has ever come from Rockaway. Or Brooklyn or Manhattan, needless to say. Tommy Sena says, "What if one tried?" He sounds doubtful and hopeful, both.

Petey Egan, 18, from Belle Harbor in Rockaway, is considered gifted. But when asked, "Have you ever thought of going pro?" he answers,

"With the winters being so cold and the summers so flat, what can I do?" Then he adds quietly, "Sure, I'd love to, but I know I don't have it."

And then there's Joe Zwick's dream, which he has nurtured since he first laid eyes on a wave that Breezy Point Surfers, at the far western tip of Rockaway, call the Avalanche. The Avalanche shows up in hurricane season. Twice. If that. A mile, maybe two, out in the heart of New York Harbor. Waves up to 25 feet high.

Nobody's ever ridden it. How would you get to it? Joe Zwick has a plan. He is going to be towed into it. By Jetskis or boat. On a surfboard with straps. Bring him right up to it and then . . . he lets go. "It would be a ferocious ride." He estimates more than a minute long, over half a mile. Out in the harbor where there is no Brooklyn, no Rockaway, just the Avalanche.

"I've gotta do it before I quit," says the schoolteacher, who has surfed these waters for more than 35 years. "Every wave is ridable."

Eric returns from his nearby apartment with some surf videos for Adam. There is a soundless TV set with a built-in VCR on the E.R. wall and Eric wants to put a video in. Adam stops him. "No, no, no. It's not our machine."

Twenty more minutes go by. Adam: "Eric, get the tape."

They ask the room, mostly elderly patients, does anybody mind if they put a surfing video on? Nobody blinks. But the VCR's too high up. Eric says, "If I had that lady's cane I could get it in." This plan dies.

Outside the hospital, smoking, Adam talks with some people he meets on the street. They all shake hands enthusiastically. Adam returns. He seems better. "They didn't know you could surf here," he says.

Finally he's called. When he comes out, it's with six stitches and a huge smile: "The doctor was a surfer and lives in Rockaway. He thinks there's something coming up from Florida."

acknowledgments

Many people made this anthology.

At Thunder's Mouth Press and Avalon Publishing Group:
Thanks to Tracy Armstead, Will Balliett, Sue Canavan, Kristen Couse, Maria Fernandez, Linda Kosarin, Shona McCarthy, Dan O'Connor, Neil Ortenberg, Paul Paddock, Susan Reich, David Riedy, Michelle Rosenfield, Simon Sullivan, and Mike Walters.

At The Writing Company:
Surfer boys Nathaniel May and Taylor Smith did most of the editorial research. Nathaniel May oversaw permissions research and negotiations. Nate Hardcastle and Wynne Parry took up slack on other projects.

At the Portland Public Library in Portland, Maine:
The librarians helped collect books from around the country.

Finally, I am grateful to the writers whose work appears in this book.

p e r m i s s i o n s

We gratefully acknowledge everyone who gave permission for written material to appear in this book. We have made every effort to trace and contact copyright holders. If an error or omission is brought to our notice we will be pleased to correct the situation in future editions of this book. For further information, please contact the publisher.

Excerpt from *Caught Inside* by Daniel Duane. Copyright © 1996 by Daniel Duane. Reprinted by permission of North Point Press, a division of Farrar, Straus and Giroux, LLC. ✦ Excerpt from *In Search of Captain Zero* by Allan C. Weisbecker. Copyright © 2001 by Allan C. Weisbecker. Used by permission of Jeremy P. Tarcher, an imprint of Penguin Group (USA) Inc. ✦ "California: Fever and the First Wave" and "The Animal" from *Pure Stoke* by John Grissim. Copyright © 1982 by John Grissim. Used by permission of the author. ✦ "Mr. Sunset Rides Again" by Rob Buchanan. Copyright © 2000 by Rob Buchanan. Used by permission of the author. ✦ "Goodbye Sunshine Superman" by Matt Warshaw. Copyright © 1994 by Matt Warshaw. Used by permission of the author. ✦ "Singular Achievement" from *Maverick's* by Matt Warshaw. Copyright © 2000 by Matt Warshaw. Published by Chronicle Books LLC, San Francisco. Used with permission. Visit http://www.chroniclebooks.com ✦ "Mavericks" by Lawrence Beck. Copyright © 1993 by Lawrence Beck. Used by permission of the author. ✦ "Life Among the Swells" by William Finnegan. Copyright © 1997 by William Finnegan. Reprinted by permission of International Creative Management, Inc. First appeared in *Outside*. ✦ "Life Isn't Fair" by Rob Story. Copyright © 2001 by Rob Story. Used by permission of the author. First appeared in *Outside*. ✦ "Something Wicked This Way Comes" by Daniel Duane. Copyright © 1998 by Daniel Duane. Reprinted by permission of Ellen Levine Literary Agency, Inc./Trident Media Group L.L.C. Originally appeared in *Outside* magazine, May 1998. ✦ "Polynesian Surfing" by Ben R. Finney and James D. Houston. Copyright © 1969 by Ben R. Finney and James D. Houston. Used by permission of the authors. ✦ "Kaku" by Bruce Jenkins. Copyright © 1994 by Bruce Jenkins. Used by permission of the author. ✦ "The Last Wave" from *Da Bull: Life Over the Edge* by Greg Noll and Andrea Gabbard. Copyright © 1989 by Greg Noll and Andrea Gabbard. Reprinted by permission of the author. ✦ "Alaska: The Land Duke Forgot" by Dave Parmenter. Copyright © 1993 by Dave Parmenter. Used by permission of the author. Originally appeared in *Surfer*, January 1993. ✦ "Alone" by Dave Parmenter. Copyright © 1994 by Dave Parmenter. Used by permission of the author. Originally appeared in *Surfer*, January 1994. ✦ "Surfacing" from *Maverick's* by Matt Warshaw. Copyright © 2000 by Matt Warshaw. Published by Chronicle Books LLC, San Francisco. Used with permission. Visit http://www.chroniclebooks.com ✦ "The Last Wave" by Peter Wilkinson. Copyright © 1995 by Rolling Stone LLC. All rights reserved. Reprinted by permission. Originally appeared in *Rolling Stone*, April 20, 1995. ✦ "Surf Dudes of Beach 89" by Charlie Rubin. Copyright © 1997 by Charlie Rubin. Used by permission of the author. Originally appeared in *The New York Times Magazine*, October 19, 1997.

bibliography

The selections used in this anthology were taken from the editions listed below. In some cases, other editions may be easier to find. Hard-to-find or out-of-print titles often are available through inter-library loan services or through Internet booksellers.

Beck, Lawrence. "Mavericks." Originally appeared in *The Surfer's Journal*, Winter 1993.

Buchanan, Rob. "Mr. Sunset Rides Again." Originally appeared in *Outside*, April, 2000.

Duane, Daniel. "Something Wicked This Way Comes." Originally appeared in *Outside*, May 1998.

Duane, Daniel. *Caught Inside: A Surfer's Year on the California Coast*. New York: North Point Press, 1996.

Finnegan, William. "Life Among the Swells." Originally appeared in *Outside*, April, 1997.

Finney, Ben R. and James D. Houston. "Polynesian Surfing." Originally appeared in *Natural History*, August-September 1969.

Grissim, John. *Pure Stoke*. New York: Harper & Row, 1982. (For "California: Fever and the First Wave" and "The Animal.")

Jenkins, Bruce. "Kaku". Originally appeared in *The Surfer's Journal*, Fall 1994.

London, Jack. *The Cruise of the Snark*. London: Seafarer Books, 1971.

Noll, Greg and Andrea Gabbard. *Da Bull: Life Over the Edge*. Berkeley, CA: North Atlantic Books, 1989.

Parmenter, Dave. "Alaska: The Land Duke Forgot." Originally appeared in *Surfer*, January, 1993.

Parmenter, Dave. "Alone." Originally appeared in *Surfer*, January, 1994.

Rubin, Charlie. "Surf Dudes of Beach 89." Originally appeared in *The New York Times Magazine*, October 19, 1997.

Story, Rob. "Life Isn't Fair." Originally appeared in *Outside*, June 2001.

Warshaw, Matt. "Goodbye Sunshine Superman." Originally appeared in *The Surfer's Journal*, Winter 1994.

Warshaw, Matt. *Maverick's: The Story of Big-Wave Surfing*. San Francisco: Chronicle Books, 2000. (For "Singular Achievement" and "Surfacing.")

Weisbecker, Allan C. *In Search of Captain Zero: A Surfer's Road Trip Beyond the End of the Road*. New York: Jeremy P. Tarcher/Putnam, 2001.

Wilkinson, Peter. "The Last Wave." Originally appeared in *Rolling Stone*, April 20, 1995.